Shore Stories

*An Anthology
of the Jersey Shore*

Edited by Rich Youmans

For information, address:

Down The Shore Publishing Corp., Box 3100, Harvey Cedars, NJ 08008
The words "Down The Shore" and the Down The Shore Publishing logo are a registered U.S. Trademark.

Printed in the United States of America. First printing, 1998.

This book is printed on recycled paper — 10% post-consumer content.

10 9 8 7 6 5 4 3 2 1

Library of Congress Cataloging-in-Publication Data

Shore stories : an anthology of the Jersey shore / edited by Rich Youmans.
    p. cm.
    ISBN 0-945582-50-1
1. Atlantic Coast (N.J.)--Literary collections.   2. Seaside resorts--New Jersey--Literary collections.   3. American literature-
-New Jersey--Atlantic Coast.   4. New Jersey--Literary collections.
I. Youmans, Richard, 1960-   .
PS548.N5S48   1998
810.8'032749--DC21   98-6923
                                                       CIP

Book and jacket design by Leslee Ganss.
Original jacket photograph by Serge J-F. Levy digitally altered by Leslee Ganss.

To my parents,
who first brought me
to the Jersey Shore,
and, as always,
to Ann

Table of Contents

Introduction

When I was growing up in Philadelphia, summers were not complete without a trip to the Jersey Shore. At least once every season, my parents would pack me and two or three suitcases into our '62 Chevy and go cruising over the Delaware. Once in New Jersey, we'd travel along busy Route 73 for a while until, like cedar water finding its level, we'd wander down onto the backroads of the Pine Barrens. For several hours, we'd pass little more than pine, weathered farmstands, and the occasional campy monstrosity (like a 20-foot spaceman before the entrance to an amusement park). Finally, when the air turned cooler and took on the tang of salt, we knew we'd arrived. As we crossed the bridge into Ocean City, the water of Great Egg Harbor popping with sun below us, the sky seemed to grow larger and brighter, and summer officially began.

We were Down the Shore.

It's a phrase that has nothing to do with directional accuracy and everything to do with place — and promise. When I was ten, Down the Shore meant sandcastles on the beach, rides and miniature golf on the boardwalk, and wave upon wave on which to ride, until my parents had to force me back to our rented apartment. When I was eighteen, Down the Shore meant clubs and girls: the fever of youth. By the time I was 23, the Shore had become my home, but the lures that attract so many visitors — the beaches, the boardwalks, the cool sea breezes — seemed no less wondrous for their familiarity.

Fifteen years later, I no longer live along the shore, but those three words, Down the Shore, still conjure scenes and sensations that remain as vivid as the day they occurred. Of course, my experience is by no means unique. It is shared by the countless numbers who migrate each summer to that 127-mile stretch of coastline from Sandy Hook to Cape May Point, as well as by the many who have decided to make a piece of that stretch their home. For all of them, the Jersey Shore is an idea, a way of life, a region that moves to the rhythm of the waves. It is not Utopia — just ask anyone who has seen an ecosystem disrupted by explosive overdevelopment, or have had their lives upended by a tropical storm or hurricane. But take a walk along the beach and, more times than not, the problems of daily life disappear over the dunes, replaced by the endless sweep of sunlight, sea, and horizon. This is life along the Jersey Shore, and it is what this anthology tries to capture.

The stories, poems, essays, and photographs in this book are a diverse lot. Some give a child's-eye view of the shore: the awe in crossing a bridge or standing on a deck, high above water. Some present that period when teenagers first cross into the responsibilities of adulthood, while others show adults facing those responsibilities — and accepting them. There are works that focus on the natural environment, and works that take their cue from historical events. William Wharton's novel *Pride*, for example, was inspired by an actual event that occured in October 1938, when a lion named Tuffy — part of a motorcycle act on the Wildwood boardwalk — escaped from its cage and killed a man. And the series of stories and poems about Atlantic City (the largest section of the book) cover much of the 20th century, from the days of rum-running to the current era of legalized gambling. There's even a good old-fashioned ghost story, with plenty of local color and history.

Yet, as different as their styles and subject matter may be, all of these works share the spirit, the romance, of life by the sea. I and all the writers, poets, and photographers represented on these pages would like you now to experience that spirit for yourself. So relax, sit back, and enjoy the trip — Down the Shore.

— Rich Youmans

Shore Stories

Scheinman's Deck

by Wendy Patrice Williams

How I longed to go up on Scheinman's deck! It was high off the ground and hung clear out over the Shrewsbury. One time a hurricane swept the river right up over the deck into Scheinman's parlor. Standing at his door once with my father, I saw that the metal legs of his TV stand were rusted five inches up from the floor.

I never passed Scheinman's bungalow without wishing I lived in it. How could we have ended up in a bungalow next to the road and the U.S. Navy guard house! Every summer for two weeks, we lived in my aunt and uncle's bungalow across the river from the Highlands and next to Sandlass's Beach House at Sandy Hook, New Jersey, a long wide sandbar bordered on one side by the Shrewsbury River and on the other by the Atlantic Ocean. Lying in bed one night, I heard the ocean waves pound the rock seawall, one after another, a deep, powerful thunder that I felt inside my body.

But Scheinman's was right over the water. The gray, sea-weathered boards, the deck jutting out over the river like the bow of a ship. If I could just get onto that deck, sit on the railing, hang my feet over the great, green, swelling water below. If I could just run out onto it whenever I heard the bridge towers clinking and see the roadway split open, its two huge halves rising slowly till they pointed straight up into the sky. If I could just sit on it quietly before bedtime and watch the green and red harbor lights of the cabin cruisers slide by each night, and be soothed by the gently humming, almost soundless motors chugging at slow speed. But a sign hung from the deck railing that read "No Trespassing" in red letters. *Oh give me the waves and the water, my mate…give me the song of the sea.*

❂

Scheinman was a thin, dark man with the skin pulled taut over his jaws. His chin was grizzly with white stubble and he had no teeth. Scheinman didn't wear dentures like my Uncle Frank, so his lips were drawn in over his gums; they were puckered and dry, deeply creviced at regular intervals all around his mouth. He never spoke to me, not even to say hello, and when my Dad and I walked past him, he nodded at Dad but not at me.

When I imagined him speaking, his lips made a little "o" and a long, low howl flowed out — "oooooooooo" — like a skeleton come alive at midnight. His nose arched down at a sharp angle and his cap always caused a rim of shade to curve under his eyes. He was bent over and so thin that I thought he might be dying of cancer.

My father and Uncle Frank consulted him daily like they did the sky each morning for boating weather. They always said things at the dinner table like "Old man Scheinman says…" or "Just ask Scheinman, he'll tell ya." My dad disappeared through Scheinman's side door evenings or stood next to him at dusk near the bulkhead as the lights were coming on across the river. Scheinman must be some kind of sage, I thought, an ancient mariner that had defied death and had earned the right to speak.

Once Dad took me along to call on him. There was his name, SCHEINMAN, raised up on a black metal plate nailed onto his screen door. Dad knocked. Scheinman's wife came to the door and told us he wasn't home. She asked us in but Dad said no. I shoved my hands into the pouch at the front of my sweatshirt. I wanted to be inside the house where the water had been, look out onto the Shrewsbury from the kitchen windows. And I wanted to hear Scheinman talk.

❂

One day, sitting on my front porch behind the cool, dark screens of afternoon, I watched Scheinman and his wife file past, heading for their old Chevy station wagon parked along the road. As the dust flew back from their tires, I raced down the sidewalk and up Scheinman's stairs holding a pretend errand in my mind. At Scheinman's door, I looked down onto the sidewalk and along the beach — no one watching. I scrambled along the railing of the deck to the far corner and popped up. Damn! — what if someone saw me from a boat? Luckily, the only presence seaward was a gull poised atop a nearby piling. I had made it onto Scheinman's deck!

Across the river, the Bahr's Restaurant sign loomed, huge neon letters that flashed on and off at night. Above Bahr's, at the top of a high ridge, the two brick towers of the Twin Lights Lighthouse stood guard. And over the waterway, the bridge — "That dramatic arch of civilization," as my mother called it — spanned the river between the Highlands and the Hook. Thick ropes hung down from the girders. At the end of the ropes, huge knots dangled above the surface of the water where whirlpools swirled their dangerous circles. Boys sometimes swung from the knots and dropped off.

I thought of the way my father, Uncle Frank, and I raced home in the motorboat after a day's fishing beyond the bridge. I perched right up on the prow pushing full speed ahead through the whitecaps, breaking into those waves and splitting them open. Suspended in mid-air till the boat dropped down onto the next wave — wham! — like a belly flop. Slicing right through those dark whirling pools beneath the bridge. It always amazed me how we didn't get sucked down to swirl and spin like Dorothy and Toto in the tornado. "Hold on!" Uncle Frank yelled over the *grrrrrrr* of the Evinrude, the waves spraying and soaking my hair.

The green water swelled and slapped at the pilings holding up Scheinman's deck. My parents told me there used to be a huge boardwalk here with a roller coaster. I remembered how my father snagged his foot on an old piece of amusement fence that stuck up from the bottom.

We were drag netting, pulling the seine net taut between us into the rushing tide, me close to shore, he farther out, the river covering his chest as he leaned back to drag. Then his shoulders emerged as he pulled in closer to shore. Suddenly he lurched forward, folded over himself like a boxer punched in the stomach. "Sonuva bitch," he growled sharply at the dark green water, wincing and snapping his head back and forth. "Go get Frank!" he yelled. I ran up the beach's slope fighting what seemed like weights attached to my legs. What if the water swallowed Dad before I found help?

Luckily, up on the sidewalk Mr. Lombard, a neighbor, was lugging an armload of beach chairs. "My father, he's hurt in the water!" I said, pointing to the river. Dropping the chairs, he ran down the sand. I followed him, saw Dad in the distance, but only his head showed now and the top of his shoulders. The tide was washing in fast.

Soon a crowd of men surrounded Dad, including Uncle Frank. They all pulled up on him, but he remained in place. Why couldn't they get him out? Wave after wave rushed toward shore, shooshing on the pebbly sand. A chill blew in off the water. It was nearing suppertime and the sand was empty of sunbathers. *Day ending, nets for mending, sailors heading home.*

Then miraculously, Dad floated toward shore as if washed in with the tide — the men pushed him through the water from behind. Finally he was free. On the beach, his bony knees leaned helplessly against each other as he sat in the wet sand. Mr. Lombard and Uncle Frank leaned down and Dad draped his thick arms around their necks. They carried him up the beach, one leg bent slightly at the knee, the foot dangling white and limp, dark blood pumping out the top. I watched until they carried him up onto the sidewalk past Scheinman's and out of sight. Then I followed the blood stains back to our bungalow, red splotches in groups of three to each cement square.

The metal spike had punctured a hole right through his foot. It had taken so long to free him, Mom told me, because the men had pulled straight up when they should've pulled at an angle — the fencing he'd stepped on was crooked. Mom was angry because Dad hadn't worn his sneakers. We left for home that evening; Mom said only quacks practiced in the nearby shore towns. At first, Dr. Feinstein thought he might have to amputate Dad's foot — it had become gangrenous. But he cleaned the wound out "mercilessly," Mom said, and with time it healed.

On the deck the wind felt cold. It plastered my long hair across my face and whipped it in front of my eyes. The buoy bell bonged loudly, rapidly as the Shrewsbury pulsed more strongly to shore. It was nearing suppertime and the tide flowed in fast. A large mass of water swelled up toward the deck, threatening to wash me away, pull me out to the tip of Sandy Hook, then out to the ocean beyond. As the boards of the deck creaked with the rush of heavy water, I ran to the stairs away from memory and the unstoppable Shrewsbury tide. *In the blustrous winds, in the great dark waters, our ship went adrift on the sea.*

✿

One morning later that week, as I reeled in the fishing line I had cast onto the sandy lawn in front of our bungalow, Scheinman and his wife passed, she walking behind him as always. Suddenly he turned and glanced at me with hard black eyes. Did he know I had been up on his deck?

I decided to stay just a little while as I flew up the wooden steps, thrilling with the sight at the top; the great expanse of water stretched all the way out to the horizon and beyond. The wide mouth of the Shrewsbury spilling into the ocean at the tip of Sandy Hook. Below the deck, the early morning water was calm. The tide flowed slowly out and by noon the beach would be wide, the water far away and the sand festooned with seaweed, necklace after necklace, tracing the different tide lines of the retreating water. I leaned over the railing, sniffing up the salty air. The water was light green and I stared into it for a long time, hoping to see fish. A red and white bobber floated by and then a long wooden plank.

I looked for the masts poking out of the middle of the river where the water was dark green and very deep. There was a sunken ship under the Shrewsbury and sometimes when the tide went way down, Eddy said you could see the tips of the masts. Eddy was a boy from the mainland who took cute older girls for rides on his speedboat. I got to go once, though I was only eight, for there was no one else out on the beach. I didn't even ask Mom for permission because I was afraid he might leave before I returned from the bungalow. That's the time when the propeller got stuck.

We were gliding with the current along the middle of the river when the boat suddenly jerked and spun around. The engine went dead and we rose quietly on the upswelling water. "It's that damn rigging again," Eddy said, looking over the side of the boat. Mom had told me that long ago pirate ships looted vessels in New York Harbor and hid in these coves. Once in a while after a storm, she said, doubloons washed up onto the shore.

While Eddy fussed with the propeller, I looked into the dark water searching for the masts. Instead, I saw a blurred, golden figurehead, a woman naked from the waist up with her arms cut off, her long hair streaming back with the current, strands writhing like sea snakes over the dark planks of the ship. Her eyes were blank but I knew she held the secret of why the ship went down. Then the water became a blue-black mirror. There I was, a dark shadow leaning over the side of the boat, floating above the rolling sea, rocking up and down with the movement of the swells, my hair blowing back with the wind.

I got scared Scheinman had returned when I heard something slam, but it was just two boys at the edge of the water trying to start an outboard motor. I leaned onto the deck railing and looked out along the length of the Hook. There was a rusty fence that I wasn't supposed to go beyond by myself. And there was the cove — the curve of water swelling with green killies and thin, silver spearing. Dad and I dragged there for bait. He never took Will, my brother, or anyone but me. He'd call my name in that certain way and I'd run for my old sneakers and the big metal bucket under the house. Down the sidewalk we headed, the huge brown net slung over Dad's shoulder, me by his side wearing my white sailor hat, the one he had worn in the Navy.

One time, we had pulled in an unusually heavy load. The net bulged with inrushing water and I could hardly pull my end up out of the surf. As we landed the net, the beach came alive with splashing and light flashing on and off the jumping fish. We grabbed all the fat-bellied killies and cool, rigid spearing and plopped them handful by handful into the bucket. Then we got to see what was left: fat, slimy, clear jellies clinging to the net; stiff brown sea horses lying helplessly on their sides; flat, round baby fluke, white on one side and gray on the other. I wanted to keep the fluke but Dad said we had to let them grow up so we could fish them out when they were big.

Then I saw the baby shark. It was only a hand long and so still in the green seaweed I thought it was dead, but when I poked it with tube grass, it curved its body in and out. There was that lipless mouth and the tiny fin on its back that would grow to poke way up out of the water and scare people. Dad said it was a nurse shark and would only get to be as long as his arm. Then we dragged the net with all its sea life back into the water and shook the creatures free. We picked up what remained on the beach and threw them back in too.

Several large waves slapped the pilings underpinning the deck, reminding me where I was. A gull screamed overhead. It was then I felt something behind me — Scheinman! He leaned toward me as if to peck my face, his body barely supported by slight bird legs. The brim of his cap shaded his eyes and his mouth was puckered and dry. I looked down at the rough, gray boards of the deck, afraid his mouth might open and the "oooooooooooo" sound come out. He cleared his throat, and I skittered like a water rat across the deck and down the steps. I ran across the beach and dove into the cool sand beneath the abandoned bathhouse. As I sat panting under the floorboards, I imagined Scheinman's gruff words: A deck's no place for a little girl, a nice little girl like you. *Each sailor lad, just like his dad, he loves the flowing bowl / The trip ashore, he does adore, with the girl that's plump and round.*

❁

That evening at dusk, as I approached the bulkhead to watch the lights go on in town across the river, I noticed yellow light in Scheinman's kitchen windows. There was the deck jutting darkly out over the high tide. On the water, light in the cabin of a cruiser filled me with a warm coziness. The boat's outline was barely visible now, only the green and red harbor lights at the front and back suggested its contours. The water was calm, gently rising and falling like the chest of someone sleeping. *The buoy bell rung long ago, sailors take ye rest.*

As the lighthouse beacons painted their dual paths across the smooth sea, the magic of Scheinman's deck came back to me. Once again I wanted to be up on the deck over the Shrewsbury like a proud gull atop a piling. But I was afraid of Scheinman — his claw-like hands, his nose like a beak pecking — and of what he might tell my dad if he found me on the deck again. I was afraid of the water too, black and hungry, sweeping over the deck, seeking to snag a little girl's feet and carry her out to sea.

The light left Scheinman's kitchen windows. The deck was the bow of a ship plunging through the darkness of the open sea. I imagined climbing to the top of the deck's steps, the great expanse of blackness beyond. No horizon — the sky, the water, and the Hook all one. In my mind, I saw the lights from Coney Island glimmering dimly, and a blink of yellow from Sandy Hook Light flashing like a faraway star. Scheinman might just now be pulling the covers up to his chin. I decided to wait just a little while before making my way to the stairs.

At the bottom step, I noticed something across the staircase at the top. A thick rope threaded back and forth like stitches to block off access. Scheinman was bent on keeping me out. I imagined his thin, rigid hands pulling the rope taut and looping it around the post again and again. I turned to go. I could have climbed over, but God, if he wanted to keep me out that badly…. As I stepped down onto the cool concrete, I heard the bridge towers begin to clink. On the roadway, bright headlights were lining up in rows. A boat! A large boat must be approaching, and the bridge would have to open to let it through! The bridge hardly ever opened after dark.

I scrambled back up the stairs and lifted one leg, then the other, over the rope barrier. The red lights on the bridge flashed on and off and the clinking hastened. I scanned the dark sea for the boat. There was the red light atop the tall mast. I saw the yellow cabin light below, and I wondered if inside there might be a little girl like me wearing a white sailor hat and plunging through the dark swells. The roadway split, each side slowly rising like two great arms into the night. They are reaching out to me, I thought as I leaned up against the railing of Scheinman's deck. I am a sturdy wooden ship, passing through.

Long Branch, New Jersey

by Robert Pinsky

Everything is regional,

And this is where I was born, dear,

And conceived,

And first moved to tears,

And last irritated to the same point.

It is bounded on three sides by similar places

And on one side by vast, uncouth houses

A glum boardwalk and,

As we say, The Beach.

I stand here now

At the corner of Third Avenue and Broadway

Waiting for you to come by in a car,

And count the red carlights

That rush through a fine rain

To where Broadway's two branches — North

Broadway and South Broadway — both reach

To the trite, salt, welcoming ocean.

Asbury Park

by R. C. Ringer

"Come on, Butch," my father says to me. He puts his large hand on the back of my head and gives me a gentle shake. "Let's get going."

He waits for me while I finish tying my sneaker laces into knots. Then we walk out to the car. He doesn't tell me where we are going — just out for another Saturday drive. I suppose that we will end up at the Ten-Two Lounge or the Alibi or some other bar where we can watch the ball game.

The way we are going, though, isn't the way to any of those places. We drive through Morristown and then we keep driving along Route 24. We are driving for a long time and the sunlight coming in through the windows is making the stale car air hot and lazy. I am drifting off to sleep. My father is whistling along to songs on the radio, tapping one hand on the steering wheel in not quite accurate time. Every so often he smiles, a great happy smile. When he does this, his whistling fades away. He seems lost in some happy memory, some hot and lazy happy memory.

I wake up because something is different.

It's the air.

I sit up straight in the seat. My wrist is sore from having been leaned on while I was napping.

It's the air. It smells like the shore.

I look around at the houses we are passing. They seem smaller, more fragile than the houses in Morristown. There is a feeling of flatness, of the low buildings, of the land. I see seagulls flying.

"Where are we going?" I ask.

"To visit a friend," my father says.

"I mean, where are we going?" I say.

"You'll like it there. You can play all the pinball you want and even eat ice cream."

I don't ask again. I know when I am not going to get an answer from him. There are some things about my father that I know, and this is one of them.

Here's another thing about him: I don't know what his job is. I don't ask that anymore, either. He's told me that he has a top secret job working for the government and will be put in jail if he tells me what it is; he's told me that he's the one who squeezes the toothpaste into the tubes; he's told me that he tests light bulbs, one by one. I don't believe any of his stories, he tells even more of them than my sister does.

I have my own ideas about his job. Sometimes I think that he's an executive. Sometimes I think he drives a forklift.

We pass a few signs that show the mileage to Asbury Park. This is probably where we are going. Or nearby.

I begin to feel uneasy. This is a long way away from Morristown. And we aren't dressed for the shore. I'm wearing long pants and sneakers. And my father, he's wearing tan slacks and one of his white shirts, the ironed-in wrinkles making it seem more clean and new. His shoes are polished. And his smile is glorious. But most of all, it is his aftershave that is making me uneasy. He only wears aftershave when he and my mother go out to dinner or parties. Never on a Saturday drive.

Asbury Park is the shore, but not the shore where we usually go to in the summer. Long Beach Island is where we usually go. And we all go together, not just two of us. My father spreads the worn green army blanket over the hot sand, my mother calls us over one by one to rub suntan lotion all over our backs. Then there are the interminable hours and hours, dull hot hours, of sitting or lying in the blazing sun. The breeze from the ocean is minimal comfort, only felt when lying absolutely still and listening to the waves. When the sun becomes too unbearable, there is the cold relief of the ocean — cold, salty, gritty relief, until my mother comes to the edge of the water and yells for me to come out, my lips are turning blue. I go back to the blanket. My sister sits apart from us on her own blanket. It's really a large white towel with a green stripe down the middle and HOLIDAY INN spelled out in green letters. Later, when it's time to go home, there is sand everywhere. I can't put on my socks or sneakers because of the sand biting into my skin. My father yells about the sand getting all over the car and the wet bathing suits ruining the car seats. My mother spreads towels out on the hot seats, checks us one last time for sunburn, and then we begin the long hot drive home. When we arrive home, the one with the most sunburn gets to take a shower first. All of the bathing suits are left to soak in soapy water in the sink. In the shower I scrub and scrub and even use soap but the sand, never visible to my eye, can't be washed away. And later yet, during the night, I wake from my dreams brushing imaginary sand out of the bed.

We don't have the blanket with us, or towels.

Besides, Asbury Park isn't like that. At least, not what I've heard. There are boardwalks and nightclubs. And the boardwalk has all sorts of rides and merry-go-rounds and games and ice cream stands. I don't remember having been here before.

We pass a sign welcoming us to Asbury Park. Looking around, I feel disappointed. This is not what I had expected of Asbury Park. It's nothing more than a town, really, with neat old houses and small front lawns of grass forever dying in the sandy dirt and salty air.

I turn anxiously, twisting on the seat, trying to see out of all the windows at the same time, disappointed with all I see.

My father is also looking out of the windows. He's stopped whistling and is looking carefully at the street signs as we drive slowly past. We turn off the main road on which we had been driving and continue straight for several blocks. My father slows down, sticks his head out of the car to see house numbers. Then he looks for a parking space along the curb. We find one, halfway down one of the blocks, and park.

He turns off the motor.

"Are we here yet?" I ask.

My father laughs.

Yes," he says. "We're here. We're always here."

He's out of the car and five or six steps away before I can unbuckle the seatbelt. I have to run to catch up to him, to keep up, to make sure I don't lose him in this unfamiliar town. He walks to a white three-story house at the corner.

It's a high, narrow house and rather odd looking. There is a wooden staircase on the outside leading to the porch and then on up to the second and third stories. These stairs feel flimsy under my feet as we climb up. I stop at the second story landing, one of my sneaker laces has come untied. I try not to look down as I tie the lace into more knots. I am afraid of these stairs, of the height.

"Come on," my father calls down to me from the third-story landing.

I have to hold my breath and not look down or anywhere except at the whitewashed walls of the house as I continue climbing up. The steps are worn smooth, some of them are loose. I would close my eyes except for fear of missing a step and falling all the way down to the ground.

Somehow I make it up.

My father is not waiting for me on the landing. He's gone into the house and has left the door open for me to follow. I can't quite see in there, the sunlight outside making it difficult to see anything inside. I hold onto the wooden railing and turn to look out, away from the house. What I see are the roofs of other houses stretching along for blocks and blocks and after the roofs I see some larger buildings, some with flags on them, and a Ferris wheel and the top rails of a roller coaster. And beyond that I can see the ocean; an enormous flat gray-green expanse with toy-like clouds hanging in the blue sky above it.

From inside the house my father calls out to me, "Hey Butch, what are you doing out there? Aren't you coming in?"

I go in.

The first thing I do is sneeze. This room stinks of perfume.

My father is sitting on a sofa drinking beer from a glass. He looks relaxed; one leg crossed over the other, his arm stretched out along the back of the sofa. He is alone on the sofa, we are alone in this room.

"Sit down," he says.

I look around for a place to sit. There are a few armchairs, mismatched colors, the white stuffing falling out of the cushions. There is a folding card table with some dirty glasses on top of it. On the floor is a stereo, with records scattered nearby, some of the records in their cardboard sleeves and others not. The floor is partially covered with a rug. Nowhere is a place that I want to sit.

A woman comes into the room.

A woman comes into the room from one of the other rooms. She is wearing a long green velour bathrobe. There are no buttons on the bathrobe and empty loops where there had once been a velour belt. She is haphazardly holding the bathrobe closed with her hand. Under it she is wearing shorts and a blouse that doesn't match. Her hair is wet and matted down but her face is almost fully made-up.

She smells of this perfume.

Everywhere is the smell of this perfume. It is inside the furniture, the walls.

It makes me sneeze again. I squeeze my nose between my fingers to keep myself from sneezing some more.

My father gets up from the sofa, but he doesn't go anywhere. He just stands there.

"This is Peg," he says. "She's an old friend of mine."

The woman, Peg, laughs and says, "I'm not that old."

I look closely at her, at her eyes and mouth and hands, to see if I can see how old she is. This light, and her make-up, make it impossible to guess. She's old enough, I'd say. She's an adult. And then it occurs to me that she might not have meant age.

"Can I get you something to drink?" she asks.

She giggles at that, raises one hand to cover her mouth as she giggles. "A soda, I mean."

I shake my head.

She says, "Just help yourself if you change your mind." She waves her arm toward another part of the apartment, where I suppose the kitchen is. Her bathrobe falls open. Both my father and I look. She pulls the bathrobe together. "You two boys will have to excuse me while I go make myself decent."

While she's gone, my father gets up from the sofa and bends down to the floor to put a record on the stereo. He gathers all of the albums together into one large stack. Once the record he has chosen is playing, he gets back up and goes to the kitchen. He returns with a can of beer for himself and a glass of soda for me.

A little while later Peg comes back into the room wearing a light green dress, stockings and high heels. She's carrying a black pocketbook. She stops at the doorway and looks at my father. My father looks over at me. I look down at my sneakers, at a spot on the floor three feet in front of me, then back at my father. He's already looking at Peg.

"That's nice," my father says. "That's real nice."

"Thank you," she says.

My father turns to me. "Hey, Butch, how's about a walk along the boardwalk. And that pinball I promised you?"

Peg says, "Butch? I thought you said his name was John."

"Butch. Everyone calls you Butch, right?" my father says. "Let's go out to the boardwalk and see those pinball games they have here."

Peg turns off the stereo. The three of us leave the apartment. We stand on the landing while Peg locks the three locks on the door. Then we go back down the nearly collapsing wooden steps.

My father goes down fast. Peg is slower, grabbing onto the railing so she doesn't tip over on her high heels. I follow behind, two steps, three steps, four, slowly making my way down. They are waiting for me on the sidewalk when I reach the front porch. I hurry, afraid that they might leave without me.

When I catch up to them, my father says, "He wants to be a mountain climber, except he's afraid of heights."

Peg puts her hand on my shoulder. "He's adorable," she says. When she takes her hand away, I can smell her perfume on my shirt.

We walk along in the direction of the ocean. The sidewalk is narrow. The smells of salt and fish get stronger with each step we take. There are few other people walking along the sidewalk, mostly old men and women. Certainly no one we pass looks like they would spend their time sitting on the beach had it been twenty degrees warmer. As we pass these people, we huddle on our side of the sidewalk and they on theirs.

It is not long before I can see the end of the street and the steps leading up to the boardwalk.

The buildings that had seemed so far away when I was standing on Peg's landing are now so close. I can see that most of them are amusement halls, with big indoor merry-go-rounds and Skee Ball games. There are cotton candy stands, ice cream stands, and salt water taffy shops everywhere.

On the boardwalk itself are even more shops and amusement halls. There are wheel of fortune games where it is possible to win cartons of cigarettes (18 or older only) and coin toss games and more ice cream stands and salt water taffy shops. Everything looks like it belongs in a carnival.

There aren't many people around and not all of the stands are open. This place has a half-deserted air about it. It looks like an empty, abandoned carnival. And the fading, peeling paint of the once jolly decorations on the buildings and stands make everything seem even more abandoned and decaying.

My father and Peg walk along the boardwalk in front of me.

Peg is holding onto my father's arm. Every so often one of her high heels catches or slips and my father puts his arm around her waist to hold her up. After this happens a couple of times, he keeps his arm around her waist.

We stop in front of one of the amusement halls. Inside are pinball games and the latest electronic and video games. There is a shooting gallery along one wall and Skee Ball games in the back.

"How's this place look to you, Butch?" my father says.

I don't say anything. He reaches into his pocket and pulls out some money. Not coins, but bills. He stuffs them into my pants pocket, then pulls up my pants so they don't sag below my waist.

Peg watches as he does this.

He says, "Peg and I are going for a walk. Don't worry about us, we'll be back for you. There's plenty of money there to keep you occupied for a couple of hours — even enough for a hot dog if you get hungry."

I don't know what to say. Certainly I am not hungry.

"You'll be okay," he says. "Just don't leave here or we won't be able to find you when we come back. Okay?"

I nod.

They begin walking away. Peg turns around, comes back. She leans down and hugs me, surrounding me with perfume. She kisses me on the mouth.

"You're a dear," she says. Then, walking carefully on her high heels, she catches up with my father. Together they walk along the boardwalk back in the direction we just came from.

Two and a half hours pass by and I am still here. I may not know left from right, but I have learned how to tell time. I have also learned that two and a half hours does not always equal two and a half hours. Sometimes it is forever.

I still have plenty of money to play pinball. I have eaten two hot dogs.

Every fifteen minutes, according to the large clock in here, I go back out to the boardwalk and look for my father and Peg. I walk in the direction that they went, but not too far. I am afraid that they will be coming back the other way and I'll miss them, so I hurry back to the amusement hall.

The man who gives out the change has been keeping an eye on me. Whenever I return from the boardwalk, he asks, "Find them yet?" When I shake my head no, he says, "Don't worry, they'll be back soon."

He's given me some free games on the pinball machines. And he even let me play the water shoot for nothing. I had been watching people at the water shoot for some time before I got to play it. What it is is you aim a water gun at the mouth of a wooden clown's head, and the water makes a balloon on top of the clown blow up. The better your aim, the faster the balloon blows up. Whoever's balloon pops first, wins.

I won twice.

Even so, the time passes slowly.

I am about to walk down the boardwalk to the hot dog stand for my third, when I hear my father yelling to me.

"Hey Butch!" he yells "Wait up."

He's half walking and half running along the boardwalk. He's alone. He's waving to me and smiling and I wave back. I can't help but smile. I run to him and he catches me in a great big hug.

"I'm back," he says. His breath smells of beer and he smells of her. "I told you I'd be back. Did you have a good time playing pinball?"

I tell him that I did. I tell him about eating two hot dogs.

"Two!" he says. "How about if I buy you an ice cream to top it off?"

We walk to the nearest ice cream stand and he orders two large soft ice cream cones with sprinkles on top. Vanilla ice cream.

I watch my father while he pays for the ice cream. I am looking for a clue, something that will tell me what has changed. Something has changed.

I look around to see if Peg might be anywhere.

Between licks of my ice cream, I ask where she is.

"Peg? She wasn't feeling well, she had to go home. But she really liked you. She said you were 'a good little soldier.' That just what she said, 'a good little soldier.' "

We walk along the boardwalk toward the street where Peg lives and the car is parked. My father messes up my hair with his hand.

"Don't tell your mother about this," he says. He winks at me. "We'll both get into trouble for it."

I say I won't say anything.

"Promise?"

I promise.

"Cross your heart and hope to die?"

I hold up my hand. "Promise," I say. I would say anything he told me to say. He's my father.

A Day in the Life of Vincent Lucciola

by J. F. Battaglia

On the boardwalk at Brighton Avenue beach, the weedy dunes updrawn like knees behind him, Vincent felt the off-shore breeze ruffle his shirt, tapping the fabric against his nipples. The ocean beckoned him, waves belligerent and bright, beyond the waves an orange buoy that signaled a diver's presence leeward of a crewless skiff, the *Caterina*. He hurried to the high-tide line, left his sandals and plum-colored beach towel and shirt and cut-offs in a little mound of jetsam on the sand, strode into the surf and dove over a wave, plunged through the next, swam over the next then out into deepening water toward the diver's buoy where he paused, arms sway-paddling, felt himself rise on a swell and saw following swells, each mirroring a sunny gash.

He dove, glimpsed a sea trout gliding through the fluid jade, then a chevron of mullet and following these a greenish form that turned like a shark closing in, flippered and goggle-eyed, air-tanked, bubbles upfloating as if her necklace of pearls had parted. They surfaced. He faced the diver, her smile taupe-lipped, cheeks puffy, her swimsuit wonderfully out of fashion with embossed flowers like welts in the white latex.

"So sorry," she burbled, water pooling on her tongue. "Thought you to be someone I know, but you're too *old*."

He gave up breath to laughter as she cleared her air regulator and sank, left him squinting sunny blossoms, muted purples, yellowish white. He dove, saw the diver's legs scissoring as she swam deep, speargun ready, heels aglow in orange flippers, strings of pearls upwavering. He surfaced and swam farther out, each stroke long and leisurely, confident that he could swim for miles. Farther and farther. He swooped underwater like a seal, flexing, hair pulsing at his temples, the bubbly effusion from his nostrils tickling his lips.

It would stay with him all afternoon, this joy of being unsinkable, for clock-time unwound in the ocean, and such sane swimming slowed all the wheels. No numbers out there, where bright water bathed him as if never before, where like a loom's shuttle the solitary swimmer interweaves sea and sky. Now beneath maple trees he stood, beach towel wedged under his arm, salt crystals tingling the backs of his legs as he raised a hand to his ear to tug at the lobe, felt hot water pop and dribble down his palm. Cool blades of grass tickled his ankles. From a coupling between two lengths of garden hose arced a thread-thin jet, within this arc a diminutive rainbow.

Ann stood immersed in foliage, cordiform leaves rocking on their stems, her vinery of nasturtium and begonia deeply shadowed by the maples. She wore office clothes, was home for lunch and had not expected his return, yet she spoke without looking up.

"I sold our soybean futures," she told him, holding out a leaf like a voucher. "How shall we use the earnings?"

He shrugged. "Six-month CD."

"Another one. No mortgage." She turned toward him.

"Didn't we decide that?" he said, and discerning her cash-gray skirt among the greens, the incurvation of her waist aglow within the smudgy whiteness of her blouse, "You *look* like money."

She smiled. "You're sort of cute yourself. Suppose I call out for the afternoon and we go up to the beach." A flicker of sunlight struck the crescents on the fingers of her left hand, three rings: the gold-cable wedding band plus the chromium loops of the scissors.

"I've been," he said, wriggling his toes to loosen clots of sand.

Ann pruned with decisive motions, tug of the leaf stem away from the stalk of the plant, scissors-snip, thumb and forefinger parting to release the leaf, watching it settle to her feet. There in a basket lay some zinnia cuttings, feeble blooms for the Delft vase on the kitchen table, this being her garden's mid-summer yield, promissory buds among a plethora of leaves.

"Too much shade," said Vincent. "I told you that."

She examined a sparse begonia vine, thumb to her lips, fingers touching her left cheek above which, in a petal of sunlight, the temporal artery pulsed.

He said, "Stopped off to shower, then I'm going by the market. Then Cate's."

"I should call her!" Ann remembered. "She needs to diversify her portfolio."

"After that I'm meeting Tom. Like you agreed this morning. Today is *my* day."

The greenish blades of the scissors parted to a thumb-thick notch.

"Yours alone," she said.

He crossed the patio and entered the apartment, slid shut the door and leaned, felt the cool glass against his brow. His towel unscrolled, grains of sand spattering the floor as the odor of brine came up to him like a surfacing swimmer.

✲

Beneath the Plymouth's tires clam shell crackled, layer upon layer of shell. He parked behind the market by the rusting dredge and the empty slip, walked around to the front door. The feel of its handle, a worn brass bow-cleat hot from the sun, kindled his puerile grin as he stepped inside where, centered in a wedge of light on the floor beneath the window, lay the foreshortened shadows of letters:

F. Esposito

FISH

"Vinny!"

Frank stepped out from behind the cold-case, the top of his apron banding his chest like a collar slipped down. From his shirt pocket protruded knife-sharpened pencils. Rough hands made a sandwich of Vincent's hand.

"How's the fish business, Frank?"

"It stinks."

They chuckled at the old joke.

"Vinny, you on vacation?"

"I am today. Went for a swim. The *Caterina* was offshore, no one else aboard, guess-who below."

Frank nodded as if he had known this and was not surprised, for with some people, said his nod, there are few surprises.

"Your other half, Vinny, she still going to business? Still nursing widows' fortunes?"

Vincent pictured Ann at her desk, steadfast and assured, on her computer screen a green grid of data, then him at his desk, sheets of paper swooping like gulls because he'd flung up a file of memoranda.

"We're doing good, Frank. Almost enough in the bank for the new boat."

He walked back and entered the walk-in, glad to feel refrigerated air dampen the heat in his lungs. He flattened his hands on a canvas-covered block of ice until his fingers began to numb. As always, the chalk was hanging on its string, the ice pick stuck into the frame of the blackboard. Notes printed on the board showed a pair of three-pound lobsters in the tank, some two-and-a-halfs, plenty of chicks. The wood slats of a crate of littlenecks sagged like weathered bulwarks. He lifted a tub of oysters, stepped out of the walk-in and shut the heavy door, felt the iron handle at his hip, the thunk of the bolt into its keeper.

Fist-size chunks of ice rattled and clicked over the oysters as he carried them to the cutting table. Frank smiled approvingly.

"Go on, shuck a few."

Vincent picked up an oyster and cradled it in his hand, the outer edge of the shell snug to the heel of his palm as he wedged the blade of the shucking knife into the hinge of the shell, pressed and twisted. Cold liquid trickled through the crotches of his fingers, the blade flashing down and back to lay the oyster open. Its puddled body squirmed and pursed. He opened another. In one motion both men raised half-shells to their lips and sucked, the sea swelling in their throats.

"Protoplasm," Vincent said.

"Dead lover's tongue."

The emptied shells rocked on the table like little cradles, blue and white inside, soft gray, purple. Vincent opened two more oysters, his voice one with Frank's voice:

"*Salute.*"

They swallowed. Vincent looked around.

Above the cash register, among several other postcards tacked to the wall, was a different one. He removed it, ignored the familiar script but read the message printed in the upper left-hand corner of the card:

> Majestic palm trees overlook the Gulf of Mexico.
>
> In the foreground, luxuriant five-petaled blossoms
>
> of a native Royal Poinciana (red) and the beautiful
>
> Hibiscus (orange).

He returned the card to its place on the wall and reseated the tack, exactly.

"Your parents," Frank said, "are in paradise. They want for nothing."

"What they want is a grandkid to take to Disney World."

"So?"

Vincent faced him.

"Look at me, Frank."

"The sandals?"

"Higher."

"The shorts? So you're the beach bum today."

"My shirt. See, Frank, how white? All my shirts are. Fucking corporation-white."

"So?"

"So this shirt's a gift from her, and a striped tie, nice conservative number. Christmas a watch."

Frank folded his sleeves to the biceps and crossed his arms. Above one wrist glowed a tattoo-like scar in the shape of a *C*, the color of old metal, some wayward hook having left its hue.

"So yours is a desk job, Vinny. Regular income you have, all seasons of the year. Two salaries."

"Two sets of books!"

Vincent leaned on the table, hands flat, knuckles little knees, his head low as if he had discerned deep some long-lost shape rising, being brought anew into the air and the light.

"You were almost a godparent, Frank. Few years back. We scuttled it. Weren't ready then. Now...."

He swallowed sand.

Frank turned away, brown hands coming round to tighten and re-knot the apron strings, then he lifted the wide lid of the freezer box. Elbow-deep into the box, his back and buttocks rounded to the work, fog roiling down his thighs as he pushed frozen things back and forth inside, grunted with final effort, straightened, lowered the lid and turned.

"Guess you'll go by your grandma's," he said, blotting his face with the hem of his apron.

"Yeah. It's my birthday."

Frank placed a foot on the metal crate, forearm resting on his knee as he turned one hand within the other. "I know that, Vinny." He opened his hands, palms x-ed with scars. "Same day I got these. Thirty years and a whole hell of a lot of fish from the sea ago."

Vincent shucked more oysters and set them in a row along the edge of the table. Frank grinned.

"When your grandma opened the restaurant, when this place was first mine. Ten years old you were, just starting to tug at the front of your pants and already you could shuck as good as anyone. Maybe not as fast but as good." With three fingers he plucked oyster meat from its shell and flicked the gray flesh into his mouth, chewed once and swallowed.

Vincent sauced his oyster with Tabasco. "Did you know Cate's husband? My grandfather?"

Frank turned a chunk of ice in his hands to clean them. The meltage dribbled from his wrists.

"Nobody did, Vinny. People knew your grandma as herself and her son, your dad." He dropped the ice into the oyster tub and dried his hands on his apron. "Sometimes in rough weather, while we was mending net, there'd be a little wine and she'd talk some. You've heard the story, how she left him in California and got a new start here in Jersey right after the war. This part of town was still a fishing village then, not like Fulton Market where she found me shoveling ice. 'Come down to the shore,' she said. 'I'll feed you. Maybe I'll pay you.' Hah! Something, your grandma. First a share in a scallop boat and the next you know she owns three trawlers, then this place, then the restaurant. Even them Italian olives — 'Frank's Famous' — her idea. Now I have the store and a thousand problems while she dives all by herself and gardens. Not what I bargained for. Damned business. Aching bones, line-burns, dreams crashing into foam."

He pointed to the last oyster.

"Mangi."

Vincent complied, then hoisted the tub and carried it into the walk-in. His breath made smoke. The perspiration on his chest flashed cold, so he replaced the tub hurriedly and turned to leave but found the door shut, had to work the iron plunger to spare himself the chagrin of twenty-some years before when they'd found their little Vinny blue-lipped and waiting for release, unable to open the heavy door from inside, unwilling to knock or call for help. Wiser now, here now, washing his hands to conceal his shuddering, hot water running through his fingers like dreams flushed out the gunnels, he spoke over his shoulder.

"My grandfather, I never knew about him, but you did." Water tickled his wrists. "He and I are alike, I think."

Frank kicked aside the crate, its metal edges rasping on the concrete floor.

"Your nonno was a fool, Vinny. Got up too many skirts and loved a bet."

Vincent gathered the oyster shells, tossed them rattling into the bone box, then held still, riding his anchor. Frank's bottom lip protruded.

"Lost his livelihood that way. She said once how he bet heavy on a race from Point Reyes to Half Moon Bay." Frank made angles with his hands. "He was on the weather side to keep the wind, which was the smart place to be, and he figured to tack the leeward boat into his shadow but misread the sky. The wind shifted a couple of points and put him under a corner of the other man's trawl. See?"

One scarred palm slid past the other.

"The leeward boat pulled up and won it clean. He lost."

Vincent wiped his hands on his shirt, streaks like gray fingers bleeding into the white cloth. He took a false step, sandal wrenching wrong, stumbled into his question — *How much did Nonno loo...*

Frank stood with hands on hips, feet apart.

"What did your grandfather lose? His best boat. Your father. Your grandmother."

From outside came the crackle of tires on shell, then the slam of a car door: afternoon customers, people coming to purchase seafood for their dinners. They would ask Frank questions about the season, about the luck of the fleet, and they would look through the slanted glass of the cold-case to see what was there, in one tray fillets of fluke, in another gutted whiting. On a bed of parsley lay two rows of soft-shell crabs, beside them three tubs of headless shrimp, next whole, hard-eyed bass thicker than a man's arm, each with a pink thread bottoming its belly.

He tasted oil, salt. Why on his tongue this imagined flavor, this biblical food? Frank clapped his hands hard as a wave broadsiding the jetty, snapped open a pink carton, filled it with olives and sacked it, passed it over the cold-case.

"Your favorite, Vinny. Go on, take! A little something for your birthday."

The market door opened. Vincent stepped aside. A customer approached the counter looking like a scarecrow out of its cornfield, asking Frank if this were the right time of year for cod.

"Cod and love," Frank said, "always are in season."

The sack of olives crinkled in Vincent's hands. Frank spoke aside to him, winking the near eye as if Vincent had snitched an olive to munch while they worked through the afternoon, as if he were fifteen again and this were just another Saturday in the fish business.

"Tell your grandma," Frank said, "I got in some nice birds, good weights." He nodded toward the ocean. "Like we used to catch right out there."

Vincent hurried to his car. Shifting into reverse, feeling the steering wheel of the Plymouth resist his hands, hearing the *tick-ick* of shell beneath the tires, he glimpsed snug in her slip the *Caterina*.

✪

He pressed the button below his surname, heard the channel buoy-bell on a foggy night. From within the shadow of his palm, Vincent peered through the screen door.

"Nonna?"

He walked the slates to the sunny side of the bungalow, stepped leeward of the beached dory spilling purples — heliotrope and sweet alyssum, petunias and wishbone — stood among the gladiolus to look in the open parlor window. On the sofa lay a wedge of sunlight, in it the shadow of his head and shoulders. She would be out back then, the pockets of her sun-bleached denim smock bulging with whatnot, damp crescents at the neck and armpits, plaits of white hair to her shoulders and, yes, there she was, stepping between a row of young tomato plants toward the neighbor's fence.

This fence! The loop-wire had become interlaced with vines, a chest-high wall of roses, every pink whorl aglow like some marvelous confection that he must approach slowly, as if air had the consistency of cake batter and his legs were wood spoons stroking through it. Then his hand was in Cate's hands, hands that hauled and mended net, fingers able to knot cord that became whales or butterflies or the heads of babies. He pictured Cate with Frank at dock's edge, him too, their crab lines taut, later the three of them laughing and joking astride the bench at her table of blue dishes, silver nutcrackers to crack the claws, slender forks to dig out the juicy meat, heels of bread to get the salty broth.

He opened the sack and the carton within.

"'Frank's Famous.' Got in some nice birds, he said to tell you. Good weights."

She took two olives, black and wrinkled. He took one, pressed it with his tongue against the roof of his mouth for the flavor of the oil, the basil. Chewing slowly, they pared the olives down with their incisors, turned like dance partners to spit out the pits. She pointed to an old half-bushel basket which he obediently took up as she stooped and lifted a pair of hedge shears then stepped toward the rose fence, legs apart for balance, feet spilling from the split insteps of dusty felt slippers. He considered the basket he was holding, unsure what she wanted him to do with it as her fingers tightened around the wood handles of the shears. Sunlight glinted along the blades.

"Ann tells me never mind futures." The second olive pit arced from her lips. "Diversify, she said. What do you think?"

He shrugged. "Ann's usually right about those things."

Cate jammed her shears into the rose-fence. As the blades clanked, a dozen roses somersaulted brightly. Again the blades clanked. Roses leaped and tumbled, the ground began to pinken, so he filled the basket and carried the roses to his car and dumped them into the trunk, not knowing why, not yet, then huffed back past the flower-boat, shirt damp all over, and knelt to refill the basket. Rose thorns glinted like sparks at his wrists.

The shears quit cutting, the lapped blades descending as her arms straightened, wrist bones nodulose. Now, he knew, would come a story, liberated as usual by some burst of common energy — out-hauling net, the wedding, his parents' departure to Florida. Then the story would come. He sat crosslegged like a boy with a pup. Her eyes, her mouth edged with glistening lines, the flesh at her throat loose as a chicken's wattles, she told him how it happened.

"Frankie caught a dud torpedo in his trawl. Shark, he figured, and hauled it in. Might have blasted him back to Brooklyn, though Frankie always was lucky. Till he got ambitious.

"That afternoon, I was on the market dock squaring away. All Frankie could do was cuss his luck and walk in circles squeezing chunks of ice. Your father rings and he says, 'What time is it, Ma?' Eight-oh-five, I say. He says, 'We'll call him Vincent.' Never thought to use your grandfather's name again. Then I figured what the hell, a baby is a baby no matter how it's called. Or when it comes."

She looked toward her kitchen as if hearing laughter.

"Frankie and me celebrated pretty good that night, him holding his wine glass with two bandaged paws. From hauling the torpedo. Even with the winch, he got line burns, deep ones. Couple of weeks and they scarred, went from purple to gray, gray as old nickels. Months later it still felt like leather straps when he touched me."

She plucked at the shoulders of her smock, shook herself free inside, and hoisted the shears.

"Your father stopped by about midnight. We all got drunk. Baby boy and a dud torpedo. U-boat, we figured. Nazi."

The shears cut vines, yanking out knotted rose stems as though they were the innards of fish, lengths of them snagging in her smock and dangling from their thorns like hooks on wire leaders. Gaping holes had opened in the fence of roses, and through these openings passed sunlight for the young tomato plants, each clutching a plentitude of bright green gibbous moons.

"Now we'll have sauce," she said. Her elbow poked into his chest; he stumbled back. "You can't make sauce from flowers, *capisci*? Only fruit. Here." She kicked at a heap of roses. "Here." They splashed pink up his legs. "Here!"

He rushed to his car with another basketful.

✿

Late afternoon, tide in, most of the forward slips vacant, the wharf of the Belmar Marine Basin had become a row of empty chairs, all the party and charter boats out, fishing offshore. Vincent tossed a rose. Gulls swooped low to eye these pinks on the river. *Roses Roses*, cried the gulls.

He sat legs adangle and looked between his feet into the water. A school of killifish swimming as one edged out from the shadowy dock, each killie a day in the life of the school. Somewhere below a snapper with a mouth the size of a human's took a killie and the school swerved up, the swiftest bursting from the water then plashing back like pebbles cast by a child.

He tossed a rose. Several roses blossomed astern of Tom's boat, a Leuhrs. Good blueing boat. Come August, a mile or two out, the blues would be ferocious and the trolling would be excellent while the weather stayed cool. Blues run deeper in the heat.

Vincent gazed across the river to Shark Island, once natural refuge and habitat, these days sparsely ringed with eelgrass. Awful change. Under the baby-blue sky stood thunder-cloud gray buildings, condos stacked like lobster pots, affluent couples and privileged singles trapped in their boxy investments, unable to get free, unwilling to see that they had no business on the island but to ruin it. Too many people at the shore was the trouble. Too much money at the shore.

Beyond the highway bridge, a north-bound Shoreline commuter slowed for the station, silver cars glinting sunlight. Tomorrow morning he'd be aboard. He'd be city-bound. Desk-bound.

Thunk-unk of footsteps along the wharf, then Tom stepped down, ducked into the cabin of the Leuhrs, brought out a bottle of Canadian Club, opened it, handed over.

"Happy thirtieth, Vince. Half your life is gone."

In the mirrored lenses of Tom's sunglasses Shark River tilted, then Vincent's face swelled as Tom took the bottle, drank, handed over, and his words came as if along the water.

"Tonight we'll be gaming men, Vince, aboard one granddaddy of a Skipjack. Ocean-going antique. Wide-bottomed beauty. She'll lie offshore and the games'll go on till dawn. Complimentary drinks served by mermaids who want to lose their tails. Wait and see."

Vincent reached into the basket, uplifted two roses, one as pink as the other, tossed.

"I'm a statistician," he said. "I know the odds. Why gamble?"

"To beat them is why," said Tom, his thumb riding up the bridge of his nose, boosting the sunglasses to his brow. "Vince, Vince — our families are here three generations. I work the water for my living while you make yours calculating liabilities, only you've had too much of that." He knelt, tapped Vincent's thigh. "What you need is a good dose of open sea."

Aslant through the greenish water swam a crab, as if suspended by its pincers on a string. The bottle tipped high, taste of Canadian grain afire.

"True," he answered.

Tom revived their favorite plan.

"We'll shove off after hurricane season, follow the sun, lay over in the Keys. Fish for a living. All those island coves! It's the long reach for us, Vince, if ye be willin'."

Vincent swigged, nodded. "I be willin', matey!" Whiskey tickled his chin. He wiped away the whiskey with a rose and tossed it. "Guess who I met today below the *Caterina*. Spearing mullet."

"That's Cate for you," Tom said. "Her own crew."

"Own crew, yeah. Thing is, she confers wi' me stockbroker."

They drank, looked downriver. Tom stood, saw the long outgoing line of roses. He nodded toward the nearly empty basket.

"How many of those things have you chucked?"

Vincent grinned.

"I calkilate one per con-ju-gal co-i-tus." He counted his fingers and stood up and kicked his sandals into the Leuhrs and counted his toes. "According to Masters and Johnson, 'bout three years' worth of roses out to sea. Plus the first one, the rose that sank."

Tom guided him onto the transom.

"Eat much today, Vince?"

"Three oysters and an olive. Where we go?"

The engines rumbled. Tom cleared the lines and edged the Leuhrs toward other boats grouped in the channel. Above them Route 35 traffic stood waiting. They rode the ebb till the bridge went up, then quickly passed through and went past the train trestle, its disconnected rails aimed skyward, at the waterline greasy pilings long deep in the mud. The old dock slid by, then the fish market, Rudy's garage, the Main Street bridge with its trapdoor flung up.

Aft, facing west, Vincent squinted into the descending sun, twin wakes astern like legs beneath a yellow sheet. Along the Belmar side receded terraced lawns with white benches and ornamental shrubbery, in the wide windows of the fine houses colorful, comfortable rooms. Paralleling First Avenue to A Street they passed under the Ocean Avenue bridge, its palm-like spans cupping dusk. Then came the jetty, which could have been the platform of the railroad station, people waiting on it, one a child waving. Vincent waved back.

They cleared the jetty, entered the ocean as if launched into space, a sidelong yawing moment then the stern descending as the Leuhrs mounted a roller to its crest, swayed and plunged. Vincent crept forward along the deck, his knees thumping hard, spine rubbery. He could see far, pale green light all across the water dotted pink and the moon rising, a big birthday cake of a moon heaving up from the sea.

Tom called from the flying bridge.

"Look leeward, mate! There's our game-ship headed out to ole Rum Row!"

Leaning into spray, Vincent beheld the wonderful vessel, Chesapeake oysterman, the ship's boom-sail and aft-raked mainsail swollen and ruddy, pressing her forward, broad hull cradled in lavender foam, roses like sparks on the water.

Two woman waved from the afterdeck, one with her sweater and one with her bra, between them a full-bearded man.

Vincent crouched on the bow, reached moonward.

"It's my gambling Grandpa Vincenzo!"

The Leuhrs nosed up, veered off into the chop, swayed, fell, again, bow high then down again as Vincent fouled himself, spat into the wind this bitter effusion of what all day he'd thought and what little he'd eaten. He dove overboard. Plunged deep. Rose.

The Leuhrs began to circle. He scissored his legs. Tom called down to him, voice starlike, head small among the early constellations.

"Ahoy lubber — Come aboard! Fortune awaits us!"

"I'll swim in!"

"The current's against you!"

Tom was wrong, Vincent thought. The ocean was supportive, warm, the water parting to help him forward, his every stroke sure and decisive. He went under, scissored, bubbles streaming from his nostrils and tickling his lips. He surfaced, saw far ahead beneath haze the beach like a purple blanket ready to receive him. As he swam, the light of the moon silvered his hands.

The Northern Shore

by Joe Paduano

Top and left: Allenhurst Beach
Bottom: Spring Lake Beach

Top: Ocean Grove
Bottom: Sandy Hook

Top: Bradley Beach
Bottom: Asbury Park

45

Ringolevio

by Dulcie Leimbach

W̲e stayed for two months with Great-Aunt Sophie, in her white stucco house in Spring Lake, when I was eight and my sister Mary was ten.

Aunt Sophie and her house were mammoth; they loomed above us as we made our way up the front steps, under the blue-and-white striped awning, to the verandah. Our Aunt Stella, our mother's sister, had just dropped us off. We were going to live with Great-Aunt Sophie for as long as we could.

Actually, she wasn't that large. The faded photographs, circa 1950 and earlier, are witness to that. She had merely blossomed from the same Bavarian stock our mother's mother, and to some extent our mother, had grown from: generous, roaming bosoms and hips, wide, smooth faces, and arms and legs as thick as the columns on Sophie's porch. She wore her hair the same way our grandmother had worn hers: bouffant-style, with long silver-colored bobby pins placed here and there.

"It's Teresa's girls, of all people to arrive at my front door," she said as we reached the top step. I hid behind Mary, who was a good three inches taller than me. Sophie had on a blue-flowered sleeveless dress. Just looking at her made me shiver.

"You've never met your Great-Aunt Sophie, now have you? She's a legend —

you ask around," she said, curling her hair behind her ears. When she moved her arms the fat jiggled like tiny bracelets.

"We met at our daddy's funeral a year ago," Mary informed her. "You had lunch at my grandfather's that day. I know who you are, you're my mother's aunt, not our aunt, and that's why we have to call you Great."

"Jah, that's one reason. I'm the oldest of the five Lutz girls, so everyone always puts me on a pedestal. Not that I mind. I'm eccentric, you know, living here alone in a big house on the ocean year round. But we must go inside now, before the little one turns blue."

We followed as she walked to the wide screen door and flung it open. It was a clear Saturday afternoon in January; across the street from Sophie's was the Atlantic — only a wide boardwalk and a low sand dune separated Shoreline Drive from her front lawn.

"She doesn't look like us," Sophie said, gazing at me. I kept my head steady to the ground, but she grabbed my chin and studied me, her heavy brown eyes like Ma's, luminous and sad. "Mein Gott," she said, shaking her head. "Not a drop of Lutz blood in that face." She dropped my chin and shepherded us past the glassed-in foyer and into the hallway. Yellow stains, like urine, dotted the walls. I thought the ocean had mysteriously left them there.

"I never use this part of the house past Labor Day," she said, moving quickly, swishing past the french doors enclosing the living and dining rooms, all the mahogany furniture and Oriental rugs within.

She swung open the pantry door, as if she were a saloonkeeper. "I'm fond of cooking and eating — an understatement. Did your mother tell you two that, did she tell you anything about your Great-Aunt Sophie?" She looked directly into Mary's face, as if counting her pores.

Mary didn't respond — my cue to talk.

"My mother said you were huge," I managed. I never liked doing the talking for Mary and me. "She said you never had any children." I had never made it to my father's funeral. Until now, Sophie had been unknown to me.

"Yes, I am huge, but that's what happens to all Lutzes after thirty," she said, not pronouncing the *h* in huge. "Come, I'll try to be warm and loving, like I should. God knows it's been a decade since a child stepped into my house. Your mother, many decades ago. She was just as scared." She moved across the kitchen, which was roomy and clean and a faded yellow, with high ceilings and tall windows, and washed with clear winter light. We sat at the broad table, where we drank tea for the first time, and sampled *pfeffernesse*. I tried to be careful with the crumbs.

"You girls will love the ocean. We Lutzes have always lived a step from some body of water, a lake, the salt water. It's as if we were born in it. Ha! We are, you know, we all are!"

A smile drifted into her eyes, but she couldn't look at us. "Your other half, the Irish of your father, is what you've got to look out for. What a bold temper he had. That's what gave him the stroke. Ach, but why do I bring that up with you two?" She poured more tea into our pink-and-gold teacups. "I never go out of the house past September. But you two must, you must use the boardwalk out front. It's much too windy for your Great-Aunt Sophie's body."

We were quiet, undoubtedly thinking of the wind, how it could knock us down, gather us up and toss us into the ocean. Except for the lulling of the grandfather clock above the table, the only sounds were of us blowing on our scalding tea.

❂

Being at the ocean was something Mary and I were used to. After Daddy died, Ma sold the house, packed our suitcases and us into the Anglia, and drove from hotel to hotel along the East Coast. We spent the longest time in towns on the Jersey shore, where Ma had spent her summers as a child.

For those three months, Ma had seemed fine, singing to us every night, talking in the kitchen to Mrs. McCarthy, a family friend we stayed with for two weeks. But one day she refused to get out of bed. When she turned to us, she looked through us as if we were shadows. They took her to the hospital, and we were driven to the only relative who would have us: Great-Aunt Sophie.

❂

"Do you think Sophie's going to die soon?" Mary said, nudging me as we lay in our queen-size bed a week later. It was musty and damp in our room and old, like Sophie. "Aunt Sophie's probably not going to live too long, you know."

It was true that everyone we knew was, or had been, sick or dead.

"Maybe she will, you can pray to stop it," I said. When Mary got nervous, I got nervous. I wished she wouldn't ask questions, because then I'd ask questions, like, What was going to happen to us? "If she dies, then Mom will come and get us. She'll leave the hospital."

"No, Louise, she's never leaving the hospital. She's going to die, like Daddy. We're stuck here."

Outside, the waves, like the grandfather clock, beat in and out. I liked the sound, it helped me sleep. We had been given this room together, at the far end of the long hallway on the second floor, in front. More bedrooms were on the third floor, and at least three were in between our room and Sophie's, in the back. The ocean, Sophie had explained, sent gusts through the front of the house, but she put us there anyway. There were windows on two sides of our room, and the wallpaper was yellowed, too. Despite the drafts I felt safe, if not comforted, especially when the early light bled in from the white ocean in the morning, when my black thoughts disappeared. Mary hated the room, she slept with the covers over her head. I worried she might suffocate and pulled them down off her when she was asleep.

The bed was mahogany, covered in a pink chenille spread with pompoms we plucked absentmindedly — we stored them in our underwear drawer, afraid Sophie would find them. On the large, claw-footed dresser was a lace runner, and a silver hairbrush, comb, and mirror set that badly needed polishing. The initials SLL were engraved on them: Sophie Louise Lutz, her name for most of her life, until she married Rudy Knott, who died ten years into their late marriage. Even the mirror above the dresser was cloudy, and the two months we lived on Shoreline Drive I stared into the mirror, trying to see why I didn't resemble a Lutz.

Sophie was always in the kitchen, sipping tea, kneading dough, stirring batter, chopping meat and vegetables, whipping meringue. This Saturday morning, a few weeks into our stay, she was making streudel, like every Saturday. She'd fill it with pecans and apples for our regular Sunday brunch.

"Your mother is not better," she said brusquely, as if she had merely asked Mary to hurry and break her an egg. "Shock treatment — they're hoping it will bring her about. Just like your grandmother, dying of a swollen, saddened heart. Mein Gott, why does He make us suffer so?"

I looked over at Mary, who was stirring oatmeal on the cast-iron stove. The spoon turned methodically, her body frozen. Was this good news or bad?

"Ach, you must know, I must tell you: you girls will suffer from this, scars will appear," Sophie said, wiping her hands now in a damp dish towel, picking pastry bits out of her nails. "Come, come, mein Louise," she said, extending her rubbery naked arm toward me. She rarely hugged, I had to give in.

"Ah, the Lutzes, what a sorrowful lot. When Rudy died, I thought I could never ever cook again. Nothing helped. But eventually all that happened was that I stopped going out of the house in the winter."

She squinted at me, as if she were trying to read my future in my brows. "We Lutzes have far too much Bavarian melancholia floating in our veins. Ach, perhaps it's a godsend to be half Irish." She swept her arms about my chest, and I caved in, as if my stomach had moved to my back. I held my breath, but had to exhale soon, and when I did, I melted into the wormy folds of Sophie, the way the butter melted through the layers of the streudel dough. Like the ocean waves, her bosoms rose, her breathing stopped, then broke.

I tried to see what Mary thought, but she turned away when I caught her eye.

✪

"I can't stand the wind," Mary said, trying to retie her scarf for the third time. It kept hitting her in the face. After breakfast on Saturdays, we'd go out and search the silent streets, looking for life, but never finding any. The houses were boarded up, no children abounded.

We strolled along the boardwalk, which bore life: bicyclists, people walking dogs. They were from other towns, having come to Spring Lake to fill their sights of the ocean.

"I can't stand any more streudel," Mary went on. She complained when she was worried. "Why can't she at least put cheese in it, like you're supposed to."

"Ask her, Mary, but she'll get her feelings hurt. I like it, but I know what you mean." I was beginning to like Sophie, who could feel as warm as clothes just out of the dryer. At the same time, Mary was beginning to bother me more than ever.

The waves thundered in translucent green, they danced out gold and silver, collecting the sand and shells along the way. Farther out, the sky matched the blue-gray of the ocean, and I thought Sophie might like to see this, if only the wind didn't bother her so.

"What does it mean, shock treatment?" I suddenly blurted. I hadn't wanted to ask Mary, but there it was.

"They put needles in her arms and legs, to make them move. She's paralyzed."

We both looked over at the beach again, as if this conversation required it. "Hey, Louise, look at that dog!" Mary said, pointing to a Labrador who was chasing a piece of paper across the sand. "He thinks it's a big duck, he thinks he's got a big delicious dinner coming."

The dog galloped through the windswept, eddying sand, chasing paper whirling in the wind. "I bet the dog's going to go crazy if he tries any harder," I said.

"That's what Mom is, Louise. She's crazy and dying."

I tried to keep walking as my knees shook and the wind, suddenly a big fat hand, pushed against me. In the distance, the waves smacked up against the jetty, and the spray leaped up like a giant crooked claw.

"I'm sorry, Louise, those are facts. Mom isn't normal anymore. All Lutzes aren't. You heard Great-Aunt Sophie."

An old man on a bike, wearing a windbreaker which blew out like a burst tire, passed and nodded. Was he crazy too? Did all grownups end up that way? Or only the Lutzes? How could I stop myself from growing up and going crazy?

"I'll die before anything happens to me," I vowed. Being half-Irish *was* good. "I'll swim in the ocean until my body freezes, then I'll drown. I don't care."

"I'll go with you, Louise, but it's cold way below. Dark, too, no light."

"Mary, you're ridiculous. Who cares if it's cold or dark?" Mary was smarter than me, but sometimes she seemed very stupid. "By then, you're dead and with God."

"I guess so," Mary said, unconvinced.

We wandered over to the Essex-and-Sussex, a white, towering, columned hotel, closed up for the winter. It rose four stories, had hundreds of large and small windows, and dying ivy draped its brick facade. We walked up the wide front steps, to the deepest front porch I had ever seen, a ballroom of a porch. Mary sang her song, "Ringolevio, Ringolevio, where art thou?" She made it up in August, when we were in Cape May, spending long slumbrous days at the beach. The song never made sense to me. When I asked her who Ringolevio was, she was so upset she refused to answer. "Why doth thou leave me, Ringolevio?" she sang now. At the far end of the porch were chains that held swings in the summer. We climbed on them, banged into each other.

"If Mom is crazy, and Aunt Sophie is crazy, then we should pretend we are, and everything will be okay," Mary said sagely.

Mary could make sense in the shortest period of time, as if her pulse and brain registered all the feelings and thoughts of the world, and they came out of her head like a straight, pure line — a tickertape. That's when being near her was worthwhile, when I admired her. Up on the chain my vista was of the ocean, and I could understand why the Lutzes, why anyone, including me, needed to watch it. Like the constants of summer — the bang of a screen door, the chill of ice cream running down your throat — the ocean, with its pattern, its heave and push, left you feeling certain about people, your life.

"Aunt Sophie's had shock treatment, too," Mary said. "That's why she's got those bumps under her arms. The needles are long and sharp."

Sophie had nodes of dark, warty flesh under her arms. "So what?" I said, trying to skip around this fact. "If it makes her better, then big deal." Maybe all grownups got shock treatment, maybe it kept you from going totally crazy.

"Louise, don't tell Sophie what we talked about," Mary said as we drifted back to the house. "She might get the idea that we have to leave. She gets so nervous about any little thing."

Aunt Sophie's hair was curled up at the sides from the humidity in the warm kitchen, where the smell of cinnamon and butter baking overpowered the room. Lunch on Saturdays was either lentil soup and wurst, or wurst and cabbage soup. We preferred to call them hot dogs, much to Sophie's disdain.

"Where have you two girls been?" she said, fussing with the pot of soup on the stove. "Your Great-Aunt's blood pressure was sky high. You're never late for lunch. Ach, the gouda. You can't eat lunch wihout gouda." She moved about with one hand under her left breast. Perspiration collected on her upper lip.

"I was seized with worry, young ladies — ach, we Lutzes have been known to surrender our wills quickly, impetuously, to give up. When I realized you were too young to know about your mother's sickness, well, I regretted what I said, you see." She stared at us sharply, as if to see whether she had ruined us.

I looked to Mary, but she was slicing her wurst, dipping it in a puddle of mustard on her plate. She nibbled some brown bread. I wondered how much damage we had done to Aunt Sophie, to our staying here.

Later that evening, Mary and I settled in the insulated sunroom off the kitchen. We watched TV and did our homework in there, while Sophie would remain planted at the kitchen table, sipping brandy, reading cookbooks, praying. This night, though, she disappeared to her room early, mumbling something about Schiller.

"She's in another world, she hardly ate any of her applesauce," Mary whispered as Sophie walked up the back stairs. We heard her huffing at the top step — a sound we had grown accustomed to hearing.

"I didn't eat mine, either, dumpkopf," I said. Great-Aunt Sophie made applesauce from Sprys and Cortlandts. She served it with heavy cream, schnapps, and raisins on Saturday nights, a snack she revived from her days with Rudy.

"Maybe she can't stand it anymore, like you hate the streudel," I said, thinking that Sophie had eaten it for ten long years.

"Young ladies?" Sophie suddenly called. She was back in the kitchen, wearing a flimsy nightie. Her bosoms were like inflated rafts, each ready to carry several passengers down a river. "Say your prayers, young heathens," she said, almost angrily. "Say them with gusto. Say them and mention me."

We slipped off to bed later than usual. Neither of us was sleepy, but it seemed extravagant staying up beyond midnight. Besides, the house seemed extra eerie with Sophie upstairs for so long.

"Louise, keep your toes away from me," Mary said as she turned out the light. "You make me want to scream sometimes." We tolerated each other better when the four walls around us seemed tight and secure. But tonight, as the wind battered the storm windows, as the ocean treaded close to the boardwalk at high tide, the house seemed ready to launch offshore.

"You fidget and I'll kick you hard," Mary said, complaining more than ever.

"You have more room," I protested. "I always have to sleep straight as an arrow."

"You'd fidget if the Pope was lying next to you, Louise."

She pulled the coverlet over her face. I said my prayers, as earnestly as I thought I could. Then, listening to the pound and roll of the surf, I wondered how I would ever sleep without it.

❂

"Guten morgen," Mary said as we entered the kitchen. We were late for mass. Aunt Sophie, who never once strayed from the house during our stay, enforced churchgoing on us. Our Lady of the Sea was a few blocks away, so we could dash out at the last minute.

"Guten morgen," Sophie said, looking up from the funnies; she had the newspaper and the groceries delivered. Mary and I had taken up some German expressions. Sophie used them more now, too. It pleased her to hear us use them, it was like having Rudy back, talking to her in bits of German, bits of English. At first, she told us, she had been wary of saying anything in German. "I thought it would depress you, such strong, serious-sounding words."

"Now frauleins, I'm sure you said many prayers last night, but at church, you must say more, more than you can imagine." She looked at us warningly. "I slept very badly last night. The wind…."

When we returned from church, we were stopped at the back door by sounds — gutteral moanings, low hums like a radiator bringing up the heat, noises as deep and quiet as the oil burner, just turned on.

"Ghosts," I said, but Mary shushed me.

The walls, the floorboards, and the ceiling all seemed to move from these sounds.

"It didn't take long," Mary said. "I predicted this. She's gone crazy, just like Mom. And it's our fault."

I wasn't sure what we had done to cause Sophie to go crazy this soon, but I was convinced that this was the case.

"Who are you girls spying on? Are you afraid of a little Gregorian chant? Come, come, they won't bite, you half-Lutzes." Sophie beckoned, but told us to tiptoe. "I can never get enough of this music under my skin." Her hair was unbrushed, though pinned up. Some of the pins were falling out. Tendrils of hair floated across her forehead.

"Your Great-Uncle Rudy, he played this record every single Sunday morning, instead of going to mass. Such heathens we were. I knew you two wouldn't like it, but you see, I was forced to play it. I'm feeling all in a muddle."

We nodded, anxious to make Sophie feel right. Her eyes were red in the corners. At the table, everything was laid out — the strawberry jam, caramel buns, streudel, sausage — but we could tell everything was cold, including the eggs.

"Eat, eat. You must eat in times of stress, when it seems the very house you live in will crumble and be swept away. Did you remember to pray for me, Louise?"

"I prayed to Jesus, Mary, and the Holy Ghost," I said. How else could I reassure her? "I lit two candles."

"Ach, but you had no extra quarters! Now I'll pay for that sin!"

Mary dug her knife into the jam, as if it were a heart and she had to stop it from beating. Her face was clenched, like the swirls in the caramel buns, and I wondered who might scream first, Mary or Great-Aunt Sophie.

But Sophie got up and changed the record in the sunroom. Soothing music, warm and soft like hot blowing air, as gentle as the ocean on a still morning, slipped across the room.

"Ah, my favorite — Mahler. Listen, mein Louise, even you, Mary. You two will appreciate this, after all you've been through, after what you still must go through." She dashed back and turned up the volume so the music now sounded like ocean waves having crept through the front door.

She didn't touch any food once she sat back down, but a glow threaded its way across her already flushed cheeks. Mary chewed on a piece of toast; I was afraid to swallow the bits of streudel in my mouth. It was like the day Ma was driven to the hospital, the day the world seemed a restless and unsafe place.

"You two, ach, you've seen it all, haven't you? It wasn't enough to have your father die, your mother turn upside-down, but now you see the Great-Aunt Sophie worked up, breathless and sweaty, out of kilter, a big ship with all her lifeboats overboard." She sighed, buttered a piece of streudel, and put it back on a plate. "I can't help it. Your lives, Gott, so dreadful, so sad they're turning out. And me, unable to take care of you." She raised up her arms, then dropped them loudly in her lap.

"You girls do understand, ja?"

"Ja," we said, not quite understanding at all.

She laughed like a little girl. "Your mother, in her chaos, yes, even she would be proud of the two half-Lutzes. Such maturity."

"Ja," we said again.

"Repeat after me, if you really want to know some German. 'Mein Kopf ist eine dampfere Dussel.'"

"Mein Kopf ist eine dampfere Dussel."

"Do you know you said, 'My head is a wet noodle'?"

I touched my head. We all laughed.

"'Ich liebe dich,'" she said sternly.

"Ich liebe dich," we replied, as somberly.

"I love you too, forever and forever," she said, sighing more. "I *am* a lucky Great-Aunt. Gott heard your prayers. He won't let his two rabbits think badly of Sophie Louise Lutz, jawohl?"

"Jawohl," we said, tiring of this game, knowing now that we would have to leave.

"You two will never forget her, nein? You won't forget to come back and visit her in her big old house, nein?"

"Nein, nein," we said, the words lost in the Mahler and the feelings of chaos and abandonment swirling around us.

The Jersey Shore:
Three Essays and a Poem

by Frank Finale

To the Shore Once More:
Point Pleasant Beach

Always, with the salt air, an aroma of sausage, peppers and onions, and God-knows-what sauces drifted up and down the boardwalk. It was one of those sea-scintillating summers, every weekend an arcade dealer's dream. I had turned twenty-one, and everything seemed right with the world — I even thought I understood Browning, who believed only God could. I drank martinis, busboyed at Martell's, and listened to Sinatra sing over and over, "It Was a Very Good Year."

Each evening after work, I would put on my best clothes and go back to the boardwalk, looking for the company of girls. Most times I would just pick up the *ping-ping* sounds of pinball machines and the wheels' spinning promises of dolls and teddy bears for a quarter down. The games of skill and chance lured me in, every stand ablaze in neon and crackling its shuttle of numbers.

By day the boardwalk became a different world. In early morning, joggers, bicycle riders, fast walkers and dog walkers thrived. Some mornings people stayed for about ten minutes to sit on a bench or lean against the rusted railing and stare out at the sea as though waiting for a revelation. Before the beach opened to vacationing throngs of bathers and sun-tanners, old men went beachcombing; their metal detectors vacuumed the tops of sand ripples like gulls skimming waves. Here and there kids searched for shells, dodged their dogs and the waves, or threw stones into the ocean just to test their reach.

Once a dead whale washed up onto the beach. By the time we got there, people had carved their initials into it, put their cigarettes out against its side, and taken chunks of flesh away. One young man climbed on top of the beast and beat his chest like Tarzan. There's something about a dead giant that sometimes brings out the worst in people. Because of the smell, the whale was later dragged out to sea and blown up, much to the relief of the people who lived nearby.

Other things washed onto shore by the hundreds: blowfish, pink, puffed, and prickly, looking like strange balloons left over from a novelty store; starfish, dry and brittle, which herring gulls liked to strut with in their beaks; and horseshoe crabs, strewn over the tideline and looking from a distance as though some ghostly cavalry had galloped by, leaving only those grotesque shapes.

Storms delivered much of the wreckage. Meanwhile, my own inner storms also drove me to the beach — the types of storms that rack many young people on their rites of passage into adulthood: Should I marry the high school girl as my mother urged me to? What would I do when summer ended? What kind of work should I devote my life to? But whatever problems I was weathering dwindled when I brought them before what the poet Hart Crane called "this great wink of eternity." Standing on the shore at night, listening to the hollow boom and hiss of the waves, I stared at the legion of stars processioning the sky. Absorbed by the immensity of space and time, I was struck by the preciousness of life in all its varied forms, and exalted in being part of that procession.

Last Stop

Bay Head Station. End
of the line for New Jersey
Transit. Only a thousand
three hundred residents
year round. Katherine
Hepburn once visited,
living here awhile. The
bygone Lorraine movie house
is specialty shops now, but
All Saints Episcopal and
the Yacht Club endure
into the new century.
The salt-white clock tower
and cross of the Sacred Heart Church
shine over Route 35 blacktop.
Sea and wind sculpt
this beach of high dunes,
and tourists still come
to sun and praise.
The Northern Cross takes
its place in the August sky
just as it did when
the Lenni-Lenape looked up
from their longhouses
and all things
possessed a spirit.

A Walk along the Beach

It is early May, and the temperature is in the seventies. Our yellow school bus pulls into the Ortley Beach parking lot, empty except for one car with a Pennsylvania license plate and a shark-like surfboard on the roof. The bus door shutters open, and we file out: myself, my class of twenty-seven excited fourth-graders, and school environmentalist Walt Doherty. With our lunches and jackets on the seats, we set off to explore the natural wonders of the Jersey shoreline, carrying with us nothing but ourselves.

A few surprised early sunbathers look up from their novels as we climb onto the wooden boardwalk and descend the few steps to the beach. Our first sensation is an abstract one: Freedom. The visual constriction of highways, buildings, and traffic abruptly lifts. There is a rush of light and a sense of space. The hard angles of buildings and houses are replaced by smooth curves: dunes, the tideline, waves, the rim of the horizon, the sweep of the gulls. The light on the sea dazzles the eyes, and the waves glitter with a thousand small suns.

By the boardwalk, along the dunes, strands of tall grass have taken root in this loose world of sand. Here is our first stop. Gathering around a dune, Walt asks what life we see. A small white butterfly flutters from the grass.

"Insect!" cries one boy.

"Yes. Any other kind?"

Raising her hand, one girl shyly says, "Plant life."

"Good!" Walt says. "That beach grass spreads out its roots underneath the sand, and holds the dune in place."

As I look at the dune and a yellow wildflower peering from the grass, William Blake's lines rise into my thoughts: "To see a world in a grain of sand,/And a Heaven in a wildflower...." The sand is multicolored, shiny, and varied in texture and size. Much of it appears to be smoky quartz. I consider how rock is a symbol of durability, and how quartz is one of the hardest minerals. But while rocks wear away and break, a particle of sand is nearly indestructible. It is what remains after years of attrition by the weather and the sea. It is the heart of the rock itself —

true grit. Perhaps *it* should be the symbol of durability.

From the grassy dunes, we walk down to the tideline and along the shore between the sea and its high-water mark — a sinuous strand varying from four to eight feet wide, with driftwood, clamshells, molted claws, seaweed, and shells of crabs and mussels as far as the eye can see.

It is here we search for other signs of life. We find the cuneiform tracks of a gull on wet, darkened sand. Above us we hear their mewing cries. In the strand we discover gull feathers with their hard, hollow quills and soft barbs — even a gull skull picked clean by beetles, its sharp, yellow beak still intact and menacing.

Farther ahead we spot sandpipers running from the breaking waves. There is a roar, then a cat-like hiss. The sea quickly slides downslope again. The teeter-tail sandpipers turn, searching for small fish and crustaceans as they rapidly chase back the Atlantic. This comic game of tag goes on until we get too close. The skittery sandpipers fly off.

We scatter then, too, each of us making individual forays. We regroup at the next jetty to share what we found: a razor clam, a white sand dollar, a skate's black egg purse, scallop and oyster shells, numerous clamshells and carapaces of crabs. Walt tells us that the coastal Indians made wampum from the white and purple parts of some of these shells. The parts were made into beads and woven into belts or short strands used for trading. One boy holding an overload of clamshells says, "Wow, I could have been rich!"

Walt laughs, saying, "Yes, but it took a lot of work and craftsmanship to make those shells valuable."

Again we go off on our individual excursions. The sun is higher in the sky. The waves are scales of light, and the sky is as clear and distinct as the smell of the salt in the breeze. It is a glorious morning as the children dance back from the waves that rush at their feet.

Just before turning back for lunch, one of the boys finds a horseshoe crab, its underparts exposed to the sun and the gulls. We gather around as it tries to upright itself with its tapered spike. The horseshoe crab has not changed in the millions of years it has been on earth, but this one probably would have died if we had not happened along. Walt points out its feeding parts, and mentions that the Atlantic Coast is the only place you can find these creatures. "As frightening as it may look, it is actually quite harmless," he says. Picking it up by its spike, he tosses it back into the Atlantic.

Just past the white foam of the breakers, we can see the crab's dark shape moving out to sea. I sense its force for life, and how we are all intricately and invisibly linked in this ancient world of the shore. The children look on for about half a minute, then turn their attention elsewhere. Above us a laughing gull goes into its noisy "Hah-hah-hah." Walt and I linger for a few seconds more, then begin walking with the children back to the bus. The long rhythm of the sea in our ears, the salt air prickling our lungs, we carry with us a renewed awareness of life; somehow our world has grown larger.

The Legend of a Tree: Toms River

L eo's Landscaping is located in a two-story wood frame house that looks as if time had passed it by. The house stands on a hill of oak, maple, and pine, surrounded by the used car lots, gas stations, and fast food restaurants of six-lane Route 37. Its screens are patched but in place, the red paint is faded but not yet peeling, and a few roof shingles are missing. In spots the rain gutters overflow with pine needles and leaves.

Leo had called the sign shop where I work, saying, "With all this traffic, my house needs a sign that'll catch the drivers' attention." So Ray and I drove out to see what we could do for him. Picking up speed after the last traffic light, we nearly missed the place. Turning sharply, I navigated the van up the dirt driveway and came to a stop in a billow of dust, next to a great tree stump spiraled with rings. From the yard near the driveway several pine trees eclipsed the sun, leaving our van in a pool of deep shade.

We knocked on the weathered screen door; its rusty hinges rattled. Behind us, traffic whooshed loudly; inside the house, nothing moved. We knocked once more before going back to the van, with Ray swearing about lost time and the heat.

As I turned the ignition key, a man in his middle to late sixties appeared at the screen door. This, assumably, was Leo. I cut the engine as he ambled over to the van. "It's difficult to hear anything on that porch with all these cars swooshing by," he said. "Come on, I'll show you what I'm looking for."

Ray and I got out and followed him down to the sign, which was between two four-by-four posts about ten yards from the road. Leo, raising his voice above the methodical hum of traffic, told us the details of what he wanted on the sign. The constant breeze from the cars whipped our hair and ballooned our shirts. Mesmerized by the flow of trucks, cars, vans, and RVs, I said, "I remember when this was a two-lane highway."

Leo laughed. "I've been here forty-five years, and I remember when it was a gravel road."

We stood just outside the shade of the pines. Ray took notes on how the sign should look. I tried to picture Route 37 as a gravel road, then gave up when the traffic light turned green and, like a dam, released the next rush of cars.

Working my way back into the shade, I said, "You have some magnificent trees here."

"I had a beautiful Norwegian maple out front by the porch," Leo said. "People used to stop and stare at it. The stump is still there. I couldn't pull it out because of the damned root system; I would've had to tear up the whole front yard and God knows what else."

"What happened?" I asked.

"When they added lanes to Route 37, they took about six feet from my front yard and pruned some of the maple's crown, so it wouldn't interfere with the telephone wire. A year later, a telephone worker in a cherry picker comes and saws off large chunks of the maple's branches nearest the highway. He said they do it so they don't have to come back every year to prune. I had a one-sided tree now. 'That's not a hell of a good advertisement for a landscaping business,' I thought. So me and a couple of my men cut it down — even though it broke my heart to do it. The tree was filled with so much water, we had to wipe the sawblade dry after each cut. It took three men to carry one three-foot piece."

The next summer, he said, he couldn't figure out why it was almost twenty degrees hotter on the porch. Then it dawned on him that his Norwegian maple had made the difference. "That tree was the best damn natural air conditioner around. It kept the noise of the cars down too."

Ray finished the sketch of the sign and told Leo we would get back to him. When we returned to the van, I took one last look at the stump. Its great girth had numerous dark and light rings that varied in thickness — a legend of its many years. I pictured the Norwegian maple as it must have been: a castle of deep green leaves, symmetrical and lofty with birds, squirrels, and cicadas. On clear days, its hundreds of leaves would dazzle green against radiant sky. When windy, the leaves would rustle and make the sound of rain, and in fall they'd flush with the season's colors: bright red, orange, and yellow, a show that made people stop and stare.

With a wave, we left Leo and drove west on Route 37. We passed a new fast food place with "Grand Opening" buntings draped around its eaves. Farther down the highway, workers in their yellow hardhats were laying out another strip mall. Under a once branchy sky, black clouds of diesel smoke hung above bulldozers, loaders, and huge dump trunks. Lying by their craters, giant trees bared their amputated roots.

Stopping at a red light, I looked through the heat-wrinkled air above the line of traffic and thought of Shel Silverstein's book, *The Giving Tree*, in which a tree loves a little boy. As the boy grows up, he takes more and more from the tree: shade, leaves, apples, branches for a house, and, in middle age, wood for a boat. When the middle-age man returns an old man after his many voyages, all that's left of the tree is a stump. The old man sits on it and, finally, is wise enough to appreciate what the tree has given him.

Squinting at the construction site through waves of exhaust fumes and heat, I thought I caught for an instant the faint outline of children running and playing in shade. Then Ray called out, "Frank! Light's green!" and I drove on.

The Wooden Gauntlet

by John Mahoney

During the 1950s, when my age was still in the single digits, my family and I traveled from North Jersey every summer to spend two weeks in Seaside Park. We packed the barest of essentials, plus one protesting cat, into our 1939 Plymouth sedan and headed south. I always enjoyed the ride no matter how long it took, always looking out the window at the changing scenery. I kept a keen lookout for the clues that meant we were getting closer to the shore: more trees, bait shops, sandy highway shoulders, the billboard picturing the dog pulling down a little girl's bathing suit. My heart kept time with the thump-thumping of the tires over the roadway separators. Because of heavy traffic, the Plymouth rarely shifted out of second gear, and by the time we reached Route 37 — which back then was only two lanes wide with no fast-food restaurants to offer reprieve — it felt like we had been traveling for days. But I didn't care; while the cat panted in protest in the backseat, my brothers and I looked forward to two weeks of crabbing, boating, fishing, penny arcades, and bare feet.

But first we had to pass a test.

The test seemed easy enough. To prove our worthiness of vacationing in Seaside, all we had to do was cross the wooden bridge that provided the only span across Barnegat Bay. The first-time traveler probably didn't realize what a killer the bridge was, but I was a veteran of many crossings and knew of its deception. Like a giant poisonous snake sunning itself, the bridge rested placidly on the blue-green splendor of the bay. It was only two cars wide, and only a few feet from the water's surface. The wooden planks looked like cardboard that had been soaked with rain and dried too quickly in the sun.

I remember one time in particular, when I was seven years old. My father didn't even slow down to think about our impending doom. I took a deep breath as he drove straight onto the bridge — too late to turn back. Immediately the boards came to life with a menacing rattle, like a thousand window shutters caught in the wind. I could feel them shaking loose, and I was certain they would rise up and slap against the side of the car. And if the boards didn't rise, their springboard actions would surely loosen the nails and send them flying like tiny missiles through the open car window.

"Quick! Roll up the windows!" I shouted at everyone.

I saw my father's bewildered eyes in the rearview mirror. I was sorry I had shouted. I was afraid any distraction might cause my father to veer to one side and touch the guardrail, which was also made of wood and looked about as sturdy as uncooked spaghetti. I held the cat in front of me for protection.

"Put that cat down," my mother ordered.

Didn't anyone understand the danger we were in?

My oldest brother, the Master Teaser, was quick to take advantage of my fears. "See those wooden pilings sticking out of the water?" he said, pointing a few yards away. "That's all that's left of the last bridge that was here. It collapsed from the weight of too many cars."

I sat up and started counting the cars on the bridge. How many cars were too many? How much weight was too much? I looked out at the pilings: seagulls had perched on some of them like aquatic vultures, waiting for their next victims to come crashing through the ancient boards.

I had doubts about the buoyancy of a 1939 Plymouth, and as a precautionary measure I laid on the floor so as not to make the car too top heavy; if we drove off the bridge, I figured, our car would remain floating long enough for the Coast Guard to rescue us. In my position on the floor, with the cat over my face to protect me against splintered wood and other projectiles, the rattling of the boards — and my fear — became magnified.

Not until I heard the hum of rubber tires on macadam did I dare raise my head. I looked behind us at the bridge that somehow had remained standing. We had run the gauntlet again — and survived. The smell of salt air filled the car and I settled back and heaved a great sigh. We had earned two glorious weeks of vacation.

Now I live in Ocean County, just a few miles from where my wooden nemesis once stood. In its place two bridges now stand. One is the Thomas A. Mathis Bridge, which was completed seconds before the wooden structure collapsed. The other is the well-planned J. Stanley Tunney Bridge, with its high arch that allows the tallest mast to pass beneath it with room to spare.

There's a fifty-year age difference between the car I drive now and the one I once huddled in. I drive over both bridges many times throughout the year — fearlessly. And my two young sons aren't afraid, either. I have yet to see one of them hiding on the floor or holding a protective object in front of them. In fact, they look forward to being stuck in traffic when the Mathis drawbridge is up so they can jump out of the car and peer over the railing. But it's during those times when I'm waiting for the drawbridge to go down that I look up at the seagulls sitting on the streetlamps, and I have to wonder: How buoyant is my car?

Seaside Heights

by Barbara O'Dair

Dad was a rollercoaster,
mother a soft machine
churning out a colored frost.

My ducks were numbered.
Some got knocked over and floated belly up
as I tried to ring their necks.
The oversized teacups whipped around the track,
spilling their cargo on the boardwalk.
Barkers called out five-legged goats
and the funhouse went home.

Strapped into the giant swing,
I soared over the ocean
wanting a big drink of water.

Bound by the chain and the belt,
I could not be broken.
Below, Grandfather wrung his hands.
He saw I wouldn't willingly come down.
I saw the dark green surf,
its knife-pleat skirt.

Island
Beach
State Park

by Gene Ahrens

Fisherman's Wife

by Josephine Lehman Thomas

T he wind off the Atlantic is raw at four o'clock in the morning, even in summer, and I pull my sweater closer about my throat as Tom and I walk down the sandy road between the tarpaper shacks where the fishermen live. The long low fish shed on the dock and the high round shaft of Barnegat Lighthouse are beginning to take form out of the darkness. The slightly sour smell of Barnegat Bay salt marshes is strong in the air.

The waves lap softly against the fishing skiffs tied in orderly rows along the breakwater. The fishermen, awkward in rubber hip-boots and stiff yellow oilskins, shuffle clumsily past the piles of wooden boxes and wire baskets to stow their gear and tin lunch cans in their boats. They make their preparations swiftly and with little to say beyond an occasional speculative comment about the weather.

"What you think about it, Axel?" The names one hears are like that — Axel and Olaf, Sven and Hans. Except for Tom and two or three native Barnegaters, these men of the fishing fleet are Scandinavians with the blood of seafaring Norsemen in their veins.

Axel scans the sky, the stars overhead, the faint pinkish glow on the eastern horizon. "Looks all right to me."

First appeared in Scribners, *July 1933.*

The other is getting the feel of the wind. "I don't think she shift before night."

Tom climbs down into his skiff and does something with a monkey wrench. There is a staccato sputter, and the motor starts with a roar. As it warms up, he pulls on oilskins and boots, and listens to the speculation about the weather. Axel, the acknowledged weather prophet, takes another long look at the sky.

"I think she is a good day. I shove off," he announces.

When one man starts the others follow. Tom kisses me good-bye, and Olaf Svenson in the next boat looks embarrassed and nudges his partner. These Scandinavians would rather lose a day's catch of fish than be seen in a public gesture of affection toward their wives.

Lines are cast off, motors throttled down, and one by one the huge gray sea-skiffs slip out of the dock basin. Tom's boat leaves a scimitar of foam in its wake as it rounds a bend in the channel and disappears behind the low sand dunes, and I have my last glimpse of him as he stands at the tiller, fastening his oilskins more securely. It will be wet going through the narrow inlet where the tide is running swiftly out of Barnegat Bay and meeting the big rollers of the Atlantic.

The last boat is lost in the early morning grayness, and inside me is the dull emptiness I feel every time Tom puts to sea. I walk back down the road to where the flivver is parked, beside the little lunch-room where two fish-truck drivers are going in for early morning coffee and fried potatoes. They glance at me curiously as I hurry along, and one asks the other a question. The answer comes to me clearly in the still morning air:

"Her? Oh, just one of the fishermen's wives."

When Tom and I married, two years ago, my excellent journalistic salary, Tom's business, and the interest from his inherited securities gave us an income of almost a thousand dollars a month. Now we have not that much in a year. The business failed after being nursed through a year of steady losses. My salary ceased because of sickness and an ill-timed venture into freelancing. The income from our securities has shrunk two-thirds, chiefly because the aunt who bequeathed most of them to Tom had such unquestionable faith in South American bonds.

After months of forced idleness and fruitless search for a paying job, Tom had become sallow and thin, harassed by nervous indigestion and insomnia. To add to his worries, I discovered I was going to have a baby. The beginning of summer found us with few tangible assets, not counting the kind known as frozen, except a quantity of furniture (and no place to put it), an expensive automobile we could not afford to use, and a motor boat acquired in the last year of our prosperity and still unfinished.

Tom had spent his summers since childhood on Barnegat Bay, and his boat was the same type of huge oceangoing skiff the Barnegat fishermen use. That boat was more than a hobby to him — it was practically a mistress, the recipient of secret extravagances, the occasion for numerous trips, ostensibly to "see a man in Philadelphia," which invariably were made by the roundabout and wholly illogical way of Barnegat. We couldn't afford to keep the car, but I knew Tom would rather pawn his clothes than sell the boat. He decided to convert it from an expensive plaything into a commercial investment, and join the fishing fleet.

The fishing village clusters around Barnegat Light on the long sliver of island that lies six miles off the New Jersey shore between Barnegat Bay and the Atlantic. A mile or so down the road we found a scantily furnished cottage for $25 a month, where one cooked and ate and lived and entertained in the same room. I did things to its glaring whitewashed walls with blue and red chintz, while Tom worked from dawn to dark fitting the skiff with what his optimistic nature considered the minimum of necessary equipment.

When the boat was being built, we pored over plans for trim-lined cabins and gay awninged cockpits where one served tall cold drinks in nautically monogrammed sea-going china and crystal. We made long lists of bronze and chromium fittings, chronometers, shining binnacles — all the enticing gadgets the more expensive yachting magazines advertise. Before we could buy them the money was gone, and instead of a smart cabin cruiser, we owned an open twenty-six-footer with no equipment except the powerful motor. Tom added fishing gear, three soggy life preservers, a home-made anchor, and a second-hand compass always at least four points off. He hired a native Barnegater as fishing partner, paid thirty dollars for a ten-year-old Model T flivver to provide transportation between house and dock, and in a week was ready to go to sea.

A deep-sea fisherman's day begins at a quarter past three. There is no sign of dawn when we are wrenched awake by the strident alarm clock. Half asleep, I fumble for slippers and warm bathrobe. (The peach satin negligee that cost more than the flivver is packed away in New York.) I awake by degrees as I go through the routine of breakfast. Coffee on one burner of the smoky oil stove; water for the eggs on the other. The pounding of the surf sounds ominously loud to me. As I dash cold water on my face at the kitchen sink, I am thinking about the treacherous bar at the inlet. I squeeze the oranges, fetch cream and bread and marmalade from the little icebox, and dress in snatches — woolen slacks, jumper and sneakers, a comb through my hair. Thank God I had that permanent. There is no time to put on powder or lipstick. My face looks pinched and old to me, and I hope Tom is too sleepy to notice.

The stove will not burn, and the first waves of early morning nausea make me short-tempered. "Damn it, darling, will you *please* not take my stove matches away." Tom says he is sorry, and I am ashamed. He is never irritable before breakfast or any other time.

He eats while I pack his lunch in a tin biscuit can. The four sandwiches. Two apples. The slab of chocolate cake. A bottle of lemonade. While he goes out to crank the flivver, I manage a few swallows of orange juice, but my stomach revolts at coffee. I put on an extra sweater and ride with him to the dock to bring back the car.

If I am too ill, or do not want the car during the day, Tom goes alone. I stand at the window and watch the red rear light of the flivver until it is lost around a curve. A fish truck returning from a night trip to Philadelphia rumbles past and disappears, its clatter drowned by the boom of the surf. Then there is nothing but the dark empty road and the thundering Atlantic. "Please God, don't let the bar be too rough," I pray, as I prayed for things when I was a child. I put the butter and cream into the icebox and try to go back to sleep. The bed seems wide and empty. In the east are the first flaming streaks of dawn.

Slowly and laboriously, I grew accustomed to the new routine. For two months I was wretched and ill most of each day, and given to morbid brooding over our poverty. In my heart I knew that Tom's smile and the way he writes "Anndear" as one word meant more to me than all the money in the world — but as I dragged miserably through the morning housework, every domestic task seemed laden with reminders of another life. Washing the blue and red breakfast dishes brought back memories of Prague and the day my Vienna-bound plane was halted there by fog. Ironing my best embroidered napkins and table runners, I saw the crooked sun-drenched street in Rome where I paid three times too much for them. And emptying the ash trays with the crossed-sabre trademark invoked a gay picture of the January day I bought them in Dresden — afternoon coffee and *belegtes Brotchen* at a table overlooking the ice cakes floating down the Elbe, the orchestra playing the latest seductive tango. All that was another existence, and that young woman was someone else, someone whose confident plans for the future had nothing to do with being a fisherman's wife on a barren island off the Jersey coast.

Lunch and a cup of hot tea usually induced a more cheerful mood. In the afternoons I walked far up the beach to lie in the sun on the hard white sand, alone except for a steamer crawling along the horizon, the gulls wheeling overhead, and the flocks of solemn little sandpipers, wholly absorbed in their own pursuits, running stiff-legged over the sand. I spent long drowsy hours there by the dunes, content to listen to the sound of the surf, captivated by the changing moods of the sea, until I grew to understand the lure it has for Tom, to comprehend how one can both love and hate it as one loves and hates a mistress who holds him in her spell.

One day is much like another. By four o'clock I begin to look for Tom. I go back to the cottage, prepare vegetables, try to read. By six o'clock I know he will be there any moment, and I put the potatoes and dessert into the oven. Forty minutes later I turn down the fire to retard the cooking, and sit at the window watching the automobiles coming around the bend in the road. By eight o'clock my imagination has encompassed every possible calamity that could beset him. I remember the two Norwegians, veteran fishermen for twenty years, who were lost when their skiff capsized on the bar last year. I think about the bad heart Tom has had ever since Belleau Wood. It begins to rain, and I go down to the beach to see if the surf is heavier.

By nine o'clock I am numb and choked from worrying, and when at last Tom strides in, ruddy and glowing from the rain and preceded by a strong odor of fish, I cry weakly down his neck and search futilely for my handkerchief. He offers me his own, one of his best monogrammed ones, which has evidently been used to clean out the fish bin.

"Never mind, honey, let 'em drip. You can't make me any wetter. I'm sorry I'm so late, Ann. We had a swell catch and I didn't want to leave."

I light the stove again and bring his dressing gown and slippers while he peels off his wet clothes and drops them out of the window to air.

"My God, I'm hungry. Is that brown Betty I smell? Come back here; you get another kiss. Look, Andy, do I have to wash all over first?"

The fishy odor he exudes makes me deathly sick, but I compromise. "All right, just your hands and face then, and finish afterward." I hurry to put the food on the table. "You shouldn't go so long without eating. It must be ten hours."

"Thirteen."

"Thirteen what?"

"Thirteen hours since food." His voice is indistinct from baked potato and omelet. "I got hungry as a bear at nine o'clock this morning and polished off my lunch."

"Oh, Tom, all of it?"

"Well, no, but I gave the rest to Bill. He didn't have any breakfast."

Bill is another fisherman — a tall young Finlander, hair unbelievably yellow, shoulders unbelievably broad, and the coat of arms of Finland tattooed in violent blue on his powerful forearms. Tom brought him home to lunch one day. He speaks English slowly and carefully and pleasantly, but was ill at ease and inarticulate at first, and had to be urged to eat. He was puzzled by the cold jellied beef consomme, and embarassed by the extra spoon and the napkin. Both Tom and I liked him immensely.

Bill came often after his first shyness had gone. On rainy days he and Tom burrowed into our collection of yachting magazines and marine catalogs, and spent hours discussing trawling and squidding, self-bailing hulls, clinker construction, and other subjects unintelligible to me. Bill could not understand anyone's being afraid of the sea, as I was, and despite warning glances and surreptitious kicks from Tom he innocently divulged in his conversation all the nautical mishaps my well-meaning husband tried to conceal from me: Tom's rudder unshipped by a heavy following sea on the bar, the dead engine twenty miles at sea and the four-hour wait until a Coast Guard cutter saw his distress signal (his pale blue B.V.D.'s flying aloft), the number of times he went out without a compass or life preservers. Tom will never learn to take life preservers seriously.

Tom was anxious for me to go on a fishing trip to convince me it was merely a prosaic day's work. After waiting weeks, a day finally came when the weather report and my internal state were simultaneously favorable. We were off in the flivver together, through the daybreak scenes that had grown so familiar — the stunted cedars and silver-green bayberry bushes ghostly and shadowy on the white dunes, Barnegat Bay flat and calm to the west of the island, the pounding surf and rosy sky to the east, and the red and white buildings of the Coast Guard station with the charming name of Loveladies.

We shoved off as soon as we reached the dock, rounded the end of the island under the long beams Barnegat Light threw far out to sea, and approached the bar. There was just enough daylight to see the buoys. Tom was at the tiller, and Jim, his fishing partner, stood at the motor controls to adjust the speed at Tom's orders to meet the incoming seas. The big skiff breasted them beautifully, and ten minutes later we were riding the long even swells of the Atlantic. The throttle was opened wider, and a compass course set for the "Ridge" — the shallow banks twenty miles offshore where the schools of bluefish run. It takes more than an hour to reach there, and the fish bite best at daybreak.

We passed the lightship nine miles out at sea. Turning to say something to Tom, I discovered the shoreline had disappeared behind the horizon. We were out of sight of land, and the skiff seemed very small in the wide expanse of water. I was glad of the half dozen other fishing boats nearby.

"Are you all right, Ann?" Tom was shouting above the roar of the unmuffled engine.

"Fine," I lied, sucking surreptitiously at the lemon I had put in my sweater pocket. Tom smoked at the tiller, and Jim, lazily chewing tobacco, began cutting up moss-bunkers, the oily fish used as bait. They were moss-bunkers that had been dead a long time, and I moved to windward of them.

We sighted the high masts of the big sailing smacks that come down here from New York, and altered course toward them. After cruising around to see which of the other skiffs were "pulling," we selected a spot not far from Axel, who has an uncanny instinct for finding fish if fish are to be found. The engine was stopped, the anchor lowered, and Jim began "grinding," putting the moss-bunker bait through what looked like an over-sized kitchen meat chopper attached to the starboard gunwale of the skiff. The nauseous mess that emerged was thrown overboard a handful at a time. The oil in it smoothed the water and made a slick on the surface. Then larger pieces of the bait were put on the two lines let over the stern into the slick. Tom attended to the lines and Jim to the grinder. We waited five minutes, ten. I was eager and impatient, and anxious to help. Another five minutes. There was a flash of brilliant blue just under the surface, then another and another. The water became radiant with streaks of bright color. We had found a big school of bluefish. They were attracted by the slick, and darted greedily at the largest particles of bait in the water — the ones with the hooks inside.

The fish bit as fast as they could be pulled in and unhooked. Tom put on a pair of old leather gloves to protect his fingers from the wet lines and also from possible bites from vindictive victims. All about us, other boats were pulling in fully as many. The fish were biting so fast Tom could not attend to both lines, and I helped him bait the hooks, in my excitement and enthusiasm forgetting my distaste for the moss-bunkers. Even the stoical Scandinavians grow excited over a catch like this.

"Look at the size of this baby, Ann." I admired it and Tom tossed the big blue into the bin.

A six-pounder lunged off Jim's hook, and the lanky Barnegater spat a resentful stream of tobacco juice after it. "God damn, there goes fifty cents."

The fish bit steadily until the bin was more than half full. Then the flashes of blue in the water grew scarcer, and it was several minutes between bites. The three of us amused ourselves throwing bits of bait to the flocks of Mother Carey's chickens twittering over the water. Watching the little birds catch the tid-bits in mid-air, I realized I was very hungry, although it was still long before noon. We opened the lunch tin and ate sandwiches ravenously out of unspeakably dirty hands.

The mid-day sun was warm, and after the last sandwich had disappeared I took off my heavy hip boots and yellow oilskins and stretched out forward for a nap. When I awoke, a half dozen more fish had been caught but none of the skiffs had repeated the luck of early morning. Toward five o'clock, one boat started for shore, and the others raised anchor and followed.

A stiff westerly breeze had come up. We began to ship water, and I put on my oilskins and boots again. The waves grew higher as we neared the bar. I was very tired by this time, and worried about going through the inlet. Tom showed no apprehension, but his remark that "it's always worse coming back than going out" did nothing to allay my fears. I started to go forward — because the life jackets were stowed in the bow.

"Stay back here,"Tom called sharply from the tiller. He knew the bow must be light to help the skiff ride the seas and keep her from burying her nose as she slid down into the trough of the waves. I clutched the gunwale in unconcealed terror as sea after sea rose into high curling crests and crashed into churning foam around us. This was the place where the two Norwegians were drowned. In that pounding surf even a good swimmer would have little chance.

Then suddenly we were through, and rounding the lighthouse into the bay. Throttles were wide open as each boat tried to reach the dock first. There was the noise of the ice crushers as we nosed in and tied up. Heavy baskets of fish were swung lightly from boat to dock — not only bluefish, but flounder and weakfish and seabass, and squirming gray lobsters making futile slaps at their captors with their claws. The news of the big catch had been brought in by the first arrivals, and already trucks were backed up to the dockshed to load the fish and start the night drive to Philadelphia and New York.

The smell of fish and gasoline sickened me, and I walked down the road while Tom made fast the skiff. Around me the lobster pots and buoys were stacked everywhere, nets were stretched to dry, and boats lay pulled out to have their bottoms copper painted. I sat on an overturned lobster pot and listened to the sounds from the waterfront — broken clam shells crunching under foot as the fishermen hurried away to hot food and coffee, the chopping of ice, the thump of heavy boxes, the snorting trucks. The sound of the surf on the other side of the island was faint and dull. It was good to be on land again.

We brought in 1,100 pounds of fish in that catch, more than a half ton after they were gutted, but the wholesale price was only four cents a pound. After paying for ice and boxes, shipping and commissions, gasoline and oil and bait, and sharing the proceeds with his partner, there was less than ten dollars left for Tom for the day's work. And that was a good catch, one of the best of the season.

Often Tom did not make expenses. There were days when the bluefish could not be found, other days when they refused to bite for some reason known only to themselves. Or the sea was too choppy for fishing, and the end of a sixteen-hour working day would find Tom coming home exhausted and white and seasick, with nothing to show for seven dollars' worth of bait and gasoline except three small bluefish and a worthless young shark.

"And I used to do this for fun," he marvelled.

There were long stretches of squally weather, when no boats ventured outside the bay, and the fishermen overhauled their engines and mended their gear, talking of the old days, two or three years ago, when bluefish sold in Fulton Market for fifty cents a pound, and five-hundred-dollar catches were not unusual.

For three weeks Tom did not have a catch big enough to pay expenses, and there was one weekend when we had nothing to eat but boiled rice and apples. As a last resort, he offered himself and the skiff for hire, to take weekenders deep-sea fishing. A party of Philadelphians engaged him every Sunday for six weeks, and were satisfied if they caught one bluefish apiece to uphold their piscatorial reputations. They paid Tom twenty dollars a trip, and once they brought him a gift of old clothes — a half dozen coats and trousers of the type known ten years ago as "cakeeater." I was first amused, thinking of the excellently tailored suits hanging unused in Tom's wardrobe, then indignant.

"How could they? Can't they see you're different?"

"The only way I'm different is that I'm not half so good a fisherman as the Squareheads. I don't look any different, you know."

He was right. In disreputable dungarees or oilskins, face and hands smeared with grease and perspiration, all men look pretty much alike. Tom's hands were never wholly clean any more, and his nails defied the stoutest mechanic's soap. He grew careless about shaving, and had his hair cut only when the tendrils began to curl about his ears.

These things no longer seemed important to me. I was content that he was growing strong and brown again, that the whites of his eyes were white instead of yellow, that the box of bicarbonate of soda stood neglected on the kitchen shelf, and that he slept the sleep of healthy fatigue and grinned at me when I shook him awake.

My own attacks of illness began to abate, and keeping house grew less laborious. The same grim satisfaction I once felt over scooping a rival foreign correspondent was now aroused by achieving a perfectly cooked meal, or ironing Tom's shirts without leaving a wrinkle in the collar. Doing my own washing and hanging clothes out on a line seemed a balder admission of poverty than any we had yet made, and at first I hung the wet things over an inadequate five-foot length of twine above the stove, where they remained damp for three days. After a month of this I said "What the Hell?" and put everything out to flap in the sun and wind and dry in two hours. After the first time, I didn't mind.

When the Sunday fishing party came no more with its weekly twenty dollars, I learned to practice economies I would have considered flatly impossible two years ago. I understood that the United States Army ration allows twelve cents a meal for food, but the best I could do was thirteen. Searching for sales on rice, butter, flour, and sugar, I dreamed of a shopping list that would again include mushrooms, Camembert cheese, sweetbreads — luxuries that are outlawed when every nickel is counted for staples.

By September I was reduced to my last pair of stockings, even though I had gone bare-legged all summer. Three-dollar face powder and thirty-dollar French perfume were merely memories, and my toilet articles came from the five-and-ten.

We learned to take pleasure in simple things — our nightly extravagance of ice cream cones (the small five-cent ones) from the general store, an occasional movie, Tom being at home for a leisurely Sunday morning breakfast of waffles and both of us trying to get *The Times* book review first, the yellow-haired Bill bringing us a basket of succulent baby lobsters. They were "bootleg" lobsters, below the minimum legal size, but we asked no questions.

It was a gala day when Tom came home with a bunch of golden calendulas bought at a wayside stand on the mainland, for few flowers grow on this sandy island. Their tawny brightness recalled the Talisman roses that played a persuasive role in his courtship.

"They only cost ten cents a dozen," he admitted. "I remembered you liked yellow."

The ten cents was the amount he allowed himself daily for the cheap cigarettes he had substituted for his favorite brand.

The months passed. The scrub cedars that cling precariously to the white dunes turned a duller green, the bayberry bushes grew brown, the summer bathers were gone, and the long white beach was left to the gulls and sandpipers. The wild ducks and geese began to fly south, and the sound of firing was heard all day from the shooting blinds in the marshes across the bay. Heavy autumn fogs hung over the island, and at night the hoarse uneasy rumble of the fog horns of passing steamers punctuated the boom of the surf.

One day there was an ominous sky, a long ground swell, and an uncertain wind that veered and shifted. The barometer fell steadily, and the surf pounded more heavily. In the afternoon Tom brought his boat from the fishing dock and anchored it in a cove of the bay near the cottage to have it within sight.

That night the first northeaster came howling out of the Atlantic. The cottage shook and quivered in the sharp gusts, and the rain dashed against the panes like handfuls of gravel. The electric current was off, and Tom stumbled about barefoot in the dark, closing windows, swearing fluently when he stepped on the sharp heels of my overturned bedroom slippers. In ten minutes he was asleep again, but I lay awake listening to the wind, and plagued by the vague worries and forebodings a pregnant woman has in the night. I knew this was the beginning of winter, and we had to plan what to do when we left the island — to face again the disheartening search for a job.

Tom heard me stirring and turning, and asked if I was all right. "I can't sleep either," he lied. "Let's play rummy."

He lighted a candle, wrapped my bathrobe around my shoulders, and dragged out a hatbox to put between us in bed for a card table. It was pleasant and intimate in the little circle of candlelight, with the cards clicking down on the gay pink and black stripes of the pasteboard hatbox. The box bore the name of a great establishment in the rue St. Honore, and the 900 francs I paid for the scrap of black felt it originally contained did not seem excessive then. I lunched in the Bois that day — but Paris is far away and long ago, and Tom beside me concealing his own weariness to help me through a wakeful night is very real.

The gale raged through the night and the next day, shaking the little cottage until I feared it would be torn from its foundations. By mid-afternoon the sea was breaking over the bulkheads and through the dunes, and sweeping broken timbers as far as the post office. The high wind sent icy blasts through loose window sashes and under the doors, and I shivered in three sweaters as I stoked the little stove with driftwood.

The second morning of the northeaster the tide was over the island and the cottage was surrounded by water. In hip-boots and oilskins we waded through it to the beach, shutting our eyes and lowering our heads against the sand that whirled off the tops of the dunes and cut into the skin like powdered glass. On the other side of the dunes everything was gray and white — pale gray sky, lines of white breakers foaming to the horizon on the mountainous waves of a dark gray sea, white suds of spume and spindrift whirling over the sand. The rain lashed at our faces and the wind tore at our breath. Walking against it was like pushing a solid weight, and I made little more progress than the gulls that hovered almost motionless overhead as they tried to fly out to sea. The beach was deserted except for Tom and me and an occasional plucky little sandpiper.

The northeaster blew itself out, calmer weather followed, and other storms came and went. The bluefish season ended, and the fishermen changed to cod-fishing gear, although by this time there were only a few days each month when it was safe for the fleet to venture far outside.

Shut in together for days at a time by long stretches of stormy weather, I found it tragically easy to slump, physically and mentally, especially in the inertia natural to my condition. I had to force myself to put on a bright dress, to polish my nails and wave my hair, to cook Tom's favorite dishes, to manufacture foolish little surprises to stimulate and vivify the continual contact of marriage. Preserving an illusion of loveliness and romance is difficult when there is utter lack of privacy, when the only plumbing is at the kitchen sink, and icy draughts from outside make Spartan fortitude necessary for even the minimum of bathing. The "jolly little coarsenesses of life" are not always jolly.

Nevertheless, we were happy. It was a satisfaction to Tom to know he was providing a living for us, even by manual labor, and some answering primitive instinct made me content to cook and tend the hearth and breed. We stayed on the island until two months before the child was born, and when we left, we left reluctantly. Besides health, this simple elemental life, in all its barrenness and frugality, had given us a deeper feeling of fulfillment in marriage, the common bond of each having worked hard for the other. Something much finer was welded between us than we found in the first prosperous days of our marriage, when our lives followed two distinct paths and we couldn't afford a baby.

At the Fishermen's Bar

by Sandy Gingras

We've got hairdos
and teased-up sentences
that rely on nothing
but an air of trying too hard
to stand up. Sometimes,
we think we've overcome need,
but on nights like this we wonder
if we missed our chance at love,
if that passed us by like a boat
under our bridge of self-esteem.

The fishermen here carry their poles
to their tables, wear their hip boots
like skins. They put hooks
on their tongues, then chug beers
with throats as wide as the love

they might have for the sea,

they might make to us.

It's how these men show things.

We see the fast ripple

then they spit out the hooks.

They talk about diminishing

catch, the future as empty as pride,

then they want to play again.

It's not something we understand,

but we spend a part of our lives softening

our hands for these men.

We've kissed their hooked cheeks for nothing

better than a wound. On nights when the blues

are running, we go to the beach with them

and stand there casting away.

Barnegat Light — Commercial Fishing

by Serge J-F. Levy

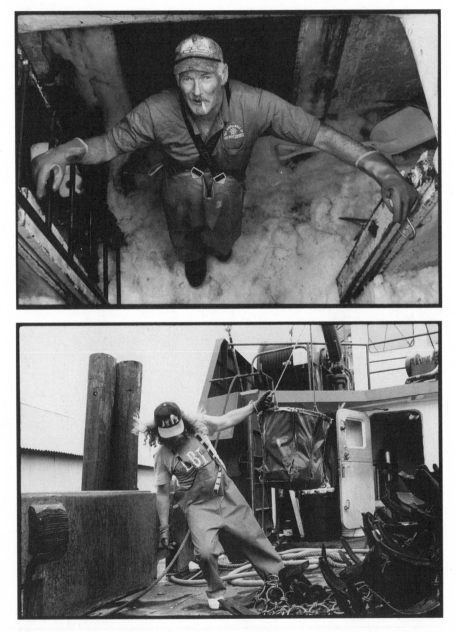

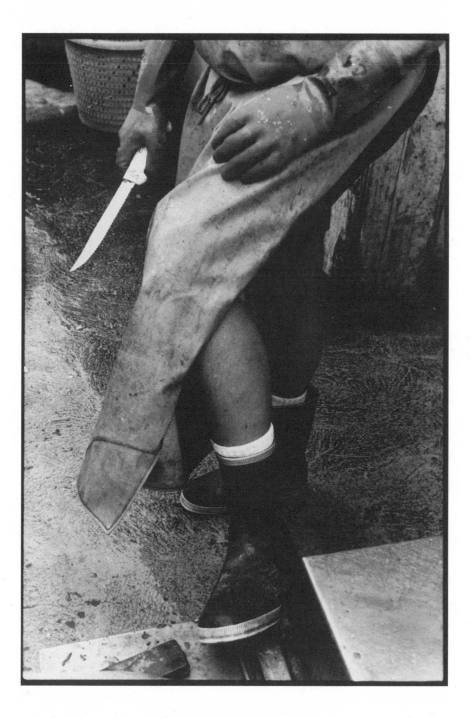

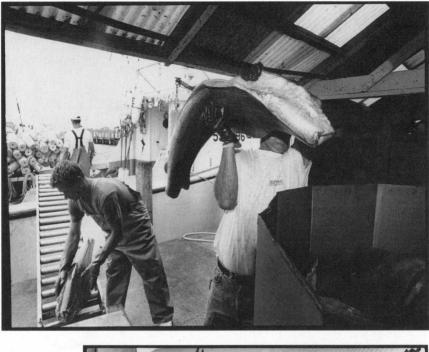

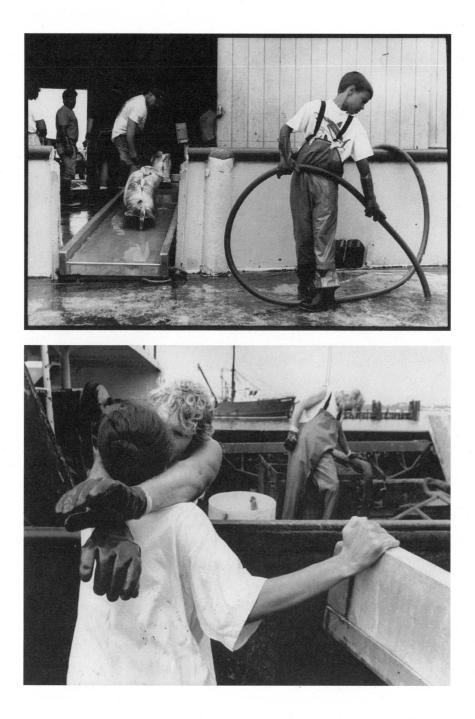

The Distant Edge of War

by Margaret R. Thomas

One evening in 1943, while trying to concentrate on my homework, I overhead my father tell my mother that a Coast Guardsman had pulled a body out of the surf; when he grabbed one of the hands to haul it to shore, the skin peeled off like a formal evening glove. Suddenly I understood the significance of the gloves, sailor caps, and uniform fragments my brother and I had picked up at the high tide line. The conflict across the ocean had reached the beaches of Harvey Cedars, the small town on Long Beach Island where I lived.

By June of 1942, just six months after our entry into the war, the Battle of the Atlantic was being fought within sight of the island. German submarines attacked shipping, and the white, sandy beach lay covered with a thick coat of black, gummy oil from torpedoed tankers. Forty U-boats prowled the eastern seaboard that month alone, sinking an average of three ships a day. Shipwrecked sailors were brought ashore, and even today the smell of kerosene recalls the time I went with my father to the Loveladies Coast Guard barracks, and saw townswomen painstakingly scrape and wipe the oil-covered bodies of rescued seamen. My five-year-old brother, Michael, and I later used the same kerosene-and-soap technique on a stranded, oil-matted wild duck.

The beach was patrolled by Coast Guardsmen on horseback with Doberman pinschers and German shepherds, which wore booties to protect their feet from the tar. That sand was my playground, and the threat of those ferocious, snarling animals left me with a fear of dogs I've never overcome. I had trouble understanding why we were using German dogs to capture German soldiers. My mother, whose father had emigrated from Prussia, explained that the Nazis were our enemies and not all Germans were Nazis. She cried as she tried to explain, but the political distinction was lost on me.

Dinner always ended at 6:45, when we listened to Lowell Thomas's news broadcast. My mother had worked for him, and this time was sacrosanct; when he went on the air we were not allowed to interrupt. We followed the war's progress on a large world map tacked to the wall. My father, a Marine in World War I, had fought on some of the same battlegrounds. He taught my brother and me to present arms using a stick for a rifle, and we sang the Marine's Hymn and the Air Corps song, "Off we go into the wild blue yonder...." (At first I thought a "yonder" was a type of plane.) I carved models of Spitfires, Zeroes, Messerschmidts, B-17 bombers, and my favorite, the twin-fuselage P-38. They hung on strings from my bedroom ceiling, and I fought many an air battle of the imagination.

As for all Americans, our food was rationed. My mother tore butter, sugar, coffee, and meat coupons from our ration books, and I planted my own Victory Garden. My poster of fat being poured from a frying pan into a coffee can won the third-grade competition. Slivers of soap melded together in a jar on the kitchen counter, and we used the slimy mass to wash dishes. All windows on the east side of the house were covered with black oilcloth blinds, and car headlights were painted with black eyelids for those times when the gas ration was sufficient for night driving. Barnegat Lighthouse was blacked out on its seaward side.

That first wartime winter, our parents turned a serious concern into a game: what to do in case of an air raid. Blimps patrolled overhead, going back and forth to Lakehurst Naval Air Station (one crashed a few miles north of Barnegat Inlet). Navy planes flew just offshore, and once a plane ran out of gas and landed on the beach. The Civil Defense directed air raid drills. When the siren let out its terrifying screech, we were to set the radio dial to 650, close the curtains, and turn out all lights. We two children had cushions under the big dining room table and kept a picture book, flashlight, and Milky Way on the crossbar. Michael liked making a game of all this, but I wanted to know what to do if a bomb hit the house, or if paratroopers landed, or if a U-boat came up and shot at us. Would we really be safe under the table? Would the German soldiers kill us if my mother spoke to them in German?

When V-mail from my grown-up cousin George confirmed his part in the invasion of Italy, Michael and I created our own Anzio beachhead on the little bay beach next to our house. We tooks turns being either George and the liberators landing in the rowboat, or the soon-to-be-defeated Italians and Germans entrenched on the beach behind the bayberry bushes. A photograph of my Navy cousin Bobby in front of his Guam foxhole sent us into the dunes, digging our own foxholes and attacking and counterattacking. We strafed and sprayed bullets with our fingers, screaming out the staccato *rat-a-tat* of a machine gun. I discovered my father's gas mask in the attic, but my mother forbade my wearing it; she said it would upset my father. After futile attempts to stop them she bore our war games, suffering their inevitability — but she allowed no gunplay in the house. On the lighter side, I cut out cartoons from the *Saturday Evening Post*, *Colliers*, and *The New Yorker*, and wrote stories and jokes. I mailed everything to my cousins' APO and FPO addresses, barely believing my packages would ever reach such faraway destinations. Eventually George's march across North Africa and up the Italian boot was lined on the map in red, and Bobby's advance from one South Pacific island to another in blue. My awareness of global relationships intensified.

By the summer of 1944, the Allies had again gained control of my ocean and the beaches were unrestricted. That's when I became a first-rate scavenger. Beachcombing yielded an abundance of artifacts: a deflated rubber raft, life jackets stamped "USN," tins of pure water, C-rations (biscuits), K-rations (biscuits and pithy, tasteless chocolate), and "yellow-bombs," the name we gave to the three-inch, tubular, sealed-glass vials containing a yellow powder that purified water. The vials made a small but satisfying explosion when thrown vigorously onto the street, leaving a white smear on the black macadam.

There were larger finds as well. When the newly installed radar on a blimp misread a whale for a submarine, depth charges were dropped and huge chunks of blubber washed onto the beach. We used the gelatinous flesh as trampolines; a lightweight child could bounce up and down without breaking through. The most exciting find, though, was a 12-foot rope ladder that my father trucked home in his 1939 Dodge pickup. It hung suspended from a friend's bedroom window until after the war, long after I lost interest in climbing in and out of his room.

The war ended and I entered adolescence, leaving behind the tomboy who carved warplanes, reveled in loud war games, and threw mud bombs from the top of a tanker's tar-stained rope ladder. I went inland to school, and when I talked about these experiences my classmates gave me blank, almost disbelieving stares. But I know now that World War II sniping at my beach shaped my view of the world; it gave me a deeply understood awareness of how a global event could affect the lives of people everywhere — even on a sliver of island off the New Jersey coast.

The Finished Sound

by Sandy Gingras

Edgar lives in an apartment on Long Beach Island overlooking Mr. Cee's Putt-Putt Golf. Mr. Cee never oils his moving obstacles so they all squeak and groan. It makes me crazy when I go over there — especially that yellow clown that keeps putting his foot down and raising it.

When Edgar first moved in, he was annoyed by the whir of the little windmill, the raucous bells when somebody won a free game, all the people bending and putting, bending and putting, as if there was nothing better to do. But now he's grown to love the sound of golf balls falling into holes. "It's a nice finished sound," he tells me. We're in my bayside apartment, and I know what he's getting at.

I close my eyes and sigh. I'm thirty-five — too old for this. I can't say, "I don't know. I can't figure things out. I'm not ready yet," anymore. Edgar wants me to move in with him. More than that, he's ready to cash in his E bond and buy me a ring.

I go in the bedroom and fake sleep. I listen to his steps approaching, the splashing noises in the bathroom, the slide of his clothes, the click of the light. He gets into the bed carefully and lies still in his own indentation. I think of a boy making an angel in the snow and forgetting to make the wings. My body leans toward his.

The next day at work at the newspaper, I have to keep taking breaks. I'm the news editor, and it's gotten so that I wish every story was just a paragraph, or even just one sentence. I can't stand all the stuff about he said, she said, all the nuance and complexity that got me into this business in the first place. Now I cross it all out. "Get to the point," I keep telling the reporters. Today there are red slashes all over the stories I've been reading; there's almost nothing left of them. I know I can't go on this way.

I call two of my married friends. I ask them how they decided to get married. Both of the stories involve wine. I write down on my "To Do" list: Wine — Red?

When I meet him for dinner, he says, "What's up?" I know what he's asking. He's given me a week to decide, and it's been four days. "You're stalling," he says. "You must know what you want?"

This restaurant is full of air plants that need no soil or pots. They're hanging on strings over our heads like puppets with no feet. They sway and rustle slightly with every air draft. I bat at one and send it whirling around in a circle. "Remember tether ball?" I ask him. He shakes his head.

Throughout the rest of the meal, I study him hard. I pretend I don't know him. I ask myself if I would want to meet him. I angle my head and squint like artists do to see contrasts. My eyes gravitate to certain parts of his body. It's as if there were magnets embedded in his cheek bones, his neck, his forearms. I know I'm not seeing the whole picture, even squinting. If there's one thing I can't trust it's my eyesight, next is my taste in men, next is my intuition. I wonder if I rely on my senses too much. I think maybe I should do those exercises that the eye doctor told me to do: focus on something close and then something far away. Then I realize I do that all the time; I can't stop doing that.

After dinner, he comes over to my place and, while we're watching TV, the screen goes blank. He fiddles with the wires behind it while I say, "No. Not yet. Nope," for what seems like hours.

He says, "I'll make a new connection for you."

I hesitate, thinking of his neat garage with shiny tools hanging on their own pegs, glass mayonnaise jars with sized bolts and screws, labels on each one. Edgar believes that living is an assembly problem. I mean, he really believes that. He thinks that if he gets the parts and follows the directions carefully, something solid will be built. I don't know anymore if this is wisdom or unbearable innocence, so I say, "I'll just wait."

"What do you mean?" he asks.

"Time sometimes works on mechanical things."

"You need a new part," he argues.

"Maybe it'll work later," I say.

"What do you have against logic anyway?" he says.

I remember my relatives telling me, "You'll know if he's the right one." They never said anything about the possibility of bad reception, of knowledge flying by me as invisibly as electricity while I wait on my couch for a clear picture.

On my lunch break at work, I make the list of pros and cons that all my friends have been advocating. I list all the things I like about him: "That blue and white flannel shirt; the gray in his mustache; the way he says 'I got you' when he holds me; the way he rubs his dog's throat...." Then I write the things I don't like: "How many wrenches he has; those geometric sheets; the persistent way he cooks dinner (i.e. the way he keeps patting things with a spatula)." These lists make my shoulders bunch up. I total them up, but that doesn't seem to be enough. I wonder if I should subtract or divide. I do both. I come up with 17 and 2.4.

I was never any good at math story problems. The teacher with the string tie had to keep me after school every Wednesday in 5th grade. He would repeat in a patient way, reassigning emphasis to different words: "If JANE goes on train A.... If Jane GOES on train A...." I'd stare down at the yellow desk and let the words choo-choo by. I'd smile regretfully, sure that this would always be a sticking point.

That night, there's a storm. The moon and tides and wind and rain align overnight, and the island is buried. I wake up and there's a flood around my house like a liquid lawn stretching out into the bay. The bay swarms over the bulkhead; it swells out of the storm drains. It's everywhere. The road is gone. My neighbor's zinnias stick their skinny necks out of the water like desperate umbrellas — red and pink and yellow. My truck's tires then doors are lapped by waves. The electricity goes quietly out.

Edgar and his dog Sammy are stuck with me in my house. They're both pacing. I sit on my plaid skirted couch feeling oddly cozy in this flimsy cottage swaying on its pilings in the battering rain. I think that this is what marriage is. Another part of me argues that this is a weather anomaly, but the other part is more sure: This is marriage. Even at low tide, the water barely recedes, and we can't leave.

Edgar has to put on waders to get the canoe from the garage just so he can put his dog in it and row her to the ocean side, up to the high ground of the dunes so she can get out and pee. He keeps coming back drenched and wild-eyed, carrying things — a large piece of a fish jaw with black teeth, driftwood shaped like a fat nude woman (there's a hole that goes all the way through her for a belly button)— giving these things to me so I can find a place for them. I line the objects up on the kitchen table like hypothetical wedding gifts.

The wind keeps shoving at the house. "Oh," I say when the house moves.

"A house on pilings is built to move," he keeps telling me.

"I know, I know," I say.

For dinner, we have canned beefaroni and canned asparagus. We light candles and spoon up our mushy food while the water rises under the house. We imagine it rising. It's too dark to see, but we know that the tide is coming in again.

"You want dessert?" I ask him.

He sticks his finger right through the driftwood woman's belly and wiggles it at me beckoning.

"What?" I say.

He just keeps on beckoning.

"What?"

He won't stop until I bend my head down and look through the hole. Then he withdraws his finger and puts his face down and looks at me through the hole. All I see is this big eye winking at me.

"I don't get it," I tell his eye.

"I see right through you, baby," he says.

"Oh yeah?" I say, and pick up the jaw bone and put it in front of my mouth. "Now what do you see?"

He reaches over and snaps one of the teeth off. A big one just comes off in his hands. I can't believe it. "So what?" I say.

He puts the tooth between his lips, and it looks like a big hole in the middle of his smirk. The he chases me around humming that "dum-dum dum-dum" shark music. Maybe I hate him a little as I throw pillows at him and hurdle over the couch into the dark living room, but I can't stop laughing either. He spits the tooth out by the time he catches me, but I swear he still tastes like something fierce when he kisses me. I could have told him then that I loved him, that I'd marry him, but I didn't. Instead, I just listened to the storm, and it sounded like it was rushing right through us.

By the next day, I guess I'm used to being surrounded by water. I don't even look for glimpses of land anymore. I trust the pilings under the house so absolutely it's a kind of purity of denial. Now I understand why people get so hooked on faith. Why it makes them want to sing. It's concentration of energy into something that doesn't deserve it. It's crazy. I vow that IF this storm is ever finished, WHEN this storm is finished, I'll get a piling sunk into my yard and paint it and carve it like a totem. I'll dance around it and sacrifice things to it. I'll worship the mad concept of having thin legs to stand on.

I expect the same of him somehow, but Edgar can't sit still. He's nervous. He doesn't know what to do with his hands. If he were out there slinging sand bags or battening hatches, he'd be fine. But he's not. He's on my couch flipping the pages of *New Woman* magazine, impatient to get somewhere.

By afternoon, the wind slows and the rain is less sheeting and absolute; the waters seem to have peaked. Now it's just a matter of waiting. I know that something in both of us is disappointed. We'll find out later that the eye of the storm didn't really hit us, that it veered off at the last moment and headed back out to sea. When I hear this, it doesn't surprise me. In my experience, most things hold themselves back like this, hint at their full potential, then tuck into themselves and wait for next time.

Edgar takes Sammy down to the beach. When he comes back this time, he says, "There's a house down on the beach." He's trying to act like it's no big deal, but I heard his feet pounding up the steps.

"You mean it fell off its pilings?" I ask

"No," he says, "washed up. In perfect shape, curtains in the windows and everything."

"Where did it come from?"

"What do I look like?" he says. "Number 112 it says on the door."

"Nobody's in it?" I ask.

"I don't know. I couldn't see from the dunes."

"What about all the closets and stuff?"

"The closets?"

"I might go in the closet if my house floated away."

"Really?" he says.

"Let's go look," I say.

"I knew it, Sammy, didn't I?" he asks his dog. "The closets," he adds.

We all get into the canoe. This is my first time out, and I know there are wires down. I hold tightly to the rim of the canoe as the wind pushes us sideways. Sammy barks at a piece of wood floating by. Everything looks shorter, cut off at the knees. Garbage can lids, wooden walkways, a mailbox with "The Lyles" printed on it go by. "Wow," I say.

"Do you know them?" he asks.

"See if there's any mail," I say, but the mailbox drifts off before he can get it with the paddle. He wants to go after it but it's sweeping toward the huge bay, and I'm afraid of letting the boat go that way. "Let's just keep going," I say.

He smiles at me absently, proudly, as if the currents are nothing to him.

"This canoe is going to your head," I tell him.

All of the houses we pass are blank, summer houses, empty in the off season. In those houses not on pilings, I know there's water moving the furniture around, opening doors and cabinets.

"This is so dangerous," I say. Edgar smiles and wiggles the boat till it tips back and forth. Sammy's paws scrabble and my hand slips into water that's swirling and very cold.

"It's not a game," I say as stiffly as I can. I'm always saying this to him. I sit up straight and look away from him. He splashes me with the paddle.

"Lighten up, profile," he says. He calls me "profile" when I get mad because that's what I give him. I've been known to walk sideways through an entire room to maintain this look. It can cut people in half; I can be cruel like that. But it doesn't work on him.

The beach, as we approach it, is loud with irregular crashes. We tie the boat up to a telephone pole. We walk up toward the dune and when our feet hit sand, I understand why people kiss the ground. He bends down and grabs a handful and scatters it like it's nothing, but I know what he's doing. At the top of the dune, we stare at the frothy ocean rolling in all directions, the piles of plastic and seaweed sloshed against the dune line, the crumpled dune fencing and wooden walkways. One huge pitted beam, maybe ten feet long, is stuck vertically in the dune as if the waves pitched it there like a spear. The dunes are gouged out and sliced like a cliff fifteen feet high. The house is pushed up against the wall of dune, its side wall just lapped by the farthest reaches of waves. The house is yellow — a Cape Cod.

We slide down the steep cut of dune on our heels swooping like kids. Sammy bounds down in two leaps. I walk to the front door and tentatively push, almost knocking. My manners amaze me sometimes, how they restrain me. "Ding dong," he says behind me.

The inside is cluttered with furniture angling in a maze; china knickknacks and lamps are broken all over the floor. Sammy nervously patters around on the kitchen linoleum. I sit down on the couch, testing it first — it's unaccountably dry. The afghan draped over the back is bright crocheted squares. I reach out and feel how warm and scratchy it is. I've got one at home just like it. I get up, and my foot kicks a can of pork 'n' beans. I pull aside the curtains to a bay window and see a wall of sand.

"What a view," Edgar says over my shoulder. The ocean is a press of noise behind us. I close the curtains and straighten the way they drape.

"This is so weird," I say. Edgar goes to check the closets.

"Where's the real estate agent?" he says. "We'll take it," he yells out, waving his arm in a grand encompassing gesture. His bravado echoes around him as he goes down the hallway, then gets smaller. I almost say I'll marry him then, but he opens a door and disappears.

I go upstairs and into the master bedroom and stand there looking around. Everything has slid over to the far side of the room. I go and sit on the double bed. He walks down the hall and says, "The tide's coming in."

He comes over and sits down on the edge of the bed next to me. He rubs my knee, slides his hand up my thigh. "Um," he says.

"Are you kidding?" I say.

"Why not?" he asks, smiling.

I look down at the ridges of the chenille spread. "Anything in the closets?"

"I don't know," he says, looking away.

"What happened to these people?" I say.

"They're OK."

"How do you know?" I say. I really want to know.

"They're in somebody's living room right now telling the story of how they got away. Having a beer," he says. "We're the ones you should be worried about." We both look around then as if we can't believe we're here, that we've put ourselves in this position. A wave hits the side of the house with such force that the whole house lifts for a moment then settles back down.

Edgar gets up and walks to the window. "Hell," he says, "how are we going to get back up that dune?"

Suddenly I feel enormously tired and lie back on the bed.

"I mean it," he says, his voice clutching. I get up and walk to the window. Up and down the beach for as far as I can see the dunes are cut into huge crumbly vertical cliffs. It's unreal that we didn't think of it before we jumped. There's no way back up.

I take his hand, but he pulls it away to bang on the window to get it open. It's been painted over. He keeps banging. "Move back," he tells me.

The house looks suddenly absurd. The bright white rooms. I'm angry at these people for putting these frames around these pictures, this vase on the table, for valuing things that are clearly too fragile. Why did they collect china and live on the ocean? Edgar's pounding his palms on the window frame like they're hammers.

"Take it easy," I tell him.

He looks at me like I have no sense at all. He pushes me back, grabs a chair and hurls it toward the window. "But," I say. The window shatters, and he bangs out the leftover pieces with the chair. He throws the bedspread over the sill and climbs out. I feel the sand grinding under the house, something shifting.

In the end, there's not even any drama. We end up climbing out the window onto the roof and hopping back to the dune. It's really very easy. Even Sammy doesn't have any trouble.

Our mistake is to look back at how fast the tide is coming in. Both of us lean over to see just how impossible the dune cliff is. The waves are slapping the side of the yellow house.

We paddle home. The oars dip like commas into the water, inserting one pause after another until we've made the whole trip in silence. "Well, thanks," I say to him as I climb out. I don't know why I say this.

Within another day and a half, the storm is over. The sun is out and the weather unseasonably warm for October. The roads are strewn with debris. The snow plows are out pushing the sand off the roads. Everyone's getting his car towed. The businesses are calling their insurance companies, pumping out their aisles, piling sodden merchandise on curbs.

Edgar can't wait to get home. His apartment is up high so it shouldn't be water damaged, but he's worried about what's happened to Mr. Cee's obstacles in the storm.

I tell him, "All those things can be replaced."

"Oh well," he says. "I like the old ones."

"They'll probably need to be replaced," I tell him.

He just looks at me.

"You didn't even talk to me through the whole storm and now you can't wait to go fix those things."

"What do you mean, I talked."

I don't know what I mean, so I say, "I hope Mr. Cee's balls floated away." I know I sound spiteful. Even Sammy looks at me with disdain.

It's hard when a storm is over. We don't know whether we wish there was more damage or less. Mr. Evary, from the next block over, has some Polaroids to show me. He's got a shot of my house during the high tide, and it looks like all the rest of the houses—a half-sunk survivor, my gaudy fish flag waving from the deck. I shake my head. I don't know what to say.

I ride my bike up to the beach. The wind is already smoothing the dunes back into manageable slopes. The house is nowhere in sight. In fact, nobody I talk to ever saw it. When I see Edgar later at Mr. Cee's, he thinks it's funny to say, "What house? Sammy, did you see a house?" I laugh with him, but I can't help feeling that maybe he's right. Maybe we didn't see it. Maybe it was just one of those mirages that spring up in a relationship — some idea of what could happen.

Edgar's helping Mr. Cee clean up. The whole electrical system is gone, but the obstacles are all still standing. I look around at the windmill, the clown, the rowboat that tips back and forth; I guess I was wishing for a clean sweep of the place — nothing but the clear greens remaining. Or maybe I hoped that the greens would go too, and there'd be nothing left but smooth sand. "Hold this," Edgar says.

I bend down and hold a loose board while he fumbles in his pouch for the right nail.

Beach Access

by Bruce Novotny

J ared opened the door of his apartment, and recoiled as the reek of
summertime disregard assaulted him. He'd had no idea how bad it had
become. The first thing he did was throw out the half-slice of meatball pizza
sitting in a box that covered his kitchen table. That was three days old, he
calculated as he jammed it into the kitchen garbage can. Next he filled the sink
with warm, soapy water and slipped a stack of encrusted plates beneath the
bubbles. This is pretty mature of me, Jared thought, maybe too mature. For a
moment he worried about that.

Then, in his bathroom, the stale stench of wetsuit overwhelmed him and he
dragged it off the shower rod. Out onto his deck railing it went, with a rubbery
flop in the long shadows. The July evening still held the heat of the day, but the
humidity might keep the suit from drying by morning.

Back in the kitchen he grabbed a plastic milk crate and set it in the middle of
the floor. He tossed a beer can into it, then another, then another, putting slick
moves on the furniture to create open shots. "Yes!" he shouted. "Yes! Yes!" as can
after can found the mark. Four, five, six, seven in a row. "And this brash kid from
the streets of Ship Bottom is on a phenomenal run!" Three more shots, each
farther and more difficult than the last, all clanked home. This was an all-time
streak for Jared. He picked up an empty Dinty Moore beef stew can. Measured its

weight in his hand. Stepped back behind the three-point line, let fly. Clank! Nothing but tin! His focus zeroed in on an empty two-liter Mountain Dew bottle across the room. A different challenge, a different game. Jared crouched down, barked the signals, took the bottle from under center, faded back into the living room and uncorked a near-spiral to the end zone. Bullseye! The green plastic container bounced off the uneven surface of aluminum and out of the crate, but it counted anyway. Jared set the bottle up on end and lifted it with his foot, gently, into the crate. "And the extra point is good!"

He straightened and took in the breeze blowing from the plastic oscillating fan by his TV. "This place is starting to smell better already," he said aloud. Now what? It was a constant question in these plentiful summer nights, and he always seemed to find answers. The answers were always good. Maybe there was a band at one of the bars. A choice of parties. Naked moonlight surfing. Just hanging out with his friend Tony. Jared hadn't stepped off the island for six weeks, and he had no plans to leave for anything soon.

A slap on the screen door made him jump. A face stared in at him, dimly lit by the kitchen light. Jared was amazed to see how dark it had become outside.

"So, life is good, ain't it?" It was Tony speaking his favorite phrase.

" 'Course it is," Jared casually retorted. "You got a problem with that?"

"I got no problem with it. We ought to do something about it, though."

"Like what?"

"Let's go riding. I just bought a new truck."

"You're shittin' me."

✪

The truck sat under the yellow street light, gleaming under a sheen of dew. Tony insisted that the vehicle was green, but it looked like midnight blue to Jared. "Big moment, huh?" Jared said. "You've been wanting a truck for a couple of years."

"This is right off the lot. Factory fresh, man. Look at that mileage."

Jared climbed into the seat and surveyed the dash. The odometer registered thirteen miles. He gripped the wheel, bounced in the seat and looked for an ignition key. Tony dangled a key chain outside the door and said, "I don't think so, boy. I'll drive."

At the wheel, Tony started the engine and eased the truck up the street toward the end at the beach.

Jared could just make out the sign that listed all the beach regulations. It was coming closer as Tony kept his foot on the gas. Finally Jared spoke. "You know you can't go this way."

"You don't want to go beach riding because it's illegal or something?" The truck engine raced a little higher. The sign approached more quickly.

"That's not it."

"Then what's the problem?"

"It's just that there's no beach access here."

Tony stomped on the brakes and whipped the truck around in a hard one-eighty. The truck slid to a rest just inches in front of the familiar sign, now plainly visible, that stood guard over a narrow path over the dunes. "Not bad, huh?" Tony offered hopefully.

"Not bad," Jared allowed.

A big luxury car rolled elegantly past them and up the sloped driveway of the house against the dunes. Tony slid open the rear window and reached into the bed for a couple of beers. He handed one to Jared and they both cracked them open. Behind them, lights went on in the house, including a corner turret that overlooked the ocean.

Tony put the truck in gear. "Let's go pick up Tucker," he said.

❂

Minutes later Tony and Jared were sharing the cab with Susan Tucker, a year-rounder who could party step-for-step with the guys. Although she wasn't really pretty, Jared found her sexy. He had never admitted it to any of his friends, and had never shown Tucker any interest. But he kind of liked being squeezed up next to her now, pinned by the door. The crowded, purring truck rolled up Eleventh Street to where the dunes opened into a funnel that led to the steep slope of the beach. They stopped at the top of the dune. Tony and Jared climbed out to release air from the tires, leaving Tucker in the cab to keep watch for cops and play with the radio. Once they prepared the tires for the soft sand and the three adventurers were in place, Tony gunned the engine and the truck rushed over the dune, plunging into the near-perfect darkness on the other side.

"Yeehooo!" Tony yelled as the truck surged ahead into the unseeable. He threw the headlights on. Jared's shoulder smacked against the window as the wheels dropped in unseen low spots and the headlights swung wildly across the eerie black and white surfline.

"Damn it, Tucker!" Tony yelled. "You got beer all over me!"

"Well, stop bouncing the truck so much!"

Suddenly they were all thrown into the dash as the truck dove into deep sand and bogged down. The engine whined and the wheels spun.

"Is it in four wheel drive?" Jared asked.

"Of course it is. We just gotta work it."

Jared and Tucker reluctantly climbed out of the cab and began digging a track in front of the tires. Then they set themselves behind the tailgate and shoved as Tony let out the clutch. The wheels were digging in further when Jared shouted for him to stop.

"The front wheels aren't turning!" Jared called as he crept up to examine the hubs.

He adjusted one, then the other, and hopped backed into the cab.

"Wasn't in four wheel. Sorry," Tony said sheepishly.

"Right."

Tony revved the engine, let the clutch out slowly. The wheels bit the surface and carried the truck gingerly over the trap. With solid footing he raced again across the nightscape. They were a couple hundred yards down the beach before Jared asked, "What about Tucker?"

Tony broke into laughter and revved up again, speeding away from where they had left her. He steered toward the water and cranked a big power turn in the wash, sending a plume of spray behind them. Bottles clanked in the truck bed. "You're getting salt all over this beast!" Jared yelled when he stopped bracing himself between the dash and the rear window. He nervously drained his beer, then crawled half-through the rear window to get another.

"The case tipped back here, bud. There's beer bottles all over," Jared called. He grabbed one as it rolled by and opened it up, still leaning out the window. A whoosh of foam covered his hand. A flash of light down the beach caught his attention.

"What was that?" he asked.

"What?" Tony yelled.

Jared yelled back over his shoulder, "Searchlight. Coming this way. Maybe another truck."

"Can't be. No one's allowed on the beach in summer."

Jared slithered back inside. "Cops are."

Tony's eyes got wide and his grin got crazier. "We can't get caught." The truck went faster.

"What are you doing, man?" Jared barked. The pursuing vehicle was making up ground. "Yi-ha!" burst Tony. "If I get caught on the beach and driving with an open beer, I'll lose my license, dude. They're not gonna catch us. Can you tell if it's cops?"

"No. Yeah. It is. I think. So we're just gonna blow off Susan like that?"

"We were just havin' some fun. And it's *Susan* now, huh?"

"Let's just stop. If it's the cops, it's only gonna get worse. They're gaining on us. They're gonna catch us."

Tony switched off the headlights and they raced into absolute darkness.

"They can't catch us. Besides, I don't think it's the cops."

Red and blue lights started flashing behind them, reflecting off the rear-facing surfaces of the truck. Their left wheels plowed through the surf with a sound like a saw cutting aluminum, slowing them down. The following vehicle made up more ground. Tony swung the wheel and bent a hard right turn, throwing Jared into Tony's lap and beginning a precarious climb through the soft sand across the beach to the top of the dune.

Jared recognized the light in the turret ahead of them. "You can't get out here!" he screeched.

"We'll get out," Tony laughed as they bounced uphill.

"This is my street, Tony. We can't make it through."

"I think we can make it. I think we can," Tony chanted desperately. The police truck made a wider turn but still followed the dark spray of sand from Tony's wheels. The dune rose ahead of them. Jared could see the upstairs decks on the houses. The house on the south side had lights on. The wood-slat dune fence was visible against the gray sand and it grew closer and the gap that Tony was aiming for grew narrower.

"We were just here, Tony — on the other side!" Jared shouted.

"Oh shit!" Tony yelled as this registered with him, but too late. The truck crunched forward, splaying the dune fence, forcing its way through. Then they were on the other side, rolling downhill, and Tony had to jog the wheel to avoid the beach sign. Jared saw something in front of them, movement or a shape. It was dark and they were on it quickly and there was a heavy thump of metal on his side, then the wheels bit the pavement and they cruised down the quiet street.

"What did we hit?" Jared yelled in a panic. "It looked like a kid or an animal!"

"We didn't hit nothing," Tony insisted, visibly shaken.

"Maybe it was the sign."

"No, I definitely missed the sign." Tony looked back. "Well, anyway, the cops didn't make it through."

"Yeah, they weren't stupid enough."

"Let's get off the street."

Tony eased the truck into the driveway of a darkened cottage and killed the engine. He sat at the wheel for a moment, then said in almost a whisper, "I'm afraid to find out what we hit." He opened the door and slid out, and shuffled over to examine the fender on Jared's side. "Oh, shit," Jared heard him moan.

Jared jumped out of the passenger seat and headed toward the beach without a backwards glance at Tony or the truck. At the top of the street he found their tire tracks, and broken slats from the fence that lined an opening much narrower than the truck's wheelbase. "Hell of a truck," he thought briefly, until he realized that he could not find what had produced the awful, ominous thump. The tracks veered away from the signpost, so that wasn't it. There was nothing. A chill slid up Jared's backbone. It had to be something.

"What the hell was it?" Tony called from down the street.

"Don't know. I don't see anything."

Tucker! flashed through his brain. He struggled with what he should do. Maybe he could find Susan, maybe she was still on the beach. Where had they left her, he wondered. He tried to scan the darkness but saw nothing as the ocean dampness swept over him on a gust. He trudged down the dune to hunt for her, keeping low in case anyone else was out there looking for him. But it wasn't fun now. They could be in trouble. Maybe the banged-up truck would be the worst thing they had to deal with. He hoped. Fog floated in and seemed to thicken with each step he took, and the night air turned cold.

A Strange Incident at Bond's Hotel

by John Bailey Lloyd

A t two o'clock on the afternoon of Friday, July 16, 1897, a woman bather drowned in the surf in front of the Engleside Hotel at Beach Haven, New Jersey. There was a coroner's inquest, and some local laws were bent to get her out of town as quickly as possible. Her remains were put aboard the 5:15 train to Camden for transfer by ferry to Philadelphia, then onto the night train to Pittsburgh, where news of her death would bring scandal to two socially prominent families.

At precisely the same time as the train carried her body out of Beach Haven, I had a harrowing encounter in the ruins of Captain Bond's hotel in Holgate, two and a half miles south of town. Thirty years have passed since then, and in that time I have never breathed a word of this experience to a soul.

Until now.

❂

I turned 35 that summer, the last season of a long and pleasant bachelorhood. An established architect in Philadelphia, I had the habit of taking frequent vacations for hunting and fishing on Long Beach Island, where I had inherited the family cottage in Beach Haven. That summer I had set aside the third week of July to fish for sheepshead and weakfish. But when I arrived, I found to my dismay that an unseasonably bad nor'easter was just beginning. So while the wind howled and the rain slashed at every east window, I made the most of it and spent the fifteenth of July playing cards, shooting pool, and drinking beer with my friends in the game room of the Hotel Baldwin.

Just as it does today in 1927, Beach Haven had two major hotels at the turn of the century, the Engleside and the Baldwin. Both had a great measure of class, and both were good fun. But the Engleside, for all its elegance, was a bit straitlaced for me. Robert Engle Sr. forbade alcohol on the premises and wouldn't even allow card playing on Sundays. The Hotel Baldwin, a few blocks away from the Engleside, was more to my taste. Its principal backer was Charles Parry of the Baldwin Locomotive Works, and his son-in-law, James Baird, was spending tons of money to make it go. The social arbiters of the place were all men like my father, who traced their friendships back to the good old days just after the Civil War, to Bond's Hotel about two miles below Beach Haven. That was when Long Beach, as we called our island then, was a sportsman's paradise. The Baldwin in the nineties was trying to carry on the traditions of the old Bond place, and that was one of the reasons why I liked it.

My father, a lawyer, had been a senior partner in the Philadelphia firm that represented not only Charles Parry's Baldwin Locomotive Works but also the Pennsylvania Railroad. It was he who drew up the charter and did all the legal work for the Tuckerton and Long Beach Land and Improvement Company, and he was also one of the select group of mostly railroad men who founded Beach Haven in 1874. I mention him here because he had died the previous winter, and thoughts of him undoubtedly influenced my decision on the still-stormy sixteenth to walk down the beach and visit the abandoned hotel of Captain Bond in Holgate.

Clad in a big, hooded oilskin, I set off southward at around one o'clock with the wind and rain at my back. It was high tide, and each crashing wave raced to the edges of the dunes. Being barefoot, I took care to sidestep the heavy driftwood I spotted gliding swiftly in the foam. Halfway to the Life Saving Station (which in those years was still on the beachfront), I chose to take the dune trail used by the surfmen in winter storms. From that vantage point I could see in the distance, over near the bay, the rambling ruin of the old hotel.

Long Beach Island's south end was almost a mile wider in the nineties; the dreadful erosion at Holgate was still a generation away. From the dunes I took a cross-island trail, which eventually led me onto a narrow footbridge that crossed a deep pond. Bond's place, its clapboard siding worn to a dull gray, loomed before me on the edge of the bay meadows. The three-story, L-shaped structure stood alone, save for a few decayed outbuildings and a badly humped dock. Through the driving rain, I approached.

This was not my first visit here; the hotel had been abandoned for years, and I'd explored it at various times with sailing parties and once with my father. I stepped onto the broad porch, which no longer wrapped nearly all the way around the building, and found the big front door partly open. Once inside, I pushed the door shut against the wind and rain, loosened my oilskin, and stood in the gloom of the old lobby. Before me, a stairway rose to the second floor. A door to my left opened onto a long, empty dining room, and to my right was the old bar with its blackened fireplace and a bowling alley badly warped by dampness. Rain dripped from countless leaks, and gusts of wind whistled through the upper floors. Still, I associated it all with my father, and for a time I wandered nostalgically from room to room, looking for anything that would remind me of him — even initals carved into the doorframes.

Since before the Civil War my father had been one of Thomas Bond's regular guests, and from him I had heard no end of stories about the Long Beach House when it was in its heyday back in the fifties and sixties. I knew all about the gunning and the fishing and the endless round of practical jokes everyone played on each other. Dad's best friend in those years was Ross Ingraham — Doc Ingraham. They were inseparable ever since undergraduate days at Penn. Both married late in life and at about the same time, and they brought their brides to Bond's the last summer before the war. One of the stories I loved best was the time, one rainy night, when Dad and Dr. Ingraham waited until everyone had gone to bed, then led Captain Bond's cow into the hotel lobby. They tied thick gunny sacks onto the cow's feet to muffle the sound of the hooves on the wooden stairs. Then, with much pushing and pulling, they got the beast up onto the third floor, which had been divided into two huge dormitories: one for men and the other for women. Dad and Dr. Ingraham pushed the cow into the women's dormitory and raced back down the stairs to the bar, where they had a nightcap and waited for the screams to start when the confused animal began bumping into beds, pulling at blankets, and upsetting chamber pots.

There were other antics and adventures, but all that good fun was to come to a sad end one hot August morning when Ross Ingrahm collapsed while descending the hotel's front stairs. Someone caught him as he fell, but he was dead before they could lay him onto the lobby floor. That was in 1872, two years before the new Parry House opened in Beach Haven and ended the great days of Bond's. I was only ten years old and at home in Philadelphia, but I went to the funeral in New York. Dr Ingrahm had one child, a beautiful little girl about my own age who cried the whole time. We had never met before because very young children did not go to Bond's in the old days.

Outside the storm raged unabated while I, deep in reverie, could think only of those lost times. I climbed the stairs. Most of the rooms on the second floor had been stripped of useful items; little remained but rusted iron bed frames and handmade wooden washstands. Broken bowls, pitchers, and other crockery littered the floors. Duck and goose feathers from dozens of old mattresses had drifted like snow into lee corners.

On the third floor, the two long, open dormitories met at right angles on a north-south and east-west axis. I shook my head; it was no wonder that the place soon became deserted after the better appointed Parry House and the Engleside opened in Beach Haven. Bond's would have seemed too primitive and old-fashioned, particularly for the women. I stepped to a window and, looking out over the rolling dunes toward the ocean, I became aware of a change in the weather. The storm was now alternating between sudden bursts and short periods of calm, a sure sign that it was almost over. The rain and the cloud cover were, however, bringing on an early dusk. To my right, framed in a big empty window at the end of the long attic room, I could see the winking of Tucker's Light at Sea Haven two miles down the beach. It was getting late.

Suddenly the whole building shook, and I realized that the front door had slammed open with incredible force. I dashed from the third level and was just making my descent from the second floor to the lobby when I saw a darkly clad figure at the foot of the stairs, looking up at me. By its long, black hair I could see it was a woman. She stood there in the waning light, enshrouded in a swirl of rain blown through the open door.

I must have shouted a greeting, but she did not seem to hear me. As I got closer I noticed that she was not even looking at me, but at something behind me on the stairs. I turned, but could see nothing. I continued down, and near the bottom of the stairs I had the distinct feeling that I had seen her before. Her loose, shoulder-length hair was wet, as if she had been in the rain a long time. Her dark clothing was really a jersey knit bathing suit with a skirt, stockings, and a sailor's collar. She had beautiful features, but I cannot remember them clearly because I was so drawn to the power of her eyes — which continued to look through me, as if I were invisible. When I was within five feet of her she opened her arms wide, as if for an embrace. Then, smiling radiantly, she looked directly at me for the first time.

The instant our eyes met I felt a dreadful chill — very much as if I had entered an icy current while swimming in warm bay water. But this was colder, far colder, and it cut to the bone. I gasped and clutched the bannister. The chill passed in an instant, and the woman closed her arms around something I could not see. She smiled one more time — and vanished. It was as if she had never been there, though I could still see the footprints of her wet bare feet on the wooden floor. The wind died away to a whisper, and I heard the faraway whistle of the departing train at Beach Haven. It was 5:15.

Vowing never to return to Bond's again, I hurried home up the old wagon road used by the people of Sea Haven on their trips to Beach Haven. I arrived at the family cottage within the hour, got into dry clothes, and went back to the Baldwin for dinner. But I was too late even for the second sitting, so I instead went to the bar for sandwiches and beer. My friends found me there.

"The fishing captains are out on the porch taking reservations," one of them announced. "The storm's's over, and we've signed you up with our party. We sail at seven o'clock tomorrow morning."

"Fine with me," I said.

"Where were you in all the excitement this afternoon?"

"Took a long walk. What happened?"

"Well, there was a drowning around two o'clock. It was a woman. She got her bathing suit out of one of the bath houses and went swimming alone, and the Engleside bathing master never saw her until it was too late. She must have been struck with a big piece of driftwood, a railroad tie maybe. She was dead when they pulled her out of the water."

"Where did she come from?"

"Pittsburgh. She'd been staying at the Engleside since last Tuesday with some

Pittsburgh mill owner. Lots of coal and steel money. That's what we heard. And guess what else? It was adultery. Both of them were married to other people out in Pittsburgh. Plenty of money on her side, too."

"What did Bob Engle think of a love tryst in his place?"

"He was fit to be tied. You know how picky he is about his guests. The inquest was over in a half hour, and they got her out of here on the evening train. That Pittsburgh chap didn't want to stick around at all. Poor guy. Think of all the explanations he's going to have to make tomorrow." I agreed that it would be very unpleasant.

"Say, Harry, do you know who she was?"

I felt a vague uneasiness. "Who?"

"She was Dr Ingraham's daughter. Remember how your dad used to talk about Ross Ingraham? He was the one who died on the stairs down at Bond's old place about twenty-five years ago. Isn't that a coincidence?"

I felt the hair rise on the back of my neck, and a chill swept through me — as if I had entered an icy current while swimming in warm bay water.

"Harry, you better drink your beer. You look like you need it.... Harry?"

Woo

by David C. Bruton

t the time we met, this one particular morning, I was practicing my
pitching. I played Little League baseball for the Braves, of course. As I
recall, at the time of this one particular morning meeting, I was
practicing my pitching, as I said, by hurling heavy cherrystone clamshells at the
hard outside crusts of dozens of horseshoe crabs that had coincidentally been
stranded to die by Mr. A. H. Aggerman, a coastal land developer and bulkheader of
the wetlands. Mr. A. H. Aggerman was in a hurry to beat the building moratorium
of the Wetlands Act, so he bulkheaded in his fifty acres of marshland and began to
fill it with sand transplanted from the mainland.

In his haste to beat the activation date of this legislation, Mr. A. H. Aggerman,
land developer and juggernaut, had coincidentally enclosed hundreds of horseshoe
crabs inside his new ten-foot wall of creosoted bulkhead, which I helped build
through an abusive child labor arrangement known as summer employment. As
the weeks passed, the big sand trucks began to fill up the marshland habitat like a
sandbox, forcing the horseshoe crabs to one corner of the tar-dripping bulkhead in
search of the last 100 feet of lowlands, where salt water from the bay was still able
to seep through the planks and provide a few inches of brine for the crabs. Mr. A.
H. Aggerman's bulldozers and tractor trailer trucks, with his name advertised on
their sides, were working around the clock, no doubt being paid time-and-a-half in

this battle to fill the bulkhead with thousands of cubic yards of imported mainland sand.

This was a Sunday, this one particular cloudless morning that I was practicing my pitching. It was silent as a seaside grave, except for the occasional chortle of sea birds and the washing of the bay through the slat spaces down in the only area where the crabs could still touch salt water. So I saw these trapped animals and began to hurl the heavy clamshells, which fit so well in the hand, through the crowns of these 250-million-year-old creatures, hearing the whirl of velocity as each shell crashed through a round brown head and liberated the blue goop of the crab's lifeforce. Shell after shell I fired, and the death count rose. I was "taking out" the men, women, and children of a stranded village, stranded by Mr. A. H. Aggerman's now sleeping machinery, which would be doing this tomorrow anyway. I was just adding the personal humanitarian touch and getting some good pitching practice in the meantime, on this cloudless Sunday morning.

Then quite suddenly my pitching practice ended. My friend Woo, who was two years younger than I, had seemingly materialized out of nowhere and walked directly into the line of fire. He was standing in the midst of the spilled blue ooze of the piles of dead or near-dead bodies, the men, women, and children of this land-locked habitat, who had given their lives in the name of my pitching practice, my Sunday morning pitching practice.

Without a word, Woo knelt down and began to search carefully for survivors, which he would find and then carry by the tail and transplant over the bulkhead and into the safety of the deep brown bay. As I watched him carry the first two horseshoe crab survivors away, one tail in each hand, I looked into the hecatomb. Things were suddenly not so clear. In the heap of bodies, I saw the legs of mortally wounded men, women, and children moving instinctively to escape from the cherrystone clam barrage that I had embedded deep in their brains in the name of pitching practice on a cloudless Sunday morning. The last clamshell fell out of my hand. I stood for a moment, frozen in this hopeless, heartless, lifeless testimonial to my own insanity. There were no words. Words did not exist to explain or excuse. I remember crying as I helped Woo transplant the remaining survivors to the safety of the deep brown bay on the other side of the ten-foot bulkhead, which I had helped build for four dollars and fifty cents an hour. These creatures had been around for 250 million years, the bulkhead for two weeks, the dead bodies in the pit for twenty-five minutes, Woo for five minutes. My remorse, which had just set like a rusted hook in my soul, would never leave me, not ever.

I have always deeply regretted this brief and previously unknown detestable murderous cruelty; but Woo, who was two years my younger, and who never spoke or reminded me of this incident again, had by gentle example shown me something to which the words "thank you" and "I'm sorry" are so pitifully, pitifully inadequate. Woo, my surfer buddy, known as Doug to his parents, died in 1983, just thirty-two days after he was married. I didn't find out about it until two years later — which sometimes happens when people lose touch.

Woo will never grow old but will rest youthfully, in silence, without the fanfare of a groveling and obsequious world. He will rest under the pine straw on rainy summer afternoons, and his memory will be touched by nothing more than raindrops unless, as happens once in a while, I think back and remember my friend.

A footnote: Mr. A. H. Aggerman and his mountains of monogrammed machinery, his thousands of cubic yards of mainland sand, and his additional overtime, succeeded in beating the moratorium, beating the clock, and beating the environmentalists. Mr. A. H. Aggerman, coastal land developer, had converted a piece of worthless swampland into several millions of dollars. Mr. A. H. Aggerman died two years later of emphysema due to his lifelong habit of smoking Camels, one after another. So down the road all runners run, Mr. A. H. Aggerman, millionaire land developer and chain smoker, is now — after suffocating at the breakfast table one sunny Sunday morning and falling headlong into his scrambled eggs — himself a part of the ever-changing landscape. Now when it rains, on a warm summer afternoon, men, women, and children will remember Mr. A. H. Aggerman with profound vocabularies as their high-priced waterfront homes sink, along with the gradually settling imported mainland sand, slowly into the bay where the 250-million-year-old horseshoe crabs look up from the bottom at the big stinking tar-dripping bulkhead and laugh like hell.

Long Beach Island in Winter

by Ray Fisk

The Refuge

by Stephen Dunn

The snow geese took off in fours,

sometimes in fives, while the great blue heron,

singular and majestically weird,

complicated a rivulet. An egret,

fishing, did its lascivious Groucho Marx

walk, only slowly, neck and head

in odd accord, and hundreds of black ducks,

driven by memory, readied themselves

in the curious calm of New Jersey

for that long flight beyond winter.

This was the safe place,

famous for these birds and meetings

of adulterous lovers, everything endangered

protected. Turtle Cove was closed

to humans; the dunlin and the swan

acted as if the world weren't harsh, maniacal.

Absecon Bay stretched out toward the Atlantic,

the very ocean Burt Lancaster said —
with the wild accuracy of a saddened heart —
wasn't the same anymore. The horizon graphed
the ziggy, unequal stretch of casino hotels,
and in front of us on the hard, dirt road
gulls dropped clam shells from a height
so perfect they opened.
 I had come with my sister-in-law,
nephew and niece, a familial gesture, not exactly
my style. My brother was back on the couch
watching football, my wife cooking
the Thanksgiving dinner that soon would bring us
together. Which one of us didn't need
to be thanked, and eventually forgiven?
A herring gull swallowed an eel.
Walking, the great blue heron
lost all of its grandeur. In a few hours
my brother would say grace at the table,
and we'd bow our heads, almost seriously,
but for now it was red-wing blackbird
and Canada goose, it was marshland and sky,
all the easily praised, the nothing like us.

Atlantic City Proof

by Christopher Cook Gilmore

I was nineteen in 1919, the year I fell in love with Annie Bloe. She smoked cigarettes, wore powder and paint, had short hair, and wore black stockings on the beach. She was a nice girl, only her father was a drunk, and she had to work in Dutchy Muldoon's saloon to pay his debts. Beautiful and worldly, only a few years older than I, she could speak right up to the swells with all the latest slang. I made her laugh; she made me frantic.

Muldoon's was the highest class saloon in Atlantic City, the town where I was born. All the politicians from Philadelphia went there on warm summer nights to play cards and drink. Annie served the drinks. Booze was expensive in 1919.

The war had ended the previous November and the Wartime Prohibition Law was to take effect on the first of July. The Eighteenth Amendment had been ratified, and distilling and brewing were forbidden. Everyone was going to be as sober as Woodrow Wilson, or so he thought. Even so, business at Dutchy's was booming. Fifty cents for a highball when milk was fifteen cents a quart, steak thirty-two cents a pound, fresh eggs sixty-two cents a dozen. The swells drank like it was going to last forever.

I longed to marry Annie after our first kiss one night on the end of Million Dollar Pier, where the sea spume coated her hair with a silver netting that I shook off with my fingers. I dreamed of paying her father's debts and taking her far from Dutchy Muldoon, who was a dirty skunk. But I was as poor as she, and jobs were hard to come by with all the soldiers home.

And so that June Dutchy's became a speakeasy, and Rum Row formed three miles off Atlantic City Inlet. From the boardwalk one could see the lights of the ships waiting to unload the rum, gin, and whiskey brought down from Canada. I'd heard rumors of fabulous profits that could be made by daring men with boats fast enough to outrun the Coast Guard.

I lived on the edge of Gardner's Basin and was no stranger to fast boats. As a boy I had scrubbed many a sport fisherman down after a cruise at sea. Later I became adept at handling the wheel while some rich duff sat on the stern in his fighting chair, a rod thicker than my thumb strapped to his shoulders with a 16.0 reel to haul in the biggest marlin. (Marlins were plentiful then.) At nineteen I was captain and crew of a thirty-foot Seabright skiff that could do twelve knots on the deep sea. The owner came down only on the weekends. I often slept aboard during the week in her spacious cabin. How I dreamed of bringing Annie Bloe to that cabin!

I suppose it was only natural that one night I had an idea. It looked like it would solve all my problems. I thought and thought about it, and in the morning I went around to see Dutchy Muldoon.

Dutchy was a big man with big hands and feet. He listened to my plan and looked at me hard. In the end he lent me five hundred dollars. It was more money than I'd ever seen in my hand, though I didn't let on.

That night I got my pal Garvey Leek and we started the skiff, took her out through the inlet to Rum Row.

Finding my way to the Row in the dark of night was simply a lark. Red, green, and white lights glowed from more than a dozen boats anchored end to end. I chose a smaller one and brought the skiff smartly alongside. A man threw Garvey a line and in a minute I was aboard, talking to a Canadian skipper in his warm cabin. He poured me a glass of gin, which I tried to swallow like a man. I have never had any great liking or capacity for alcohol, but after that first glass my nervousness left me. I talked of business, but my mind was on my Annie.

The Canadian sold me twenty-five cases of good gin at twenty dollars a case.

His man passed them to Garvey, who stowed them in the cabin and the cockpit. I felt wonderful, exactly like an old hand. But my glee dissolved when the scene suddenly lit up in the glare of a search light. A Coast Guard cutter was a quarter of a mile off having a look.

"No matter, Sonny," yelled the captain. "She can't bear down on you until you're a mile in from here. Run north, then cut in fast. You'll make it."

I started the Gardner engine and shoved the throttle way over. Garvey nearly fell off the stern. I ran down to a buoy that seemed to wink at me like a sleepy cat, cut it hard and headed toward shore. In a short time I was off the beach at Brigantine, the next island north of Atlantic City. I headed toward the channel, shot across the bar, and soon we were in the basin, alone and undetected. Dutchy's men were waiting near the dock with a big Reo.

Next morning Dutchy paid me a thousand dollars and I paid him back his five hundred. I was hooked. Dutchy looked at me with new eyes.

"When can I get some more?" he asked.

"Tonight."

Garvey and I made the trip again that night, and the next. On Friday my owner showed up and I had to spend the weekend baiting his hook and trolling for tuna. He didn't know I had enough money to buy his boat, practically.

This was on my mind during the next two weeks. I needed a bigger boat, a boat of my own. The sportfisherman could handle just under fifty cases; above that, she was slow and hard to handle. No one had chased us yet, but I knew if they did we would have to jettison the cargo just to match their speed. At the end of June I headed over to the Eberding Boat Works on the western rim of Gardner's Basin, at the end of Massachusetts Avenue.

I'd heard of "Old Ebby" since I was a kid. He built lap-strake skiffs of cedar, oak, and pine, all sizes. His were the fastest boats over the water. When I told him I'd like one built to certain curious specifications, he showed me around the yard. I was in for a surprise.

On the ways was an enclosed skiff of forty-two feet, about halfway completed. She was powered by a sixty h.p. Pierce Arrow engine and could do fifteen knots on an open sea, he said. He was building her for the Coast Guard. I raised an eyebrow.

"I'd like one like her, only bigger and faster," I said. Just like that.

"How fast?" he asked. Ebby had a habit of looking you in the eye when he spoke, smiling, and making you smile (or try not to).

"Oh," I said, "twice as fast."

"Fishing?"

"Cargo."

"How many cases?"

"Five hundred."

"Ah."

"Interested?"

"You bet you." The old man sat down on a nail keg and drew a picture on a pine plank.

"No cabin, no superstructure," he said. "Low freeboard, low fuel capacity. With a 190 h.p. Mianus engine and an overall length of fifty feet, she'll do twenty-two knots with five hundred cases."

"Faster," I said.

"I could take a thirty-second off every plank and timber to get her weight down. She might push twenty-four. But she'd leak."

"Would she still be seaworthy?"

"She'd make the Row with one man on the pump."

"Build her," I said.

She was launched in mid-August. Painted standard grey all round, she sat high in the water, a delightful throb to her engine. The old man and I took her out for a shakedown. She took the channel waves like a dolphin, leveled out over the deep sea swells.

The wheel was mounted in the bow over a narrow platform for the driver, another in the stern for the bailer. The rest was all open space except for the engine box. The mined cedar planks strained against thousands of copper rivets which held them to the white oak, steam-bent frames. She did an honest twenty-five knots empty. Eberding's cutter, launched two weeks before, made thirteen. I asked him why the Coast Guard didn't have one like mine.

"They have to go by government contract. That takes time. Her specs were made for last summer, not this one. But don't worry; they've had a good look at this one and they know her for what she is. They'll be coming up with a new contract."

"How long have I got?" I asked.

"Six months at least."

In those six months I made a laughingstock of the Coast Guard. They tried everything. Once they got close enough (found me in the fog somehow) to get a shot at me with their deck gun. I just laughed and set the throttle over. Often they were waiting for me in the channel. I'd turn on a dime and head south for the Absecon Inlet, or Townsend's Inlet, or north to Holgate's, Barnegat, or even Shark River.

She drank water and poor Garvey had to bail the whole time. But he was big, twice my size, and I paid him well.

Disaster struck one night in early December. Running out through Manasquan Inlet we ran aground on one of the constantly shifting, unmarked sandbars. A cutter came into view at first light, a welcome sight as the surf began to pound us to death. I stood by the bight in the bow to take a tow line. I might just as well have saved myself the trouble.

When they saw we were empty they stood far off and hailed us. They told us to swim for it. We did, but not for the cutter. We swam to shore and stood shivering on the beach, watching the skiff slowly disintegrate like a downed old gull in a windstorm.

I needed a new boat. I got another surprise at the Eberding Boat Works. On the trestles was a hull similar to my old one, but in it were two Mianus engines. The old man chuckled. He liked my custom, but he liked his government contracts as well.

I suggested three engines. We went upstairs to an office behind the loft. He had still another surprise.

"Ah, I can get you something better than three engines. Up in Jersey City the Vimalert Company is converting surplus aircraft engines. I can get you a Liberty!"

"How big is that?"

"Four-hundred-fifty h.p. She'll push you a good thirty knots, sure. More if I soup her up."

"Do it."

It was an odd scene in the yard, my rum runner sitting there next to the cutter. They were both big skiffs, beamy and deep. The cutter had two small engines, side by side. Mine had one, a monster. Everyone had a laugh.

My second boat was a dog to manuever. But she ran like a greyhound. The engine that helped to win the Great War was coupled directly to a marine-clutch, but Old Ebby never got the power-to-hull ratio quite right. She was a burden to steer.

Garvey and I became the black beasts of Rum Row. We often sideswiped the little freighters, leaving our grey paint along their hulls, splinters from our gunwales on their decks. But that silly cutter with its two engines never got close enough to us to smell our exhaust. My big Liberty, after all, had carried bombs to the Kaiser, and one quite like it had taken Alcock and Brown across the Atlantic in a single hop. There was nothing on the water that could match my speed, not even other rum runners.

I begged Annie to marry me. I never told her just how rich I was getting, but I did buy a car, a Briscoe. I still have a photograph of her sitting on the hood, her legs apart, a lit cigarette in one hand, a highball in the other. She said she was too young to think of marriage, but she did come to my hotel room (I'd taken a suite at the Union), and once, only once, she let me see her naked body. She'd had a lot of gin and wanted to know if I thought she was getting fat. She came out of the bath wearing only her step-ins, and she dropped those on the floor. She told me she posed once that way for a real artist from Philadelphia in an upstairs room at Dutchy Muldoon's. I hoped she was only joshing.

By this time Dutchy was just one of my customers, and by no means the biggest. I was bringing in the hooch all up and down the Jersey Coast, dodging the Coast Guard, the Customs Service, and the Immigration Service, delivering cases to the boys from Philly, Baltimore, and New York. Everybody in Atlantic City knew what I was doing, knew I had the fastest boat ever seen around there. Of course it didn't last.

The E. Fell Jardine Co. of Atlantic City built three chasers for the Coast Guard, each powered by a pair of Gar Wood Liberties. Ebby assured me they would make forty-four knots.

Ebby put another Liberty in my boat, souped them up to 565 h.p. each. But it was not enough. Fully loaded, we only matched the speed of the chasers. My customers were demanding shipments, and I had become more daring and not a little reckless. Garvey and I tried a run.

On a moonless night with five hundred cases aboard, a cutter intercepted us between the Row and Corsons Inlet. I headed north and soon saw she was gaining on us. Garvey and I worked harder than we'd ever had to in our careers. We threw those five hundred cases over the side in less than twenty minutes. Many of them washed up on the beach at Longport, a delight to the residents who hauled them into the bushes and split them up that night. But we were empty now, and by keeping her at full throttle with Garvey alternately bailing and keeping those damn finicky engines at top tune, we just managed to escape. By the time we were berthed we were thoroughly sick of the boat.

Eberding was ready for me in two weeks. He had plans on the board for a fifty-two-footer with room for eight hundred cases and three engines. No more Liberties, either. She would fit two 565 h.p. Wright Cyclones aft; set slightly forward was an eight-cylinder Sterling Viking with an eight-inch bore, a nine-inch stroke.

On our first run we cruised out to the Row using only the Cyclones. Loaded up on the way back, we ran at forty-two knots. Two chasers appeared and tried to run us down.

I waited until we were just in range of their cannon, then I kicked in the Viking. The bow lifted from the surge of power, then settled down. We planed off at fifty-five! The Coast Guard never quite got over that one.

In fact, they came to me with a very interesting offer. A certain officer who was in charge of the three-man installation at Longport said he'd make a deal. Three nights a week he would take over the observation shack at the base of the bridge to the causeway. He would hang a red lantern from that bridge, and while it was lit *anything* could go under it. He was willing to do this for a hundred dollars a week. His salary at the time was nineteen hundred dollars a year.

Longport is just down the beach from Atlantic City. Over the bridge is the mainland, and at the end of the causeway is Somers Point, a haven for smugglers, bootleggers, and speakeasys. Nothing could have suited me better. I chose a mooring just inside the bridge at a place called Risley's Channel. My customers could pick up the load at Hospitality Creek, which was watched over by a black man who lived there. That red lantern was the best thing any smuggler could see, and I was growing steadily richer.

And I saved it all for me and Annie. I'd decided not to reveal to her the extent of my wealth until after she'd agreed to marry me. I was so idealistic in my youth, I wanted our love to be pure. I'd never tried to seduce her, though I sometimes felt she wished I would. She said once that she was tired of being a "nice girl," and that the whole country was changing its ideas about love, marriage, and families. She'd talk and talk about it while she sipped gin.

During this period I had changed from boy to man, from hook-baiter to experienced captain. I was accustomed to being shot at, I was wary of all men. The three-mile limit had been increased to twelve, and there were now destroyers plying the coast looking for me and others like me. They were serious, too, as serious as I. The good ship *I'm Alone*, of Canadian registry, was pursued by a revenue boat for two and a half days and sunk at a distance of 215 miles from the American coast, and she had no booze aboard. Izzy Einstein, Moe Smith, and even General Smedley Butler of the Marines were all cracking down hard on bootleggers. I had become a man who could accept these challenges and overcome them.

But Annie had changed, too. Atlantic City had become a gathering place for hoods, and something about them appealed to Annie. She was often seen in the company of men like Johnny Torrio, Lefty Louie, Gyp the Blood, out-of-towners who came to the shore to relax and talk business. She sat at the bars of the best hotels and drank martinis, danced to jazz bands, flirted with crooks. Oh, they thought she was quite a lilly, lots of fun when she was "blotto."

She said I smelled of gasoline and salt water. No matter how I dressed I couldn't measure up to her thin, low-cut dresses, her stockings rolled below her knees. She said I couldn't dance (I still can't). She said I was an old fuddy-duddy, even though she was older than I.

Well, I had three engines and no Annie. I'd rather have had one Annie and no engines. Why was I doing it all if not for her? ,

I even tried to impress upon her that I was as big an operator as some of her new friends. I told her about my Coast Guard deal, but all she wanted to know was if I'd ever shot anybody. This from my Annie? I've always hated violence, and had determined early on that I would never harm anyone in the course of my illicit trade. Of course, I'd had to take precautions....

One February night in '26 I came creeping in under the red lamp, my Cyclones just ticking over. I remember looking up at the stars, wondering which ones were mine and Annie's, and if they'd ever cross. I cleared the bridge and was headed for my secret mooring when suddenly there came shots from the causeway, automatic fire. I swerved back into the bay, ran north to a cut in the marshes behind Margate. A cutter was there waiting for me. We took two rounds through the hull, through a few dozen cases of scotch whiskey. I couldn't open her up on those narrow waters, so the Viking was useless. I was trapped like a fish in a barrel, and the bullets were flying by my head.

I headed her back for the bridge, hoping to reach open waters. Garvey yelled that we were sinking. I had to make it to the bridge. If she settled in the bay she could be raised with her incriminating cargo. I'd be in jail, and God only knew what the federal agents would do to me once they got me there. But the boys on the causeway saw me coming and they headed for the bridge. It would be suicide to run her directly under all those Thompsons.

I opened up the Cyclones, I opened up the Viking. I headed her bow directly for the main span of the rickety old bridge. I figured she'd make it through without me and scuttle herself in the channel, where the currents would carry those cases out to sea. I tied the wheel, ran aft to Garvey, and signaled for him to jump. We hit the water hard, and as I came up I saw my boat plough into the pilings of the bridge. She blew, and when she blew, she took a good section of the bridge with her. Everything was on fire.

Garvey and I swam to shore on the mainland side and made our way on foot to Somers Point. We holed up there for a few days waiting to see if they were looking for us. They weren't. There was no investigation because there was no evidence. But there were a lot of bad feelings all around.

I went down to Florida while things cooled off. I wrote to Annie, but she never answered my letters. I stayed six months and came home in the summer. I drove over to Dutchy's, and there at the bar was Annie Bloe. Dutchy was sitting beside her, holding her hand. He gave me a drink and left us alone.

Before I could say anything, she told me she and Dutchy were getting married. She said she knew I was finished without a boat, but that maybe Dutchy would give me a job. She was tipsy, the little curls on her head shaking, her bra-less breasts jutting out like the hood ornaments on a Cadillac. I just let her talk.

I didn't tell her I *owned* Dutchy's, that I owned three other saloons in town, that I had controlling interest in two amusement piers, five hotels, and was buying up railroad stock. I didn't want to break her heart the way she'd broken mine.

Well, I survived the crash of '29, retired from the brotherhood of the coast for good. I married a girl from Paterson, a girl I'd kissed one night over the falls where the cold mist settled on her hair like a silver net. She died giving birth to our boy. He's now president of a local bank. I have seven grandchildren, one of whom steers my boat while I sit in a fighting chair and fish.

When Dutchy died (he turned out not such a bad sort), I gave Annie the saloon. Just before old man Eberding died he built me a twin-engined sport fisherman with a flying bridge. Now and then I take Annie Bloe out for a ride.

We're just two old, old friends now, but I can never forget her the way she used to be. She admitted to me once that it was she who'd talked too much while drinking one night with an undercover revenuer. But I'd known that for a long time.

What can you do when you love a girl who talks too much and drinks too much? You take her out to sea in a fast boat where you can smell hot oil and gasoline, where you can recall the thump of cases coming aboard, the tinkle of thousands of bottles. You open a bottle of pink champagne, and you open up those engines until they sing like the sweet angels you'd like her to be.

And it's only angels and engines that can drown out that old devil rum. And, damn it all, it's only pretty Annie Bloe who could ever catch me on the run.

Black Boy

by Kay Boyle

At that time, it was the forsaken part, it was the other end of the city, and on early spring mornings there was no one about. By soft words, you could woo the horse into the foam, and ride her with the sea knee-deep around her. The waves came in and out there, as indolent as ladies, gathered up their skirts in their hands and, with a murmur, came tiptoeing in across the velvet sand.

The wooden promenade was high there, and when the wind was up the water came running under it like wild. On such days, you had to content yourself with riding the horse over the deep white drifts of dry sand on the other side of the walks; the horse's hoofs here made no sound and the sparks of sand stung your face in fury. It had no body to it, like the mile or two of sand packed hard that you could open out on once the tide was down.

My little grandfather, Puss, was alive then, with his delicate gait and ankles, and his belly pouting in his dove-gray clothes. When he saw from the window that the tide was sidling out, he put on his pearl fedora and came stepping down the street. For a minute, he put one foot on the sand, but he was not at ease there. On the boardwalk over our heads was some other kind of life in progress. If you looked up, you could see it in motion through the cracks in the timber: rolling chairs, and women in high heels proceeding, if the weather were fair.

"You know," my grandfather said, "I think I might like to have a look at a shop or two along the boardwalk." Or: "I suppose you don't feel like leaving the beach for a minute," or: "If you would go with me, we might take a chair together, and look at the hats and the dresses and roll along in the sun."

He was alive then, taking his pick of the broad easy chairs and the black boys.

"There's a nice skinny boy," he'd say. "He looks as though he might put some action into it. Here you are, sonny. Push me and the little girl down to the Million Dollar Pier and back."

The cushions were red velvet with a sheen of dew over them. And Puss settled back on them and took my hand in his. In his mind there was no hesitation about whether he would look at the shops on one side, or out on the vacant side where there was nothing shining but the sea.

"What's your name, Charlie?" Puss would say without turning his head to the black boy pushing the chair behind our shoulders.

"Charlie's my name, sir," he'd answer with his face dripping down like tar in the sun.

"What's your name, sonny?" Puss would say another time, and the black boy answered:

"Sonny's my name, sir."

"What's your name, Big Boy?"

"Big Boy's my name."

He never wore a smile on his face, the black boy. He was thin as a shadow but darker, and he was pushing and sweating, getting the chair down to the Million Dollar Pier and back again, in and out through the people. If you turned toward the sea for a minute, you could see his face out of the corner of your eye, hanging black as a bat's wing, nodding and nodding like a dark heavy flower.

But in the early morning, he was the only one who came down onto the sand and sat under the beams of the boardwalk, sitting idle there with a languor fallen on every limb. He had long bones. He sat idle there, with his clothes shrunk up from his wrists and his ankles, with his legs drawn up, looking out at the sea.

"I might be a king if I wanted to be," was what he said to me.

Maybe I was twelve years old, or maybe I was ten when we used to sit eating dog biscuits together. Sometimes when you broke them in two, a worm fell out and the black boy lifted his sharp finger and flicked it carelessly from off his knee.

"I seen kings," he said, "with a kind of cloth over they heads, and kind of jewels-like around here and here. They weren't any blacker than me, if as black," he said. "I could be almost anything I made up my mind to be."

"King Nebuchadnezzar," I said. "He wasn't a white man."

The wind was off the ocean and was filled with alien smells. It was early in the day, and no human sign was given. Overhead were the green beams of the boardwalk and no wheel or step to sound it.

"If I was a king," said the black boy with his biscuit in his fingers, "I wouldn't put much stock in hanging around here."

Great crystal jelly beasts were quivering in a hundred different colors on the wastes of sand around us. The dogs came, jumping them, and when they saw me still sitting still, they wheeled like gulls and sped back to the sea.

"I'd be traveling around," he said, "here and there. Now here, now there. I'd change most of my habits."

His hair grew all over the top of his head in tight dry rosettes. His neck was longer and more shapely than a white man's neck, and his fingers ran in and out of the sand like the blue feet of a bird.

"I wouldn't have much to do with pushing chairs around under them circumstances," he said. "I might even give up sleeping out here on the sand."

Or if you came out when it was starlight, you could see him sitting there in the clear white darkness. I could go and come as I liked, for whenever I went out the door, I had the dogs shouldering behind me. At night, they shook the taste of the house out of their coats and came down across the sand. There he was, with his knees up, sitting idle.

"They used to be all kinds of animals come down here to drink in the dark," he said. "They was a kind of a mirage came along and gave that impression. I seen tigers, lions, lambs, deer; I seen ostriches drinking down there side by side with each other. They's the Northern Lights gets crossed some way and switches the wrong picture down."

It may be that the coast has changed there, for even then it was changing. The lighthouse that had once stood far out on the white rocks near the outlet was standing then like a lighted torch in the heart of the town. And the deep currents of the sea may have altered so that the clearest water runs in another direction, and houses may have been built down as far as where the brink used to be. But the brink was so perilous then that every word the black boy spoke seemed to fall into a cavern of beauty.

"I seen camels; I seen zebras," he said. "I might have caught any of one of them if I'd felt inclined."

The street was so still and wide then that when Puss stepped out of the house, I could hear him clearing his throat of the sharp salty air. He had no intention of soiling the soles of his boots, but he came down the street to find me.

"If you feel like going with me," he said, "we'll take a chair and see the fifty-seven varieties changing on the electric sign."

And then he saw the black boy sitting quiet. His voice drew up short on his tongue and he touched his white mustache.

"I shouldn't think it a good idea," he said, and he put his arm through my arm. "I saw another little oak not three inches high in the Jap's window yesterday. We might roll down the boardwalk and have a look at it. You know," said Puss, and he put his kid gloves carefully on his fingers, "that black boy might do you some kind of harm."

"What kind of harm could he do me?" I said.

"Well," said Puss with the garlands of lights hanging around him, "he might steal some money from you. He might knock you down and take your money away."

"How could he do that?" I said. "We just sit and talk there." Puss looked at me sharply.

"What do you find to sit and talk about?" he said.

"I don't know," I said. "I don't remember. It doesn't sound like much to tell it."

The burden of his words was lying there on my heart when I woke up in the morning. I went out by myself to the stable and led the horse to the door and put the saddle on her. If Puss were ill at ease for a day or two, he could look out the window in peace and see me riding high and mighty away. The day after tomorrow, I thought, or the next day, I'll sit down on the beach again and talk to the black boy. But when I rode out, I saw him seated idle there, under the boardwalk, heedless, looking away to the cool wide sea. He had been eating peanuts and the shells lay all around him. The dogs came running at the horse's heels, nipping the foam that lay along the tide.

The horse was as shy as a bird that morning, and when I drew her up beside the black boy, she tossed her head on high. Her mane went back and forth, from one side to the other, and a flight of joy in her limbs sent her forelegs like rockets into the air. The black boy stood up from the cold smooth sand, unsmiling, but a spark of wonder shone in his marble eyes. He put out his arm in the short tight sleeve of his coat and stroked her shivering shoulder.

"I was going to be a jockey once," he said, "but I changed my mind."

I slid down on one side while he climbed up the other.

"I don't know as I can ride him right," he said as I held her head. "The kind of saddle you have, it gives you nothing to grip your heels around. I ride them with their bare skin."

The black boy settled himself on the leather and put his feet in the stirrups. He was quiet and quick with delight, but he had no thought of smiling as he took the reins in his hands.

I stood on the beach with the dogs beside me, looking after the horse as she ambled down to the water. The black boy rode easily and straight, letting the horse stretch out and sneeze and canter. When they reached the jetty, he turned her casually and brought her loping back.

"Some folks licks hell out of their horses," he said. "I'd never raise a hand to one, unless he was to bite me or do something I didn't care for."

He sat in the saddle at ease, as though in a rocker, stroking her shoulder with his hand spread open, and turning in the stirrups to smooth her shining flank.

"Jockeys make a pile of money," I said.

"I wouldn't care for the life they have," said the black boy. "They have to watch their diet so careful."

His fingers ran delicately through her hair and laid her mane back on her neck.

When I was up on the horse again, I turned her toward the boardwalk.

"I'm going to take her over the jetty," I said. "You'll see how she clears it. I'll take her up under the boardwalk to give her a good start."

I struck her shoulder with the end of my crop, and she started toward the tough black beams. She was under it, galloping, when the dogs came down the beach like mad. They had chased a cat out of cover and were after it, screaming as they ran, with a wing of sand blowing wide behind them, and when the horse saw them under her legs, she jumped sidewise in sprightliness and terror and flung herself against an iron arch.

For a long time I heard nothing at all in my head except the melody of someone crying, whether it was my dead mother holding me in comfort, or the soft wind grieving over me where I had fallen. I lay on the sand asleep; I could feel it running with my tears through my fingers. I was rocked in a cradle of love, cradled and rocked in sorrow.

"Oh, my little lamb, my little lamb pie!" Oh, sorrow, sorrow, wailed the wind, or the tide, or my own kin about me. "Oh, lamb, oh, lamb!"

I could feel the long swift fingers of love untying the terrible knot of pain that bound my head. And I put my arms around him and lay close to his heart in comfort.

Puss was alive then, and when he met the black boy carrying me up to the house, he struck him square across the mouth.

from The Boardwalk

by Robert Kotlowitz

[Atlantic City, 1939]

Teddy acted as guide. It was his Boardwalk. He had been in Atlantic City a week longer than Erich Kessler; he would force him to see it through his eyes. He assumed a faintly priggish, didactic tone. He gave a sermon, as though he was sure of everything, somewhat holy, full of false emphases. For that, he could be forgiven. The salt air buoyed him, the company of a new friend challenged him. He would do it right. Over there, he said, striding along, hands in the pockets of his white ducks, in that dinky-looking store, books could be bought dirt cheap, forty-nine cents, fifty-nine cents, eighty-nine cents, and ninety-nine cents, thousands of them. There were a lot of great bargains inside, piled up in huge bins. You had to scramble to find them but they were there. Teddy had his eye on a couple, a Garden City Press edition of *Personal History* by Vincent Sheean, which Benedict was pushing him to try, and a fake-leatherbound *Nana* he had found himself, illustrated with voluptuous silhouettes of naked women and printed on paper that felt like satin. Erich Kessler grunted approval. "Who is Vincent Sheean?" he asked.

Then, a half block farther on, Teddy pointed out the hole-in-the-wall in which the Boardwalk's famous gypsy foretold all human events and solved every riddle. During the day, she stood in the beaded doorway, Teddy said, and invited passersby in. She wore a purple dress down to her ankles, like the old lady Eisen, seductive gold earrings, smoked long blue cigarettes. Her bare feet were always filthy, and you could see the nipples of her breasts through her dress. Only gentiles, Teddy said, repeating what he had heard at Sloan's, went in there to have their fortunes told. God knew what really went on inside; the future in a deck of cards, clouds of blue cigarette smoke, other dark, gypsy things. The boys exchanged a glance and, despite themselves, shied away superstitiously. They lingered then at a miniature golf course, bought ice-cream cones, ate them in front of the colored fountain at the Claridge. Soft mauve and green lights rose higher and higher on the hotel's deep lawn. A spotlight wavered in the air. The water hissed noisily. The crowd sighed with pleasure. There was no sight quite like it in the whole city, no lawn so even, so perfect, so deep.

A million visitors, two million, strolled in both directions. Wicker carriages rolled by, pushed by Negroes who charged their passengers by the hour. Candystands lined the walk, peanut brittle, salt water taffy, sour balls, and popcorn like pebbles; the air reeked with it. On their left, the sea was invisible, but the sound of the breaking surf split the night air. Massive piers thrust into the ocean. Stars were everywhere overhead, dense creamy galaxies that overlapped without boundaries; lovers below; husbands in for the weekend; tired children and wan mothers; a dim moon offshore; and on their right mammoth hotels styled to the vagaries of their builders: a hallucinatory Tudor, faithful romantic Gothic, Victorian, Edwardian, Moorish, twenties boom, the willfully eccentric, pridefully bizarre, turreted, towered with frosted stucco, minareted like Islam, open to the sun, closed, timbered, bricked, and some, here and there, mortared in honey-colored stone.

That, Teddy said, is Haddon Hall, and *that* is the Marlborough-Blenheim and the Morton, and *that* is the Traymore, and down there is the Shelburne and the Dennis, and you just saw the Claridge. They're all like the Cotswold. Fifteen dollars a day, without food. Lots of Baltimore people, Teddy said, stay at the Shelburne. You can sit on the porch at the Shelburne, he said, pointing in its direction, and watch the horses race on the big electric sign over the Million Dollar Pier. They could just make them out from where they stood, jittery electric bulbs combined to look like jockeyed horses, jumping erratically across an electrified track to an electrified finish line. Six horses, each a different color. Then back to the start again and another race. The Shelburne porch wasn't as big as the Cotswold, Teddy said, but it was big enough. You could sit there half the night on rocking chairs and bet the evening away. Some of his aunts and uncles stayed at the Shelburne, Teddy said; they were all rich.

It seemed to Teddy that Erich Kessler was hanging on every word. He appeared quietly staggered by the incoherent vistas, intimidated by the crowds. He looked for his cues, grunted appreciation. He kept taking off his thick glasses and polishing them. Without them, he looked like a frightened child. Every now and then, a piece of information slipped through his reticence like grass through a cement crack. He lived in Washington Heights, he told Teddy at one point. That was in Manhattan. It was nice in Washington Heights, he said. Everywhere you went in Washington Heights, you could see the Hudson River and the George Washington Bridge.

Teddy had to listen to Erich Kessler with care, had to pick his way through the sentences syllable by syllable, sound by sound, transcribing sound into sense as he went along. He was familiar enough with the German accent, had been hearing it in Baltimore for almost five years. There were dozens of Germans in Baltimore like the Kesslers, old, young, middle-aged, they just kept coming, like imported delicacies, but often their accents set up an instant antagonism, a need for special, tense attention that bred resentment out of feelings of strangeness, out of all those uncontrollable, unthinking alien signals that make themselves known through language. There were Germans Teddy had met who could barely get a dozen English words out in comprehensible order. Others sounded as though they had been trained to speak English in phonetic syllables. Their diction was so impeccable it was almost deranged. Erich was somewhere in the middle, neither fluent nor frozen, struggling courageously in a war on two fronts against an erratic Yankee syntax and the middle Atlantic vernacular. He spoke slowly, treading the cobblestones of American speech with well-made, thick-soled boots that were built for sturdiness, not grace.

He and his father, he went on, measuring it out carefully, lived in a flat on the second floor of a new apartment building. That was the word he used: flat. They had a view of New Jersey from the living room. Erich shared the bedroom with his father. There were a lot of Germans in Washington Heights, a lot of Viennese, too. Some of the Germans were from Frankfurt, a few old acquaintances. It made his father happy to be with them. Then Erich had nothing more to say. He began to scrape at a spot of ice cream on the front of his shirt.

"Joseph and Tibor Talles went to Chalfonte Alley tonight," Teddy said after a moment. Erich nodded, examined the chocolate spot. "You know where that is?" Teddy asked. "No," Erich said. Teddy pointed inland, vaguely. He couldn't tell whether or not Erich knew what he was talking about. "You know what I mean?" Teddy said. He heard a new note creep into his voice, something nervous and tight. Erich didn't answer. It was just as well. You really couldn't push those things, Teddy knew. He thought a moment of Chalfonte Alley, of Joseph and Tibor, vile images.

The conversation stopped dead. Then picking up suddenly, his energy on the alert, Teddy began to offer Erich a few statistics about Atlantic City. Like music, statistics were one of Teddy's strengths. They existed in his head like printed clusters of black notes waiting to be translated into performance, into something public and useful. The populations of each of the forty-eight states, the number of times *Tobacco Road* had been played, the height of Mt. Everest and a dozen others, all gathered inside Teddy in a single undiscriminating embrace with the scores of the *Pathétique* of the "Minute Waltz" or the *Aragonaise*. They were sometimes coequal, obssessively sprung from a shared number-driven impulse, or nerve, and, like music, they had their own compulsively seductive sound. All the information Teddy had about Atlantic City he had picked up from the little promotional booklets scattered around Sloan's lobby. His mind clicked down the pages now. Ten million people, he said, came to Atlantic City every summer. Erich nodded once again, impassively. Most of them came from Pennsylvania, it was so close by. Teddy made up a figure: 28 percent. Summer visitors came from as far as Michigan, which was halfway across the country. There were about two hundred thousand rooms for rent every night in Atlantic City. You could get a room for two dollars, you could get a room for ten, you could get a room for two hundred. It all depended on where you wanted to stay, Sloan's, the Cotswold, the Shelburne, or a dump four blocks from the beach.

It seemed to be going down well enough. Erich was giving him brisk, satisfied nods; he was taking it all in. Anyway, Teddy said, the Convention Hall, which he signaled lay just ahead, covered seven acres of ground, in all, and could seat forty thousand people at one time. He let that sink in before going on. There was not a single supporting column in the main hall, he said. The whole damn thing was held up by the world's biggest trusses. It was one of America's wonders, like the Empire State Building. At the same time, the roof of the Convention Hall contracted more than three inches every winter when the temperature dropped. Also, he said, a whisper at one end of the auditorium could be heard all the way down at the other end, the acoustics were so spectacular. Beyond all that, he remembered that 200,000 tons of sand had to be removed to leave room for a foundation for the Hall. After all, when you got right down to it, Atlantic City was nothing but a long skinny sand pit, shaped like a broken toothpick.

They could now see Miss America pennants hanging outside the Convention Hall. Forty-eight girls posing in one-piece bathing suits that fit them like satin girdles. One of them would be Queen of the whole U.S.A. soon, Teddy told his friend. He felt a surge of unexpected pride as he said it. It was the biggest, most important competition in the whole country. Only the most beautiful could enter, only the most pure, only the most truly American. The whole world paid attention to Miss America, it was like being a movie star. For the moment, as he spoke, he believed himself, fell half in love with the idea, wanting it to be true. But some wicked sense of irony rattled his words. He began to laugh a little, examining Erich's quiet profile, thick, serious glasses, his heavy Central European look of common braininess so conscious of itself. There was not much beauty there, no sense of purity. It was not at all American. Well, Teddy said, still laughing, it helped in the Miss America contest if you weren't Jewish, Jewish girls never won, Jewish girls probably couldn't win, he didn't even know if they could enter. Erich gave him a quick, tiny smile of comprehension, shrugged good-naturedly.

Anyway, Teddy went on, the Boardwalk beneath their feet was more than four miles long and cost two million dollars to build. It went as far as Ventnor, he said, pointing straight ahead. Then he finally remembered to tell Erich that there was a horse that was trained to dive into the ocean five times a day from the deep end of the Steel Pier. Erich opened his eyes wide. Can horses swim? he asked. How deep was the ocean out there? A diving horse almost in the middle of the Atlantic? It was the most interesting fact of all, a triumph for Teddy, and they both silently turned it over in their minds for a moment or two, concentrating on it.

But Teddy forced them along again, picking up the stride this time, the Boardwalk crowds a little thinner here, easier to move through. He was full of

from *The Boardwalk*

purpose, energy piled on energy. New statistics hovered in his mind, questions and answers formed behind them. There was a second glimpse of Joseph and Tibor Talles, dim flickering images now which disappeared almost instantly. The sea alongside them was a steellike blur. Salt foam broke hissing at the shoreline. The boys marched in quickstep unison, the smell of cotton candy souring the air. He was up to something, he knew. He recognized the symptoms, knew this restlessness. An eyelid trembled, an old tic. Everything seemed to wait for expression. He couldn't stop talking. He wouldn't shut up.

Would there be a war? What would happen if the Germans won? What would happen to the Jews then? What would happen to all of them? And so on. Erich remained silent, eyes fixed on the black depthless horizon ahead. He didn't have any answers for Teddy, he didn't have any answers for himself. Could the Germans break the Maginot Line? That wasn't possible, was it? No one could break the Maginot Line. It was ten miles deep, sunk fifty feet into the ground. And so on. The words flew out to sea like hungry gulls. Ma-gi-not Line, a flap of Gallic syllables. Say, Teddy said then, brought up a little short. A kind of slow huskiness filled his voice, the sound of oncoming duplicity. Say, he said again, pulling the word out, why don't we take a look at that place. I mean, Jesus, it's really something. He slowed down, so did Erich. Look at that, Teddy said, pausing in wonder. Let's walk through. Let's take a couple of minutes. Why not? Erich was agreeable. That was his temperament, trained by events. It was simple. They turned off the Boardwalk without further discussion and made for the entrance to the Ritz. As they hurried along, Teddy began to talk about the Reds and the Yankees, about the races for the pennants and the coming Series, a hopeless jumble, all gratuitous, as though someone had asked him, Europe now forgotten, Europe already dead. He couldn't wait to get inside the hotel, pushed his way blindly through the revolving doors, waved Erich on.

Once inside, standing amidst the almost silent lobby traffic, amidst the guests of the Ritz and their deskmen and servants, he had an instant sense of another life moving beside him on a noiseless, parallel track. It was different from his own, as foreign as Erich Kessler's accent, a rich, deferential, rapt pulse against which the slightest tactless move on his part would bring immediate retribution, immediate disapproval. He must not intrude. He must not disrupt. He must behave himself. No one must recognize him for what he was. Bland-faced and wary, he forced himself to move, lifted one soundless foot, then the other. There was a bar on his right, Merry-Go-Round it said over the door canopy, blue neon lights shining mistily somewhere in the dark, a formal dining room on the other side already set in blinding white for breakfast. He could hear an organ playing "Deep Purple" in the bar. He moved on ten feet, twenty, Erich alongside him, stopping when he stopped, precisely paced to keep from making an error. Whenever they stopped, Erich took off his glasses and polished them. He seemed very nervous, seemed to have no idea where they were.

At last, step by step, they arrived at the heart of the lobby. They saw a vast rectangle stretching an entire block to the west and another toward the sea. They now stood amidst a reflected paradise of chrome, plate glass, and deep-piled beige carpeting. A convention hall of a lobby, broken up by mirrored pillars. The biggest room in the world, filled with the familiar scent of money everywhere, the overpowering fragrance of luxury. Squat, contemporary chairs, with squared-off backs and crushed velvet upholstery six inches deep, chandeliers the size of baby grands, and bellhops who looked Teddy's age and wore pillbox hats like the Philip Morris midget. Where could you get a cup of coffee in such a place? "Irving Berlin stays here," Teddy whispered out of the side of his mouth. "With his three daughters." Erich look startled. He knew who Irving Berlin was.

Around them, the contemporary chairs were filled with guests of the Ritz. Suntans like cream, dresses of summer rainbow colors, white suits. The chandeliers over their heads shone like diamond suns. To the rear, there was a library filled with best-sellers, and a writing room with a dozen teak desks; nearby, a florist's with orchids in the window, a perfume shop, a French hairdresser, an arcade of sweet-smelling grandeur. Someone was being paged, someone was wanted on the telephone. A bellhop moved across the carpet, a small silver tray extended in his hand. Could Gustav Levi feel at home here, could the rich Victor Talles, his wife Thelma, could even the old lady Eisen with her silver-knobbed cane? Who at the Ritz would understand about Riga?

Then a kind of restlessness set in. The boys welcomed it. There was nothing here for Teddy Lewin, nothing for Erich Kessler. Erich was squinting through his glasses, as though he were afraid he was going to lose his vision. He wanted to escape, they both wanted to escape. They moved around delicately, politely, following each other's spoor on the balls of their feet, as though they knew where they were going. They were looking for a way out, a blessed exit to the Boardwalk and a world they were comfortable in. What had Teddy thought he would find here? He tucked the question away. Let it rest for a while. He'd deal with it later, create an unforgettable coincidence over a cup of coffee when he was better prepared, force fortune in his own way, surprise Bea and her judge another time.

He felt better, though. He felt better as soon as they hit the Boardwalk and began to head for the north side of town. He was positively overcome by cheerfulness, was full of smiles. For some reason, Erich seemed to have loosened up, too. He emerged from the Ritz with his powers of speech fully restored, and on the way back it was Erich who did most of the talking. Teddy didn't mind. He was in a sudden benign state, filled with pleasant giddiness and the languors of music. Rachmaninoff occupied half his head, long, slow, meandering melodies that opened and shut like the swelling pleats of an accordian. He could listen to Erich and Rachmaninoff at the same time, it was one of his tricks. He also knew how to practice the piano inside his head; he didn't need a keyboard. Erich was talking on in his own heavy way, releasing the words as though there were a price on each. A strange language was expensive. He was telling Teddy about how he had come to the United States a year before his father, alone, about how he had lived on West End Avenue in New York with a family that wanted to give German refugee boys a start, about how he had grown to hate them.

"Hate them?" Teddy said, suddenly distracted.

"They never changed the bed linens."

"Never changed the bed linens?"

"Yes."

"You mean just yours? Or theirs, too?"

"Mine, yes. I don't know about their own."

"You mean they never changed your sheets?"

"Yes."

"Was that because they were poor, or was that the way they lived, or what?"

"Every month they were paid for me by the Jewish Agency. It was to make money from me."

Then Erich told Teddy that the family made him say a prayer to President

Roosevelt every night at the dinner table. What kind of prayer? Teddy asked. "To say I was grateful," Erich said. He paused a moment, stared at Teddy without expression, then walked on. Things were different now that his father was here, he said. His father managed a lady's hat factory on Thirty-sixth Street for his American cousin. Felt and straw. His father was lucky to have a rich cousin with a hat factory. He and his father were happy together in their three-room flat in Washington Heights. His father did the cooking; they had dinner together every night. Without prayers. "Where's your mother?" Teddy finally asked. An agonized look washed over Erich's face, vanished like a sudden squall. He looked away. "My mother is in Frankfurt," he said. "She waits for a visa." "Ah," Teddy said, expelling his breath. They slowed down then, made the second half of the trip at a half-hearted pace, window-shopped, poked their heads into a couple of auctions. Teddy decided that he liked Erich Kessler. He liked the stolidity, the way he placed himself on his two feet as though he were made of granite. Teddy would like to lean into that. There was nothing flighty there, nothing agitated, no trembling of an eyelid. Erich Kessler would never be able to practice the piano in his head.

Caveat Emptor

by Barry Targan

Joey Rogovin swung in and out of the way of the hard platoon marching like hammers on the Boardwalk. Like one more in the vast undulant sheet of searching pigeons, he would move aside for the rectangle of men and then fold back in their wake. Like the pigeons, he was a gleaner. At fifteen, he was unsure of the shape of irony, yet he responded to the fact of it: heavy armies might trample down the golden fields and destroy Empire, but along the way they also smashed it into little pieces manageable by small scavengers. What Joey Rogovin in his own lifetime could never have hoped to share in now fell easily to his hand and wit, and he battened upon his luck and opportunity, for this was war.

Not that the Boardwalk was a golden grain field; not that Atlantic City was that sort of Empire. Rather, it had suddenly become the largest military training camp in the world. By the potent magic of supreme decree, it had been changed in a few months from the Queen of Resorts to the King of Armories. From December 1941 to the following April, the grand hotels — the Haddon Hall, the Traymore, the Dennis, the Marlborough-Blenheim, the Shelburne, the Breakers, and all the rest, as well as every modest sidestreet inn and even some of the larger rooming houses — were converted into barracks. Nothing else in America was so ready made, so in place, so quickly adaptable in 1941 to such a purpose as was Atlantic City.

Partitions divided space to multiply it. The magnificent suites such as that on the fifteenth floor of the Ritz-Carlton high over the gray-green Atlantic of the south Jersey shore, that which even through the recent summer had sheltered variously the Ludens of the Luden cough drop fortune; the Clothiers from Ardmore, Pennsylvania; the entourage of the mobster Louis "Thumbs" Mangore — that suite now housed forty common men. And now with no splendid view. All the windows facing the sea were blacked out, darkened against the lurking eye of marauding enemy U-boats, steel sharks waiting out in the ship channel not more than a dozen miles offshore.

Partitions were erected or walls were ripped out, toilet facilities were expanded, shifted, or built. Stairwells and fire escapes were repaired, evacuation plans made, elevator cables restrung — there were details. But in the main nothing could have been easier than this transfiguration. The large kitchens were ready, the crystal-chandeliered dining rooms were turned into mess halls, the parquet ballrooms cleared for calisthenics when it rained. And of course there was the perfect drill field — the wide, substantial, flat, clean, resilient, and nearly endless Boardwalk.

All day from reveille to retreat the khaki men would drill, marching north in the inland lane, south on the seaside. Between each element sufficient space was left, a hundred yards or sometimes two hundred, for the troops to be wheeled about and wheeled again, to be moved from ranks into files and back, to be dressed right, to parade rest. Order, containment — the discipline upon which unquestioned response in battle depended — was established here.

"Companeeeeeee ... *halt!*" the sergeant would call. "Take ten. Smoke 'em if you got 'em. Don't leave no butts."

Then it was time for Joey Rogovin.

The men on their ten-minute break could move about, but only within the loose shape of the unit. No one could walk back a half-block to a Boardwalk store to buy a Coke or a hot dog or gum or cigarettes. Even if they were on the beach side of the Boardwalk and the company had chanced to halt across from a store, they could not cross to the opposite side. And along much of the Boardwalk where the men drilled, that part of the Boardwalk which before December had been an elegant promenade of elegant shops (Wing Fat's Oriental knickknacks in jade) and auction galleries (Lloyd's for the finest lace, Boughton's for Wedgwood and Louis

Quatorze chairs), along this stretch there were no hot dog stands or sundries stores at all. So often there was not time enough, and every distance was too great for the soldiers to buy anything, obedience now opening a chasm between their old lives so recently shed and the soldiery they had become.

"Cigarettes, Cokes, gum. Candy. What do you want? What do you want? Let's hear it," Joey Rogovin would shout. He would wheel his rattling balloon-tired bike around them like a herder of cattle. Quickly then men who wanted something would give him money, and on his bike he would speed down or up the Boardwalk to the nearest store and back to buy for them. He lived on the change they left him. Coke was a nickel, two cents deposit on the bottle. From the dime they gave him he made three cents, for the bottle two more. Out of a dime he made half. A hundred percent profit. This was a great country. And sometimes they gave him a tip, a nickel extra. Except for the farm boys from the middle of America — Missouri, Oklahoma, Iowa; for Joey Rogovin, the edges of the earth. The farm boys would count it out. A nickel and a two-cent deposit. Nothing for nothing. As if they had come, warned by their parents and ministers, to be on guard against the slick World. But did they think he, Joey Rogovin, was a service provided by the United States Army? All he could get from them was the bottle deposit. In time he learned to spot them, the clean white-haired, blue-eyed counters, and not take their orders if he could avoid it. Time was money, the space in his basket was money. In time he learned more.

He was not alone. He was not the only boy with a Rollfast bike and a wire basket propped out over the front wheel. But, unlike the casual boys who once or twice worked an hour or a day or two at the game of it for the dollar they might not need, Joey Rogovin was filled with a mercantile vitality, driven by the entrepreneurial imagination of merchantmen such as those who sailed from Genoa around the Cape or that once propelled caravans to Byzantium and beyond. In him there was an intensity of trade that blurred any line between need or want, though he had plenty of both.

He and his parents lived in a tiny top-floor apartment on Seaside Place, a little half-street off Oriental Avenue between Vermont and New Hampshire. But his mother — his small, gentle, fragile mother — every morning opened the door expecting an old Latvia, nubbed hills, rolling fields, high trees. She never understood the whiteness of sand, the size of oceans, seagulls, and the world was round. War. Every morning she was surprised. And one day she would at last open the door to the sturdy green earth, to the pungency of manure at work in the land of the valley a hundred kilometers beyond Riga, and she would step through, smiling gaily forever after, her patience finally rewarded, and be gone.

His father, Koslo, wherever he had come from, whenever, knew nothing, could learn little. He worked in Fineberg's Junk Yard sorting debris, shifting mounds of paper and rags into larger mounds for the bailing machine to compress and strap. In Atlantic City there were three junk yards: Snyder's and Giordano's, each as big as a city block, and Fineberg's, as small as a garage. Fineberg got the junk left over from the junk. Koslo Rogovin tended it.

At night he and his wife would sit in their tiny kitchen, winter and summer, drinking tea and listening, to what Joey never knew. Certainly not to America.

Joey Rogovin listened to America. Some nights it would pulse through him like his own blood, surging, torrential with its promises, textures, strengths, words, complexities. Or he would lie in bed and on his radio listen to Byron Syamm, the voice of the Philadelphia Athletics, inventing baseball games between the A's and the Detroit Tigers, creating the game off the ticker tape just as if he were there in the Motor City. For a home run Syamm would whack a block of hard wood with a stick. ("It's going, *going,* GONE!") Joey had read about it in the *Philadelphia Sunday Record*, this casting of the illusion. But he did not care less because of that, for beyond the illusion was the reality, the game itself. Whether Byron Syamm saw it or not, it was there, going on, men endeavoring, straining, reaching, innings, runs, stolen bases. And maybe even the game was, maybe everything was, just a sign anyway, itself a signal for something else, something tough and solid and hard as gold.

Even by the middle of that first summer, soon after the Battle of Midway, he made the first important changes, the first critical business decisions. Why wait for orders from the soldiers? What, after all, was there for them to order? Cokes, cigarettes, candy, gum, sometimes a hot dog; ice cream and Popsicles after the weather warmed up. Always the same. What they could consume instantly. So why wait to hear what you already knew? Why waste half the drill break on the ride to the store?

Joey began to follow the troops prepared, his basket (larger now, reinforced) full of goodies. A master stroke. His business doubled, tripled. Not only could he carry more and supply it quicker, but the presence of the goods, the actuality of them, made customers of the men who might not have bothered to emerge from their weary boredom or reverie or hot and gritty chagrin. For those who could not imagine the frosty Coke, the nectarish Juicy Fruit, the ambrosial Mounds bar, for them Joey Rogovin would provide both image and substance out of the fecundity of his own abundant spirit and his cornucopial basket. He would give a little to get. Good business was a two-way street, was it not? A two-way Boardwalk?

And now there were risks. Where before he was little more than a delivery boy, buying with the money of others what they wanted, his gain limited to gratuities and two-cent bottle deposits, now he invested his money, set his own prices, absorbed his own losses.

His biggest problem was this: warm Cokes. He had to buy cold and sell cold, which meant that he had to time everything — the buying, the bringing, the selling — to coincide with the break.

A break was never a certainty. He could know neither the exact moment when it would occur nor even if it would occur at all. Different units at different points in their training cycles had different drill patterns. At the beginning of the cycle, the troops raw and stumbling, there were long periods of drilling and fewer breaks. In the middle, after about a month, more breaks. At the end, long periods of marching and much more double time, fewer breaks but longer ones, fifteen minutes, sometimes twenty. These late units were the best for him.

And he learned to identify his customers — the hesitancy of recent civilians, the unworn heels of stiff boots, the stab of blisters, the wince. He didn't have to ask. Idle talk could sink a ship, right? Instead he could listen to the complaints. If they complained about the drilling itself, they were new. Middle units complained about the food. By the end of the training cycle the men were quieter, more private. Soon they would be going into specific training. Infantry, tanks. Airplanes. From Missouri and Oklahoma and Iowa they had now come halfway to the ship waiting to take them. For them the giddy camaraderie of dislocation had ended. These units ate and drank and smoked more, like a last chance, or a chance ending.

And sometimes the sergeant would scream, "Awwwwlright, you mothers. No break. No friggin break till you drop down dead or get it going like it should. TeeeeenHUT! Foooohaaard, HARTCH!"

And Joey Rogovin's iced Cokes would warm, his Popsicles would melt.

Or it would rain.

There were no guarantees, only opportunities. And vicissitudes.

❊

By summer's end he had banked an incredible thousand dollars. He bought his mother a Pyrex pot to boil water for tea, but she dropped and shattered it in a week; for his father, the finest pair of leather work gloves, by then difficult to obtain. But Joey Rogovin was learning about more than soda pop. He was learning about the deeper luxuries of men and about the price of services and goods.

And finally September was in the air, equinox visible in the shifted patterns of the sand ridged on the beaches, autumn in the different angle of the sea wrack lined out by the receded tide. In the early bright blue mornings the men would shiver slightly and stamp and make a collective cloud of human breath. Sometimes a block or two away Joey would see it, the gauzy cloud hovering like mist just above them, then steaming off in the quickly rising sun.

His sales per unit were down, went down with the temperature. But volume over all was up as the military base expanded and expanded again, like an organism that only inhaled. The distances between the drilling units were shortened to gain additional space for the crowding battalions. Fifty yards now between them. And even some of the side streets — Kentucky Avenue, Tennessee, New York — were used as drill areas as well.

Joey held his own, and his own had become more. He had mechanized. Harry's Bike Shop built him a good-sized cart mounted on a bicycle-wheeled chassis that he could haul behind him. He had the box lined with galvanized metal that his father had found and saved. There was a drain in the bottom. Now he could carry ice to keep his Cokes cold, his Popsicles firm. Let the sergeants thwart him no more! With the combined capacity of the cart and the front basket, he could supply, if not an army, then at least a thirsty and hungry platoon. With two grocery stores on Atlantic Avenue he had made deals to buy their now-limited supplies of TastyKakes at double the markup. From the soldiers he could get triple that. Was this black market? Would he at last be investigated by the newly forming Office of

Price Administration?

But in the bright blue days that seemed like an endless and perfect promise of lassitude that mocked the rage of war came the first subliminal lick of northeasterly winds, the gray to come, the wash of salt scud weather that would scour the Boardwalk clear of men and their appetites. Although on clear winter days they would continue to drill as ever, they would hate their breaks, and all they would do would be to huddle and curse the blade of the North Atlantic wind slicing through them.

In early September Joey tasted the season like the other native creatures in the air and sea, and he knew better than these men what was about to end.

School was threatening him as well. Not that he disliked school; not at all. He was an apt and attentive student, and he believed in the efficacy of decimals and fractions, mixed numbers and Pythagorean lucidity, the history of his nation, the structure of flowering plants, the voyaging of Odysseus.

But Occasion had come to him specially, and it would be difficult for him to relinquish what he had made of it, what he might make of it, although none of them — the men marching on the Boardwalk, the busy people of the city, even the other students his age; yea, the world and all that it inherit — none thought life would ever be the same again. They all sensed that whatever had been suspended for the duration had been suspended for good. The concussion of enemy or Allied shells falling even now at Guadalcanal had shaken apart, would shake apart, the old fabric, tearing it beyond repair. But for Joey Rogovin this knowledge, which was new to him and not comparative, had come in a more exact, a more precisely defined shape than it had for others, than it had for most.

The exact shape of the present that seemed to define his future was $1,784. Some of it had been put into war bonds. But there was more to his knowledge even than the bank account or what he had learned that his father had never grasped: the connection between Will and Profit. He had also learned that there were rules for some and rules for others: there were always rules to human conduct, but not always the same rules at the same time or place. Who mastered that knowledge would make the future and master it. The world, just now being beaten to a pulp, would in time take whatever mold was put upon it. Joey Rogovin learned this in his way from a man who taught him — in *his* way.

❂

"Hey you, kid," Eddie Cribbins called to him. "Come here."

The profitable day was over. Friday. Fridays were always good, the best, as if the promise of the less restrained weekend awoke in the men preparatory wants. The last refrains of retreat's trumpet died. The movement of the Boardwalk, halted along its length for the ceremony of lowering the flag, started up again, but the drilling men were gone.

"Hey kid," Eddie Cribbins called to him again. Joey had wheeled his machine nearly to the top of the ramp down from the Boardwalk when he heard Eddie, his voice raspy like a small insect buzzing.

Eddie Cribbins was a Private First Class. One stripe. More than a recruit in basic training.

"I seen you working. All summer. You got a good thing," he said.

"Yeah," Joey said. But Cribbins's words sounded to him like a warning, a feint before the spring of something more.

"You work hard. You make a buck. I can see. I got eyes."

"Yeah," Joey said. "I do OK. You don't drill? You got a stripe already?"

"I'm assigned here," he gestured vaguely. Where? Joey wondered. To this building, the Chalfonte Hotel on the Boardwalk that they stood before? To the entire base? To the city itself? Who was this guy? "I'm waiting for orders. They got me lost. I'm waiting here till I get found."

"See you around," Joey said and started off.

"Wait a minute. Hey. Wait a minute. I got something for you."

"You got something for me? You got nothing for me. What do I need? See you around."

"Advice. For you I got advice."

"Thanks," Joey said. He moved away.

"Make money," Eddie Cribbins said. "That's my advice to you. Make money."

The boy stopped.

"What am I doing? What do you call this?"

Eddie Cribbins had been resting with his back against the building; now he stood straight. Even so, he was not much taller than the boy, as lean as a stretched muscle, a runner's shank of a man, but narrow, his shoulders no wider than his hips. "I been watching you. You got a good reputation, too. You hang in. You work. Reliable. Honest. Smart kid. I got plans."

"I got to get home. They're waiting." But Eddie Cribbins went on, his eyes like ball bearings in a pinball machine only dark like marble, deepest maroon and hard. Joey could see in Eddie Cribbins's eyes his own reflection.

"You want to make money? Here is how you make money." He turned and quickly ducked behind the heavy column of the arcade and out again, and in the same motion opened the lid to Joey's wheeled carrier and put into it twenty cartons of cigarettes. "So." He stepped back to the boy. "There you go. Get thirty bucks for that at least, maybe more. Fifteen bucks for me, fifteen bucks and plus for you. Fifty/fifty. What a deal."

"What do you mean? What is this?" Joey Rogovin protested, but already he understood.

"Do I ask for anything now?" Eddie Cribbins gave as an answer. "Do I trust you? Is this trust or is this not trust?"

"What'll I do?"

"Listen kid, I don't even know your name."

"Joey. Joey Rogovin."

"I don't even know your name and I hang on you thirty bucks' worth of choice tobacco. Trust. I'm telling you, if you can't trust the man you do business with, you shouldn't do business with him. Right? Is that right? You're a businessman, you should know. Right? All summer I see you. You don't give no credit, right? Cash off the top, right?" Eddie Cribbins's voice sawed at the air, making fine dust of it.

"Yeah, right."

"Sure. It's the only way with your kind of operation. And when do you know you'll see these guys again, huh? So it's cash up front."

"Yeah."

"But you and me, now this is a different operation altogether. Without trust we got nothing. With trust we got a gold mine. We got a mint. We can print money. You understand."

There was much that Joey did not understand, but he understood enough so that he knew he would be able to work out what more he needed to know. For now he knew that suddenly he had a supplier — cartons of cigarettes instead of Cokes; he knew that there was no cash outlay on his part; and he knew that now he needed a customer. So nothing had changed. Up, down, left, right, forward, backward were all the same. It depended on where you looked, where you were when you needed to know where you were. But what did not depend upon position or stance or attitude at all was this: if you sold Cokes out of your trailer, Crackerjacks if you could get them, Fleer's Double Bubble Gum (already as rare as ambergris), then you might as well sell anything else. *You sold or you did not sell.* In the insubstantial welter and flux of the human condition, there was at least this rock to stand upon.

"I understand," Joey said at last. And just at that moment he also understood that Eddie Cribbins had stolen the cigarettes, probably from where he worked.

Joey and the civilians had begun to hear about fabulous hordes of commodities ordered and requisitioned and stored by the military even as civilian goods began to disappear. Rationing was coming down — sugar, meat, gasoline, Jell-O, coffee, and more. In place of the famous brands of quality cigarettes, now instead there were such imitative shreds and remnants as Marvels and Wings. Bugler tobacco loose in cans to roll your own. New name brands for foods and other goods sprang up to mask the ersatz and the use of lesser grades of things while Heinz and Kellogg and Campbell marched off into their country's service.

Eddie Cribbins had his own access to this massive store. Now he needed someone at the other end, someone to go out into the world where he could not go himself, not with impunity. He needed Joey Rogovin. Trust is what you need to trust in.

"I understand," Joey Rogovin said and pushed off on his bike.

"Monday," Eddie Cribbins said after him. "Four o'clock."

But even before he reached Seaside Place he had sold the cigarettes. Ten cartons each of Phillip Morris to Mr. Slotkin at the Delaware Avenue Market and to Mr. Fishman at Fishman's across the street, the two sources of his TastyKakes. He left for home with money and with orders — requests — for more.

More he gave them. And others, too. There was not much that Eddie Cribbins could not provide, and frequently in amounts so brazen that Joey would have to store things in his parents' apartment, lugging up to the third floor sometimes half-cases of cigarettes, boxes of Chuckles and Mars bars and Chicklets, condoms by the gross lot, bags of razor blades, vials of perfume.

His mother said nothing, nor did his father, as if Fineberg's had followed him home, though this was not junk. But Koslo Rogovin perhaps could no longer tell the difference; or maybe instead, in the way illiterate sailors could intuit their positions at sea, he knew, in a condition beyond perception, the profound similarity of all things, the fundamental form which did not change in the passage of objects from state to altered state, from a pile in his son's bedroom to a pile in Fineberg's building. Either way, at either end of the progression, wealth was generated, born, more of it, or less: for under heaven there was a price for everything. So all there was or could be or need be of truth was *transaction*. The materials, the things in themselves, were only the grass and grain of energy exchanging shapes.

Eddie Cribbins and Joey Rogovin moved their meeting place often. Smaller goods could still be passed easily near or on the Boardwalk by dropping whatever Eddie had on him into the wheeled carrier. Larger transfers needed more cover and even extra trips. Eddie Cribbins made these arrangements with some care, selecting a small restaurant or bar, the back of a bakery, the toilets of gasoline stations, taxi stands.

And Joey's movement through the city became more noticeable. October, and then November, he peddled on against the lowering days.

Who did not know what he did each day after school and all through Saturdays? But this was a city in constant motion now, as if every day was the Fourth of July or Labor Day, the hectic, transient mood of high summer the ordinary tone of daily life. For not only had the city become a major military base; like all such places through all of such histories, it also became the center for much else and many others — whores and gamblers, thieves and derelicts, the refuse of armies. Unlike most other bases, because this was Atlantic City, where apartments or even single rooms could still be rented for a season or a day, wives could come and visit their husbands, bring the children to watch their fathers marching. Mothers came bringing bundles of food. Many others, too, were simply drawn as to any spectacle. It was, after all, a long parade, this edge by the sea that was the first line between brave America and the dark evil of the Axis powers. Whatever would happen to the sacred land of the nation would happen here first.

The impulse to come to the city was like that which had brought the bonneted and frock-coated gentlemen of Washington to observe gaily from open carriages, with baskets of food and champagne at their feet, the first battle and sunny rout of Bull Run.

And indeed there was battle. Reports of U-boat sightings were frequent. Nearly every day the swift patrol boats moored in Gardner's Basin at the end of the island would burst spuming like unleashed hounds across the seas. Local volunteers would drone out and back over the ocean like reconnaissance bees in their own spruce and canvas Piper Cubs at their own expense. Sometimes a ship would be torpedoed at night. A few days later, in an eastern on-shore wind, the oil slick would come to stain and clog some of the Atlantic beaches. Once there were bodies.

So no one bothered about Joey Rogovin, whatever they knew or suspected. If you looked closely at him, then where did you not look, where did you stop looking? So you looked another way.

Except Officer Norman, too flat-footed to enlist, too essential to be drafted, who stopped Joey one day on Massachusetts Avenue.

"What's your name?"

"Joseph Rogovin."

"Where do you live?"

"321 Seaside Place."

"You got a vendor's license? Let's see your vendor's license. And if you got a vendor's license I'll arrest you. You ain't old enough to get a license."

"So who's selling anything?" Joey said.

"What are you talking? All summer you're selling — Cokes, hot dogs, all kinds of crap."

"I took orders. I delivered," Joey said. "And this isn't summer now."

"Don't give me no shit, kid, OK?"

"OK, Lieutenant."

"Open the lid, wise guy," Officer Norman said. "Open it."

He stepped back as if in the carrier there might be, what? — poison snakes, a bomb, Nazi infiltrators? Joey opened the carrier. Nothing.

"Go on," Officer Norman ordered. "Go on, go on. Beat it."

Joey reported the incident to Eddie Cribbins.

"It's the dumb ones you got to look out for, Joey. The ones that don't know how to get something."

"What do you mean? What does he want?"

"What does he want? Whatever you got, that's what he wants. He wants some of that. He knows there's action here, but he can't figure out what to do to get his. How to get it. You got to be careful with that kind. You can't just go up and lay it on him, stick a bill in his pocket and forget it. No. He's got to wake up with it in his pocket in the morning wondering where it came from so he's still thinking he's an honest cop. But we got ways to handle dummies, Joey, we got ways. And we got to get this guy fixed up before Christmas, remember that. Christmas is going to be our big season. We make it good then. We don't need nothing messing with Christmas, right?"

The plan was simple enough, and effective. For about four days Joey stayed in Officer Norman's path, peddling back and forth across his way like a gull taking large tacking stitches across a freighter until the policeman turned finally against whatever kind of resolve he had decided upon for himself and stopped the boy. He opened the carrier lid. On the galvanized bottom of the carrier rested, out of its package, a large-faced Elgin wristwatch with the new type of expanding band. New and bright and irresistible. Norman looked at it for a long time.

"What's that?" he pointed.

"What's what?" Joey said. Eddie Cribbins had instructed him.

"That."

"What?"

"That. *That!*"

"I don't see nothing."

"What do you mean you don't see nothing. Look, *look*, goddamn it."

"Nothing," Joey said. "I don't see nothing."

*"Look!"*Norman ordered. Pleaded.

"I don't need to look. I know what I got in my carrier. Nothing. It's empty."
Then he walked off.

"Hey," Norman shouted. "Hey, where you going? Come here! *Come back here!"*
But Joey walked on, about a hundred feet away. Slowly. Long enough. When he
turned around Officer Norman was gone. The lid to the carrier was closed. Only
when he got home did he look inside. Empty. Just as Eddie Cribbins had said it
would be. So are contracts made, pledges given, bonds and covenants insured. Joey
Rogovin mounted the stairs breathing in deeply. Now truly he felt expanded and
bold.

✿

Then there was the problem with Charles "Sonny" Miller.

Sonny Miller had a candystore-newsroom on Indiana between Atlantic and
Arctic Avenues, but what he really sold was policy, numbers. He booked some
horses. And sometimes he sold other things, out of the way, like stolen goods.

How Eddie Cribbins found out about Sonny Miller he did not say, and even
then he had, as always, left the business of arrangement and delivery and collection
to Joey. Still, he knew his man.

"Forty woolen blankets. Tell him. Special stuff. White, not khaki. No insignia.
Nothing. Beautiful stuff. Five bucks apiece."

"Blankets?" Joey had asked.

"Why not? Maybe it's a long war. So should civilians freeze? See what he says."

The deal was made easily enough. But instead of Joey delivering forty heavy
blankets, they arranged for a pickup. Sonny Miller had a car and certainly he did
not want merchandise like that, so clearly traceable, in his store, even with his
expensive good will in place with the law. A hundred dollars now, a hundred
dollars at delivery. But after Sonny Miller threw the last blanket into the trunk, he
would pay no more. A kid was a kid. Where did he get the blankets? His mother
knit them? So? The kid had no leverage. What could he do? And if by chance he was
working for someone, and one day large men with thick hands showed up on
Indiana Avenue with clear demands, so then he would pay. Quickly. Where was

there a mistake that couldn't be mended faster than a broken head? You pushed what you could push. You bent when you couldn't bend. That was all. Charles "Sonny" Miller pushed Joey Rogovin, bent him. The door slammed. The car started.

"A hundred bucks is enough," Miller said. "Plenty. What do *you* need? And it's a hundred more than it cost you." And he drove off.

But in two days — Monday, a school day even — large men did not show up at Sonny Miller's store. Only Joey Rogovin appeared.

"You want more blankets?" Joey said.

"What blankets? What are you talking? Get out of here. Once is all I'm telling you." But Joey did not leave, so Sonny Miller came around from his glass-cased candy counter and threw him out.

Miller's phone rang. Business. When he looked up from the pad he was writing on, Joey was back in the store. Miller threw him out again. The third time he threw him out he hit him, a stinging smack across the face. The fourth time he threw him out, he kicked the bicycle until the chain broke and the front wheel twisted and its spokes pulled out. Ruined.

But Eddie Cribbins had taught him that there was a business to threat. You make a man know what you're willing to do, and once he believes that, then you're back in business again. Either he pays the price or you do. It's a tough negotiation, but at least there are limits, terms can get worked out. Sometimes it's better to write it off, take a loss as a loss and don't pretend. But if you want to deal in pressure, then make the pressure clear right away, just the same as if you were selling something else. This is this, this is that. Take it or leave it. No discounts.

So the next day Joey Rogovin was back at work. Earlier. Right in the middle of the early morning traffic when most of Miller's numbers business was going on, people hurrying to work placing their nickels and dimes or even quarters on three numbers, sometimes boxed, a deposit on a dream waiting at the end of the day, a chance on tomorrow.

Miller was too busy to throw Joey out of the store more than once, and too surrounded by his customers to do anything else, to scream or beat him. But he threw him out twice before lunch and three times after. And he hit him hard now, sometimes hurting him right down to the bone.

167

On the third morning, when Joey Rogovin showed up, bruised and on foot, Charles "Sonny" Miller paid up.

"Here," he said, white, defeated, a bubble of small terror even clogging his throat. "Here." He pulled the money from a bundle in his pocket and stuffed it into Joey's hand. "Now get out. Go."

"The bike," Joey said. Miller yelped as if he had himself been battered, but he pulled another ten dollars off his roll.

"Here. That's all. That's it. Now get out. Come back again and then I'll show you something. I'll break your arm. I'll break it twice, here and here, I swear to God."

But three days later, when Joey Rogovin did return with a new bike, when he entered the store late in the afternoon, Miller slumped.

"I told you. I *told* you!" he shouted, but his voice was thin and he stayed behind the counter. Joey looked around. The store was empty.

"I got ten silver identification bracelets. Pure silver. Heavy. Eight bucks."

Miller looked at him. Was this true, that he had come back?

"You're crazy," Miller said.

"I'm in business," Joey said. "I work for a living."

"Six," Miller said. "Six bucks."

Joey shook his head. He held up a fist and two fingers.

"No. Seven is too much. No. Six-fifty. Six-fifty is as far as I go."

The boy and the man shook hands across the glass counter that housed the moldering squares of Klein's Grade A chocolate and the faded blue boxes of Jawbreakers. Then the boy took a small brown bag out of his coat pocket and gave it to the man, who went into the back room and examined the contents carefully. When he returned he measured out thirteen five-dollar bills and handed them to the boy.

For Christmas Joey bought his mother the only good coat she had ever had in her life, though she seldom left the apartment and the coat was beyond her need. That was what he wanted to give her, an idea about her possibilities here, a coat that might make her dream in America. But she did not change. Maybe she imagined that someday she would use this wonderful coat trimmed with fur in

Riga, where there were winters deep and long and white. For his father he also bought clothing: workshoes with steel protected toes, and a leather jacket to protect him from the sparks that flew at him like tracer bullets and burned holes in his shirts and scarred his chest when he cut up scrap metal with the oxyacetylene torch at Fineberg's. For himself he bought a fine radio, a Zenith with a magical green cat's eye that winked and squinted as the tuning dial spun through thousands of megacycles. On the radio, which he connected to an aerial on the roof, he could hear short wave and ships at sea dotting and dashing to destinations and to each other. Sometimes late at night, after listening to the gabble of foreign voices that increased with the darkness, he would go to the roof of 321 Seaside Place and look up at the winter-brightened stars and the white constellations they etched on the black sky and he would wonder where they all were.

In his bank book, deposited at one and a half percent interest, was $3,532.18. At sixteen, Joey Rogovin was a person not only of some financial means but of some highly fluid property; he was in possession, too, of an experience as rich and patterned as a stiff brocade, as tough and durable as sailcloth.

❂

Joey and Eddie Cribbins met at Kornblau's Delicatessen. Eddie was drinking tea, Joey ate a large Kornblau Special: corned beef and coleslaw on rye with oozy Russian dressing. Eddie Cribbins had a bad cold, and it drew him in even tighter; he looked squashed, as in an accident. And maybe this is what had happened, an accident.

"They found me," he told Joey.

"What's that mean?"

"I was misplaced, now I'm found. I'm getting shipped out. To England." His body tightened another notch. He would squeeze into nothing and disappear, leaving this calamitous world altogether.

Quickly Joey looked around the restaurant. Who might have heard? What spies might there be even here in Kornblau's on Virginia Avenue? Maybe something of what he heard at night on his radio came out of such inadvertence. Maybe even this would be sent in code, tonight, Eddie's indiscriminate information. Joey had seen the war movies. A hint here, a word there, a slip of the tongue; soon enough the picture laid out across the plotting board of the Atlantic Ocean in Command

Headquarters in Berlin would be classified, and another convoy of Liberty Ships would be in danger as the sinister admiral moved a wolf pack into position with a long stick, like a croupier in a great game.

"Hey, Eddie," Joey said. "You shouldn't talk about troop movements. You never know who's listening."

"Fuck it," Eddie Cribbins said. They were silent then. Joey continued to eat, hoping Eddie would say no more, say nothing else that might endanger others and even him.

At last Eddie said, "So that means we're out of business."

Not until then did that fully occur to the boy.

"Yeah. I guess that's so," Joey said, holding his sandwich away. "We did real good, though, Eddie. While it lasted."

"We ain't done yet. I got a good idea. A last but very big score." He pulled at his nose with a sodden handkerchief.

"Yeah?" Joey waited. Eddie sipped his tea.

"Only this time it works different. We make an investment. This time we buy. Some very very very special goods. I'll need five hundred from you. Five from you, five from me. Just like always, right? Fifty/fifty."

"Five hundred," Joey said. "That's a lot of money."

"What's the matter? You ain't got $500 left from all you made?"

"No. I got it OK. It's just a lot, that's all."

"What's the matter, you don't trust me? All of a sudden, now I'm leaving, now you don't need Eddie Cribbins, the door is closed? Is that what you mean? Shit. What a world."

"I trust you, Eddie. Just like you said when we started. I'll get you the money."

Two days later he handed Eddie Cribbins the envelope. In two more days Joey would make the pickup at the Paris Coffee Shoppe on Ohio Avenue, just by the hospital. They had used it many times before.

"What am I selling, Eddie?"

"Don't ask. Not on this one. You'll see. It's very small. We'll make a bundle. But don't ask; not now. Be surprised. You'll be surprised."

Joey was surprised. Eddie Cribbins did not show up, either at the Paris Coffee Shoppe or ever. He was gone. After a week, Joey was sure of it.

✵

February, March, the British army entered Tunisia, the U.S. 43rd Infantry occupied the Russell Islands, and the first reports from spring training camps as the Dodgers and the Giants stretched their war-depleted limbs. And still Joey could not easily heal, could not shake out of himself the clutter and shards of what had broken. Not that it was simply the money; he had plenty left of that. Besides, money was only the abstraction, only another sign of a greater potency, like Byron Syamm, who would soon start to swing his miniature baseball bat against his maple block. No. There was here a violation deeper than any balm of money could touch or heal, a sundering so profound and exquisite that philosophies were born in the contemplation of it, and poets sang its history. But Joey Rogovin had no words for any of this. All he could do was throb with ache for all lost conditions, the fatal act that casts us all out into what we are. He would throb and ache and shudder but have no words to describe the birth in himself of unaccommodated man. Until, one restless night under the dawning spring sky on the roof at Seaside Place, Joey Rogovin thought maybe he had been wrong: maybe under heaven there was no price for anything. Maybe there was no value to anything at all. No strict accounting. And all was dross: the stars, the sea, the hammered gold enamelings of men. The hearts and words of men most of all. Maybe, after all, only his mother in her dream and his father pushing his life along like a bundle of soiled rags could read with any authority a truth.

The summer of 1943. The Allied juggernaut began to move like a great charger mounted with the armored knight as in a medieval tapestry of battle, the relentless pace increasing, the earth shaking with each lengthening stride. That summer Joey returned to the Boardwalk, but more elaborately. He bought five units — bikes and carriers — and hired boys to work for him; he showed them how. He set up his own distribution system, buying Cokes and Popsicles directly in wholesale amounts, and whatever else he could purchase from whoever had something to unload. There were shortages of everything now, and much was gone; but there was always something left to work with, however shoddy.

Sometimes when he examined the thin, brittle covering of bitter chocolate dipped sparingly over the spongelike marshmallow substitute, he would think of the military warehouses outrageously stuffed with Tootsie Rolls and Clark bars, the sealed and stenciled cardboard boxes of Dentyne and genuine Necco wafers. The tobacco of the millions and millions of cigarettes turning dry and dusty. Profusion. Glut. Waste. Sometimes, too, he would think of Eddie Cribbins, though not in anger. What he thought or how he thought about him he could not tell, only that his mind then seemed to grow flat, listless, as if he were looking at a picture of something rather than being alive with weight and mass and motion, as if he could rub his life between his fingers and feel nothing. He did not like the sensation, and less and less did he allow himself to think of Eddie Cribbins.

Besides, now he had much else to think about in any day or hour, not least his delicate and tenuous relationship with City Hall and its crablike minions, official and otherwise; with the Military Police; with occasional penny-ante thugs, incompetent workers, unreliable sources of supplies, price-gouging marketeers. A day's work/worth of aggravations, and a lubricious percentage of his income to calm the stormy waves of greed lapping all around him.

Now he *was* required to buy a license for his vending. He made Koslo Rogovin the head of the business, the president of Rogovin Enterprises, but only for his legal status as an adult and thus for his signature, though his father could hardly write his name. (Koslo continued on with Fineberg, another magnate.) Joey paid taxes, direct and implicit bribes, and rent on the space in the building he used to store the bikes and his merchandise. He bought a large used refrigerator for his Cokes, a little stove for hot dogs. A dollar here, five dollars there, ten and twenty to police, detectives, dangerous characters, health inspectors, and self-appointed guardians of certain streets and some choice business areas.

But Joey Rogovin took no belligerent defensive posture; he was all offense — a tactician, a Halsey, a Montgomery, a Patton of commerce. Against the complaints of the Boardwalk stores that he was illegal, that there were ordinances against vehicles such as his, that they paid property taxes and he did not, that he was hurting their businesses by unfair competition — Joey moved beyond the Maginot Line of argument (which he could lose) to the solution of the flexible strike force. He gave to magistrates their tribute and tariff as if they were his partners, gave to them before they needed to ask, as if it were their due. The merchants of the Boardwalk went to protocol and to law; Joey Rogovin went to his bank account. He did not want to win a position or make a cause. He wanted to stay in business into September. He didn't want everything, or even to be right. Who could grant him that? All he wanted was ninety days of summer. For which he was willing to pay, and pay well.

That summer was full of sun and the fumes of victory. The Russians began to move westward, pressing the Germans back. To his father, the corporate president, he gave a bank book with a thousand dollars entered. He put much of his now considerable money into war bonds and considered stocks and went back to high school. They studied Hannibal, *A Tale of Two Cities*, the theory of valences and the balancing of equations.

In 1944 the city began to change once more. His Boardwalk business declined, though other ventures beckoned to Joey now that he had a car, a 1932 Chevy coupe in good condition. But now the city began to receive back the men it had trained and sent forth. From the world's largest basic training camp it was turning, as quickly as before, into the world's largest convalescent hospital, for a broken man can lie as neatly in a barracks bed as can a whole man. The largest hotel, the Haddon Hall and the connected Chalfonte, became the Thomas England General Hospital, *memento mori*. Other barracks hotels followed as the line of war coiled across Europe and the Pacific.

Now over the worn cedar Boardwalk instead of the muffled synchronous thud of marching men came the soft, susurrant whine of wheelchairs. Instead of the broad khaki strokes of columned men, now dabs of men dressed in different colored robes walked slowly or hobbled on crutches or rode in wheelchairs pushed by white nurses, sometimes blue-caped in a sea breeze, a wind from Normandy, Cherbourg, Rheims. Through the summer the names of victories fell on the Boardwalk like drops of blood.

Some training did continue, and Joey kept two bikes at work. But mainly the wounded could get to the stores themselves, though they had small appetites and little thirst. Even the men still confined to the wards had attendants that prevented his business from entering there successfully. So many volunteers poured out of the city into the hospitals that they needed to be scheduled, given proper shifts, and they brought gifts of just what Joey would have to sell, every man a hero.

He gave it up. And he was sick of war.

In a year he would have to register for the draft. Even with the strong likelihood that the war would be over by then, still he would probably be pulled in for a time, part of the army of occupation that was already being discussed in the newspapers and among his more vulnerable older classmates. But what had he to do with that? For the first time in a long time he thought of Eddie Cribbins, of how Eddie Cribbins must also have felt this way, that he had no purpose in war. War belonged to others, not to merchants. Eddie Cribbins. To think of him now.

And then Joey saw him. A pretty, starched nurse wheeled him along. He had no left leg. Nothing right up to where his body began. Joey followed behind them, maybe ten yards. The jolt of his discovery, his excitement pushing him after them — he wanted to run up, but he kept his distance. Could he have been wrong? At Michigan Avenue the nurse turned the chair around: Eddie Cribbins, without a doubt. Only now in his face there were a few small holes, a rip or two, a rough closure of flesh, on his forehead two white streaks of scar tissue that would never again grow tan. His shoulders were so close together that they seemed to touch his chin. Eddie Cribbins passed not two feet away and did not recognize him. Recognized nothing. The tide of war had washed him out across the sea and now had brought him back, a piece of flotsam.

"Eddie," Joey called. "Eddie." He went after them. "Nurse. Nurse." She stopped. "This is an old friend of mine," he said. "This man is Eddie Cribbins, right? He was stationed here once, a couple of years ago. I know him. I know him good. Eddie? Eddie?" he said. He bent down to look closer.

The nurse said, "He doesn't say anything. He might not recognize you." She paused. "You understand?"

Joey stood up.

"Yeah," he said. "Sure." She started to push Eddie Cribbins away, but Joey put out his hand. "Can I visit him? Is that possible? When? Where is he?"

She told him he could visit and then rolled off down the Boardwalk. Overhead a Piper Cub floated out over the ocean in the last automatic patrolling, the blurred memory of a search for a fleet of danger now broken and sunk fathoms deep.

Even with the trilling of the excitement in him, Joey waited two days before visiting Eddie Cribbins on the eighth floor of Thomas England General Hospital. It was for him a grisly scene. None of the men on the eighth floor had all their limbs. They were housed together as if they should support and comfort each other in the sharing of mutual incapacity; or perhaps they were kept together to prevent the spread of a morbid infection of the soul.

Eddie Cribbins shared a room with seven other men. When Joey entered, he was in his wheelchair looking, staring, out the window, which had now been scraped clear of blackout paint. On the horizon little smudges of trawlers pulled at the sea.

"Hi, Eddie. It's me. Joey. Joey Rogovin. How you doing?" But what could he ask? What could he say? What could be done with words now? "It's been a long time. What? Two years, two and a half?" He waited. "You need anything? You want something?"

Behind him a man without an arm said, "He won't talk. He hasn't said a word since he got here. Two weeks. Not a word."

"Why not?" Joey asked, and looked back at Eddie Cribbins, who had not moved. He turned again to the one-armed man. "What is it? Is he deaf? He can't hear, maybe?"

"He can hear," the one-armed man said. "He can hear what we're saying right now. He does what he's told. He goes to the mess hall. He watches the movies. He can hear."

"He can hear us now? Eddie?" He turned again and put his hand on his shoulder. Joey was bigger than Eddie Cribbins now, a good deal bigger. "Eddie, is that right? Can you hear us? Can you hear me?"

"He can hear," the one-armed man said.

Others in the room were watching now, turning from gin rummy and dominoes, a jigsaw puzzle, turning from the tedium of a convalescence that would do them no good, the men without legs and arms, hands, feet.

"Eddie, goddamn it, *speak*. Say something." He flushed with a confusion and turned now to the audience. "What is it? Shell shock? Something like that?"

"Why don't you get out of here, kid," someone said.

"Yeah, kid, something like that," another man said.

"Shock. Sure enough," a long, heavy man with both legs gone said. "But not shell shock. All you do is wake up one morning and half of you is gone. After that you got nothing to say. What's there to say?"

"Will you shut up? Will you get out of here?" the other voice rose.

"Eddie?" Joey shouted at him now. "Eddie!"

"Get out of here. Get out of here," a new, dark, furious voice rose behind him. "This is enough of a crap house already. We don't need more of this. Go away! Leave the son of a bitch alone."

"Eddie, say something!"

"Get out of here! Leave him alone!"

But he could not. He had been too intimate a partner, and the old pain of lost worth had been wrenched up in him again from the Paris Coffee Shoppe, the old dissolution, the terrible crack of doom. Now let Joey Rogovin stand forth against the dull brute of such chaos. Gently he took Eddie Cribbins's head and turned it toward him. He looked into his eyes to end discrepancies, to give him mercy, but what he saw there — the milky cataracts of hopelessness — was obscene.

He took his mercy back to save them both. To save them all.

"Where's my five hundred dollars, Eddie? I want my five hundred dollars!" He shook the ragged head a little. "I'll give you a break. I'll forget two years of lost interest, OK? My contribution to the war effort. You hear. OK, so understand." He shook him again. Harder. "Five hundred dollars, Eddie. Five hundred dollars! This is no joke. When, Eddie, when? Soon." He took him by the shoulders now and shook him until the head jiggled and lolled.

Behind him Joey heard the strain and twist of apparatus, leather and wire, hinges, Bakelite and steel as the restive men moved to anger, but he had business here to do, a deal to complete. Anger was for warriors, the fuel of war, a fire that ate itself and then went out. But debt, not ashes, made bricks; debt surveyed the crummy deed on the land east of Eden. Joey Rogovin was not angry. He was making the only demand that could be made for what alone would last when names like Iwo Jima and Saipan and Okinawa were erased and instead reinscribed by new names, and those in time by others. Eddie Cribbins had to pay so that once more there could be asserted the worth of letters of credit, bills of exchange, articles of commerce, documents of commission — all the redeeming instruments of faith that London would honor Zurich again, New York Milan, Paris Katmandu. For under heaven there was nothing at all but what we *agreed* to.

"Five hundred dollars, Eddie. I know you. You've got it somewhere. I don't care how you get it here, but *do it. Get it.* Because you know me, Eddie. I'll get it. I'll get it out of you. Pay, Eddie. *Pay up!"*

They reached him even as their howl did, and they grabbed for him. But in the country of the maimed, what could they do to the whole man? Joey turned and knocked them down and away. His shirt ripped. A chair wheel pinned his foot for a moment, a crutch cracked down across his shoulders. Chairs spun off into other men, the card tables splintered, the dominoes clattered to the floor like hail, the jigsaw puzzle of a serene lake in Wisconsin was jolted as if a large stone had been thrown into its center. But he beat them down and grabbed Eddie Cribbins and shook him harder than ever and screamed at him above the shouting, the curses and the cries, and now the scurrying in the outer hall of the orderlies summoned to the alarm.

No more. Let there be an end. Let there be Awe that we are capable of Consequence, that it can guide if not succor us and make us human, whatever else human might be.

"You made a deal, Eddie. You made a deal, you finish a deal. Five hundred dollars. When?"

Then Eddie Cribbins spoke, redeemed at last by choice.

"Fuck you," he said, faced once again with alternatives. "Fuck you," he said. And lived.

Old Light

by Barry Targan

Her house was her studio, a contrivance of light and space around her painting. Her work was everywhere, a dominant line. Sketchbooks, canvases, tubes, bottles, jars, frames, cans of brushes, until it all joined into its own controlling logic; but she moved about in it easily enough.

She painted anything that would hold light, but she was best known, well known, as a painter of people's faces. Not as a portraitist glorifying corporate presidents and dowager heiresses (though she had painted them all in her time), but a painter who tried to see, like her betters before her — Velázquez perhaps, Rembrandt — the soul figured forth in pigments. Her work hung in the world's great galleries and museums and private collections. And now young art historians wrote her letters and were beginning to construct treatises about her accomplishments and what they fancied was her glory.

But there was a greater glory.

"Your father slept there from the time he was twelve." She pointed through one of her large windows to a small barnlike shed. "Up top. Your grandfather and I, we slept here in the main house. And your Aunt Susan, well, we were never sure where she would turn up. With her you could never tell."

It was our delight to hear this, and our envy, I suppose. Against her indulgent

178

but firm, creative chaos, we would compare the grumbling strictures we lived by. For our father, though an abundant man in all ways, was orderly, and as accurate as one of his T-squares.

"He gets that from your grandfather. He was orderly. But about the rest — meals and beds and clothing and where the children were — he never thought much about that, and I suppose I didn't, either. It must have put a mark upon your father."

And then, "Tell us about John Palmer," one of us would ask. Again. As always.

"Oh, you've heard all about John Palmer," she would say. "How about Winston Churchill? Or Eisenhower?"

"No, no. Tell us about John Palmer, how you met."

"I'll tell you about Rita Hayworth or William Faulkner. I met them, too. Or Enrico Fermi."

"No, no. John Palmer. You and John." And the three of us, her grandchildren, would chorus until she was borne back into that summer, into the salt-tanged days of war and love to come.

She had just graduated from art school in Philadelphia and now, in that summer, she went back to the Atlantic City boardwalk where she had in summers past drawn quick portraits in charcoal or sepia pencil or full pastels. She worked in a boardwalk store that had been hollowed out to allow room for the twelve artists, their easels and chairs, and for the crowds who became their customers to stand behind them and watch them work. A man, Joseph Brody, owned the store — the Artists Village, he called it.

There wasn't much other work to get then, and what she had really wanted to do anyway, had wanted since childhood, was to visit Europe, to see the cathedrals, the paintings, Picasso, the Left Bank, the Paris night. But now, of course, Europe was aflame. Just weeks ago we had invaded it. Even as she drew the soldiers and their girls, many had received their orders. They would all get to Europe before her, but a Europe she could not imagine now but could only fear for. Would the Cathedral at Ulm be standing? The Louvre. What would be left for her?

Atlantic City had been converted into possibly the world's largest military training base. All the hotels were made into barracks, and all day soldiers would drill on the boardwalk. But at night and on weekends, even with the special precautions taken to keep the lights from shining out to sea, the city and the boardwalk turned back to play, as if the daytime business of preparing for war was just that: a business, with regular hours and a set routine.

Everyone on the boardwalk then was from somewhere else — Idaho, New Mexico, Maine, the west Texas hills, Louisiana, the cornfields of Kansas. And no one was staying. Everyone was passing through, to Europe or the Pacific. Nothing was standing still.

"Time and event was in charge of all our lives, sweeping us together and apart and yet toward a grand destiny that we all had a share in," she would tell us. "It was — the *war* was — terrible; but this, this was wonderful. A mad music. A heady wine."

About the end of July, maybe early August, in midafternoon when the temperature had driven everyone off the boardwalk and onto the beach, she and two other artists were taking turns minding the store. It was a Monday, slow and tired after the hurtling weekend. Only Joseph Brody, from time to time, would whirl through and urge them to get up and pull someone in off the boardwalk, or maybe he even meant the beach. They paid no attention. This summer she was reading her way slowly through an anthology of American poetry. She had gotten to Whitman, and that day, remarkably, she had just read,

Give me the shores and wharves heavy-fringed with black ships!
O such for me! O an intense life, full of repletion and varied!
The life of the theatre, bar-room, huge hotel, for me!
The saloon of the steamer! The crowded excursion for me! The
      torchlight procession!
The dense brigade bound for the war, with high-piled military
      wagons following;
People, endless, streaming, with strong voices, passions, pageants ...

when she heard a man begin to talk to her. She didn't remember him starting to talk, just that he was talking when she finally heard him.

"You're the best one, you know," he said. "I've been watching you for two days and you are by far the best one. You should open your own place, or at least you should work on your own. Is the problem capital? There are ways around that, you know. I've been looking around. There are three stores that would rent you space. Here, I've got the figures." He sat down in the customer's chair and pulled it over to her and produced a small notebook of figures — rents, percentages, equipment, paper, mats, bags, insurance, utilities. He had it all worked out. On paper she could open her own business in a week. She was astounded.

"Who are you?" she asked. And then, "And what's it your concern anyway?"

"I'm John Palmer," he said. "Corporal Palmer for the time being. And there's no point in getting angry. You don't have to open your business just because you could. But if you ever think about it, this is the way to do it."

Just then Joseph Brody came by and saw John Palmer sitting close to her. "What is this, afternoon tea? You. Up," he said to John. John got up and Joseph Brody pushed the customer's chair back to its proper position and then he pushed John down into it.

"Now," he said. "You want to talk, so talk." To her he said, "Draw." And then he was gone.

"Go ahead, draw," John said.

"It's OK. You don't have to. Joseph is just a little crazy."

"No. Go ahead, draw my portrait."

And so she did. As she drew he talked on and on about her possibilities, about what she could do for herself. After a time she heard that it was good talk, that there was thought and fact and imagination to it, that what he had constructed for her was, indeed, as possible as he had claimed. Finally, when she got to his mouth, she told him he would have to stop talking so she could draw it. He stopped, but she could see that it was not easy for him; though it wasn't that he was *driven* to talk, it was only that he had so much to say.

By the time she had finished, a small crowd had gathered at her back, which was what usually happened. When John got up, another person sat down.

"Here," he said, and gave her the notebook with the figures and plans.

"Thanks, it's an interesting idea but I don't want to be that permanent. I've got more to do than this. But thanks. And good luck. Goodbye."

"I'll be back," he said.

Late in the afternoon three days later he returned with a wonderfully crafted artist's easel, unique and better than any she had ever seen. It was made out of a lovely mahogany, elegantly joined, with brass fittings and buttons of a contrasting wood. It had drawers and compartments and arms that slid out of slots and turned in sockets. It even had places to hold extra canvases or boards. Most incredible of all, the whole thing could fold up as if into itself and could be carried about like a suitcase.

"For you," he said after demonstrating it.

"But where ever did you get it?" she asked.

"I made it. I designed it and I made it."

"You *made* it? But I don't understand."

"I'm a carpenter. A boatbuilder, actually, but they have me a carpenter now. I'm attached to a combat engineer unit bound for somewhere. I went to the shop and worked on this until I got it right, though I can think of ways I might change it if I ever do it again. That's the way I am."

He went to her regular easel and started to dismantle it, moving the lights, the chairs, her supplies, everything. Quickly he put the new easel — more a traveling studio — in place.

"But Corporal Palmer, how can I accept this? I don't even know you."

"It's not an engagement ring," he said over his shoulder. "It's just a piece of furniture." He turned. "And I sure can't take it with me, so you either have to take it or sell it or throw it out."

"What's going on here?" Joseph Brody descended and twirled like a tornado. "What is this?" He looked at the old easel before him and the new one in its place. He spun. He didn't know what to do. "You," he said to John, "what do you want?"

"My picture. I want her to draw my picture," he said, disarming Joseph Brody, neutralizing him.

"Oh ... well ... so," he turned to her, "what are you waiting for? Draw him, draw him."

And she did. Then, and again, and again, four and five or even six times almost every day or evening right through August and past Labor Day.

As in any fairy tale, the three of us bore down upon the details, waiting to savor again the familiar, excited within our expectations the way you anticipate music that you have gotten by heart.

John Palmer would come by at odd times, day but mostly night. Like many others, he was in a holding pattern, past training and now waiting for the orders to depart. Sometimes he had duties, but often not. He would come to the Artists Village and talk to her and whenever she was not busy with a customer, and when Joseph Brody would swoop down on them, he would sit and be drawn.

He would talk about *going on*, she would explain to us. It was as if he did not recognize the war, overlooked it, *refused it*. It could claim his time, but that was all. He was busy with other things that he could imagine — so busy that what he imagined became real enough to live by, as if he could actually see and touch what he was looking at through the mind's eye. And, oh, he looked at everything.

He was a boatbuilder born and reared in Warren, Rhode Island. But more than a boatbuilder. He was a master shipwright, the youngest ever in Rhode Island. He was a naval architect without the title or the schooling. He had taught himself their math and had read all their books, and then he added to that what he knew in his fingers and with it all built better boats. He told her about his triumphs, about the racing victories of Palmer boats through Narragansett Bay and beyond. Clear over to Martha's Vineyard.

He designed and invented and built boats to any task — for racing or fishing or hauling or just to row in. He was twenty-five years old but already had his own yard "stuffed with boats," as he put it, waiting for his return. But there was no arrogance to him, not a touch of it. It was confidence, rather, the self-assurance of a superb craftsman. To be so good at something that it could speak loudly enough for you, first you must be absorbed by it, taken over and humbled by it. Finally, there had to be no room for *you* in your work. She knew what he meant. They talked about the discipline and intricacies of their respective crafts, though John did more talking than she.

And then, casually, he began to wait for her until she finished working, sometimes until one in the morning or even two on the weekends, when he would walk her home, to the boarding house on a side street far from the boardwalk. But just as often they would stay on the boardwalk and walk its length, talking about the things they had done with paint and wood and about the things they were going to do, the astonishing paintings, the magnificent boats. They did not talk about themselves, or about each other. But who they were came clear, each to each, as they talked about their love of light and of straight-grained wood.

She had one day free each week, and they would go off. John was marvelous. · He could produce anything. A car to take them away, a boat when they wanted, and just the right boat. He would rig a sail out of what he could find and they would poke about the sandbar islands and into the small inlets for crabs to eat late at night on a beach somewhere. Or he would sail them out to sea on a boat like a slab of wood with a sail not much more than a bedsheet, but he would tighten everything down and make the boat do just what he told it. She never worried then. She would have sailed around the world in such a tiny boat with John Palmer at the tiller.

Those were filling days, the sea and the light bursting together, John Palmer sitting back with the mainsheet clenched in his toes like another hand, at ease in any swell. She watched him, lean and effective, to remember and sketch later.

Sometimes a Coast Guard cutter would steam up close to them as if to board them for an inspection, but they were never stopped or questioned. The cutter would steam away, men along the rail looking at them, *glad* for them, for they were charmed.

They would fish and swim and walk through the starved sand grasses and the ground-up shells. Sometimes they would walk across the sand stained with oil from a torpedoed boat, oil that may have floated across from Portugal or hung in the sea for years before coming down finally on the beach.

And John Palmer could find anything. The moon snail alive creeping across the sand, the ripest beach plums, ghost crabs. Sometimes they would go down to Cape May, to the very point of New Jersey, and watch the birds of all sorts. John Palmer would know them all. The birds and the stars and the trees and the curve and shape of everything and how it would weigh out in water or air, how it would balance.

"Gaiety," she would say to us. "It is a word I think of when I think of then."

Sometimes they would walk before the huge hotels, grey and ornate as sandcastles, with the thousands of men in them sleeping, waiting to cross the dark sea just a hundred yards away. They would walk in the salty night, carving the air excitedly into glowing images and animate shapes so sharp and firm that she always remembered them, even as the Coast Guardsmen with dogs patrolled the beaches at the water's edge against enemies, and airplanes from the mainland droned overhead looking out.

"Oh my, oh my," she would say, "but we were affirming flames."

Once they walked right into the dawn. They were not allowed to be on the boardwalk after a certain hour, but by now the patrols knew them well enough to let them be. And that night they never turned back. They clambered out to the end of a rocky jetty and watched the sea slowly brighten into day.

It was the first time John Palmer was entirely silent. They just sat there in the darkness, listening to the sea well up and hiss through the dried seaweed. They sat quietly, thinking their own thoughts but each other's thoughts, too. When he finally did speak again he said, "Maybe after the war I'll come back here."

It was the first time he had ever mentioned the war. "Maybe I'll come back and build boats. There are special problems to water like this, different from the Bay." He explained the problems. "And there are advantages." The easy cedar he could get, the oak, the wider-ranging markets of the Delaware and the Chesapeake. As ever, he had worked it all out first, not as a daydream but as a plan as exact as the boats he would design, even if he might never build them. John Palmer went about his life doing things one way.

"But what about your yard in Warren?"

"Oh, I could sell it off easily enough. A yard's not worth much more than the man who runs it."

"But you would be starting all over again."

"I don't see it as starting over, just as continuing in another place."

She thought he was going to say more, and she thought she knew what more he was going to say, but he had not thought her out fully enough to figure her into his calculations yet. Not yet, though she was sure he was working on it. The time would come. Then what would she do?

But the war came first, swiftly. Orders. Packing up. No time for a gentle leaving. John Palmer came up to the boardwalk at a busy time. It was the Sunday of the Miss America Pageant week, and she had customers waiting in line. He took his place. She did not see him until he sat down before her. He told her he was leaving in a few hours. He talked on as if the audience at her back was not there. He had found a sawmill on the mainland that had stacks and stacks of perfectly dried planks waiting. He had made an informal contract with the operator. He went on as if the orders in his pocket and the ordering of his life were not in contention. He was, as always, *going on*.

But she could not put it all together as well as he, not nearly as well. The blue September day, Miss America in the air, the density of people everywhere, the rivulets of perspiration that ran down her charcoal-smudged face, Joseph Brody flying about like a trapped pigeon, John Palmer calmly figuring the length of his dry-dock runway against the average of the tides. And the battle lines in France, defined in the maps that the newspapers were now printing each day. She could not hold it together in a pattern.

Then John Palmer was gone. She had not even time for a proper goodbye. Before he left he gave her a portfolio of all the drawings she had done of him over the summer. And he would write. Make plans. Yes. But where? Where would she be?

But he was gone. Someone else, another soldier, was sitting in his place. She drew him and how many others she could not tell. She saw nothing more. Not even John Palmer. Only a blankness.

Only much later that night, at the bone-weary end of work, did it all come together. She fell and kept falling, into autumn and into her life alone. The war had come suddenly true; the fire that was John Palmer, that had burned the mist of the war away, was banked down now. And she grew cold.

She went back to Philadelphia and set up a studio and spent days doing nothing, hearing the radio, walking about, sitting in Rittenhouse Square for hours until it became too cold, sometimes doing freelance work that a friend would call about. Her money was running low, but she was listless, a bobbing cork. There were parties, and young men who were interested in her, and professors whose pet she had been who were anxious that she begin her promising career. But she could not take hold.

She grew cold with waiting, for what she did not know. Only sometimes the thought of John Palmer would warm her, his exuberance and confidence and energy would radiate through her, and for an hour or two or a morning she would start up, mix paint, spring at a canvas, paint at what she had talked to him about in the long summer nights and on the beaches and at sea. Then she would take courage, make plans. But the winter wore on, bore her down in the snow and the shortness of things so that even John Palmer grew vague and thin and fleeting.

The war bore down on her, too, as the terrible cost of moving the battle lines in the newspaper came clearer. By February she was as vacant as February can be, as toneless as a raw umber wash on an unprimed canvas.

What was worse, she could not say what had happened to her. She was not suffering, exactly. She was not depressed or worried, only empty, as if a plug had been pulled and she had drained out.

In late March a friend showed up at her dreary studio with a letter from Joseph Brody. The friend had worked for Brody, too, and he had sent the letter this way because he did not know how to reach her. She had given him no address, for she had no thought of returning to his Artists Village or to her indentured status. His letter thought otherwise. It was the same letter she had been receiving since her senior year in high school, a letter of instructions, work schedules, arrangement of pay. She dropped it on the table. But in his envelope there were other letters to her, six of them, from John Palmer. She opened them and arranged them in order, smoothing out the thin blue paper, and she read them, long letters, and thorough.

In the midst of war there was no war, only the intimacy of personal effort and the sweep of his imagination doing this to some building or that to some machine. The boatyard somewhere along the south Jersey coast grew more tangible in his letters even than in his talk. There were sketches, bills of particulars, lists. He even asked her to send for information from certain manufacturers whose names he included.

But he saw Europe, too, and reported to her that Chartres was intact, the Louvre undamaged though all the art was hidden away, the Cathedral at Ulm still standing. He had remembered everything, every detail that she had told him about her European dreams. As best he could, he had gone about seeing Europe for her. And he saw it clearly, not only the splintered streets, rubble strewn and broken, but also the spirit and hope and achievement of civilization. She knew enough about the destruction from the daily news. It took a John Palmer in the midst of it all to remember that there was more, and that time would come, and maybe men like him, to make life whole again.

She read all the letters, then read them three times again. And she stirred like life itself in March begins to stir. Who was John Palmer? She would see.

She found the portfolio of portraits she had drawn through the summer. She had stored them in the miraculous easel. Like his letters, she arranged the portraits in an order. There were 174 of them. Through that long March afternoon she watched herself as she came to know this man almost as if for the first time. She discovered herself, too, how she had a great magic: she could find a person's humor in a charcoal line, his wit and compassion and strength and courage and fear. Through that summer she had been discovering John Palmer layer by layer. Discovering herself, too. Though she had found neither of them until now. But now she knew what she was supposed to do.

In the easel in which she had stored the portfolio there were other things — her hodgepodge of art supplies, broken shells and pieces of beach glass, sketchbooks. Opening the easel was like opening the summer again; there was even sand. And there was the anthology of poetry she had been reading when John Palmer began to speak to her. The page was marked still, the poem at which she had stopped as he began to speak.

❂

Give me the shores and wharves heavy-fringed with black ships!

O such for me!

❂

She had fallen in love. Now what was she to do? Could she write to the APO address on his letters? The last letter was dated in January; she had answered none. What could he have thought? Did he imagine she worked at the Artists Village all year long? She had told him that she would go back to Philadelphia, but she had no address to give him then. Would he understand that she was not receiving his letters even as he dutifully went on writing them? But she decided that John Palmer would figure out whatever was necessary if anyone could, and that what he was doing was *going on*. The important figuring out was for her. What was she to do? And where begin?

She would write, of course, but she would go back to where she had stepped off into nothing. She would go back to where she had gotten off any path. Of course, she was going back to wait. With the kind of faith that comes to us once only, when we are young enough to believe *completely* in anything we want, she went back to Joseph Brody's Artists Village. She *knew* that someday John Palmer would come back there to do what he had said, and that he would come back for her, too. They would walk off down the boardwalk again, as if time had not happened, as if the bridges on the Rhine had not happened. He would come back and they would pick up their proper lives.

But he did not. The war claimed him after all. And her story would end.

In other years we would ask clamoring children's questions like after a tale by the Brothers Grimm, intense with the literal necessities of where and when and what and why, until the excitement of the story wore down and we were beckoned away by other pleasures.

But we were older now. *I* was.

"That's a sad story, Grandma," I said.

"Yes," she said. She had gone to the great window above the sea and watched the snake-necked cormorants resting on the exposed reefs. "Yes, it is. Sad. But it is a lovely story, too. I've remembered, you see. And proudly. Proudly."

I came to her by the window. My sisters had gone off. There was more to the story, this part of it now, as if she had waited until I had turned, was turning, into life myself. She had waited for me to allow her to come closer.

"He was a special man, John Palmer. A gorgeous human," she said. Then, "We all need — *must have* — someone like that, or else nothing will ever make enough sense. Do you understand?" She turned to me, hard and nearly vehement; but she was imploring, rather, and not angry, granting a trust now made good. "I love him still. I won't put that aside. I would not willingly lose him or give him up. Not in all these years. There's room in my life for him and for your grandfather and for all of this." She waved her hand around her kingdom in and out of the house. "John Palmer made it large enough for that. I've had all the luck."

Atlantic City

*Photographs from the historical collection
of Robert E. Ruffolo Jr.*

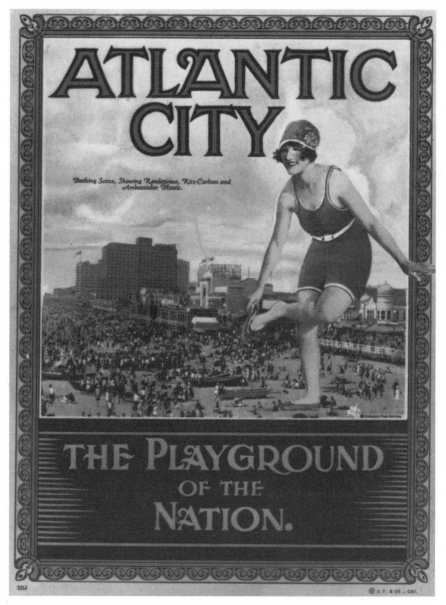

Atlantic City — 1955

by Norman Paul Hyett

Two mattresses laid out like slices of toast under the slope of my grandmother's attic, and we lie on them, my brother and I, each with our own dreams. The sheets are pulled around my fully clothed body like a Band-Aid stuck to an injured finger. It is almost sunrise. Time to go to work: anticipation has been my wake-up call since I started fishing on the pier.

I first began to sleep in my clothes when I was nine. My brother had discovered the fishing pier, and he and Dad took me there one night. It must have been August, because the weakfish were around. Just as we baited our hooks with sea worms and strips of squid, a storm came in from the south — dark clouds rolling in like smoke from my uncle Jockey's cigar. Life in Atlantic City, where storms are as common as tourists, had taught me to respect the harshness of nature but not to fear it, and this storm was not going to stop any of us from fishing. Once, my father told me that predator fish feed during the storms, and this time he was right. The ocean was a frenzy of bait fish leaping from the larger fish trying to eat them, and we could see, among the rough waves, speckled weakfish feeding near the surface. The pier lights weathered the winds, and we caught fish after fish. Every cast brought a hard strike to our lines, and most times a weakfish or a bluefish heaved over the railing to be placed in the large crate we had found there. As tired as I became, even when the storm abated, I cast out, over and over.

That was five years ago, and even though I am now thirteen, whenever I decide to go fishing I sleep in my clothes. My excitement is heightened by my desire not to wake my parents, who are sleeping on their mattress at the tip of this triangular room, especially my easily angered father. The thrill of being nearly a man, of doing a real man's work, makes sleeping fully dressed, even in the heat of an attic in summer, an adventure.

As I get out of my make-do bed, I recall how easy it used to be to stand straight when I was smaller and the slope wasn't so noticeable. For three summers now my parents have sublet at a meager profit our rented apartment to summer vacationers, and we have had to live here, where I miss my toys left in the closet, my fish tank with my soon-to-give-birth angelfish, and my too-soft bed. But I know that every dollar counts toward our getting by. Shoes in hand, I walk bent over in my socks toward the porthole of a window at the far end of the attic. I stop, as I habitually do each morning, to watch my parents sleep. The deep breathing of my father, who is never without a lit cigarette when he is awake, makes the gentle ins and outs of air from my mother's mouth almost inaudible, and I wonder if they are dreaming of me.

I poke my head out of this one hole of light in the room, looking up to see that the stars forecast a clear day; I'll need no cumbersome rain gear. I hate to wear that thick rubber; in the summertime it raises the humidity as if the space between my body and the coat's lining were a tropical rain forest. The window, unfortunately, faces the city rather than the waves, so I never know what to expect from the sea. For someone who pulls a fishing net for a living, the sky represents only half of the equation. Still, I am grateful that this room, which was never built to house a family, has any window at all. We are like the humidity; the tension of closeness is always here.

I look down at the small strip of rag I tied to my grandmother's clothesline. It tells me both the direction and the intensity of the wind, and now it is hanging like the tail of a frightened dog, straight down. It looks like it's going to be a scorcher, hot as hell and no wind.

Sometimes my grandmother takes down my makeshift weather predictor when she hangs the clothes out to dry. Every summer I look forward to helping her do the laundry in the old washer in the basement; sometimes I get to turn the handle of the wringer as her fat fingers feed the washed clothes through the rollers. I love to watch the pancakes of cloth come out the other side; big pancakes, like the ones at Mammies on the boardwalk where tourists go for breakfast all day long, and even into the night.

Slowly, I wind my way down the two flights of stairs, still carrying my shoes so as not to wake my three aunts, two uncles, six cousins, or grandmother, on my way to the enormous stark white bathroom. The large tub, held up by four talon legs each holding a baseball, takes up only a small portion of this room. It is always cold here, even on the hottest of summer days. Sometimes I use the small bathroom in the basement to brush my teeth, pee, and put on my shoes, but today I feel rushed.

It is still dark out, but a streetlight fills the kitchen with a mystical glow as I turn the round glass doorknob and open the door at the bottom of the inner staircase. Tall masts with large round bulbs, like giant flowers, illuminate the trolley tracks that run behind the house. Big trollies with magnificent straw seats and porcelain loops for holding on. I like to put pennies on the tracks and wait for the heaviness of the trolley to flatten them to quarter-sized wafers. Sometimes they stick to the wheels and are lost forever, but those I do retrieve I sell as oddities to the tourists who also buy my painted clamshells and popsicle-stick rafts. I started making my own spending money when I was eight by separating bottles into wooden crates in the back of a hotdog stand on the boardwalk. Since then, I save my coins in a glass jar and I buy comics, candy, and soda whenever I want. My paycheck is not mine to spend. I give it whole to my father. The leftover bread, as usual, is cloth-covered on the kitchen table next to the huge silver knife used to cut it. Two slices will do me until the concession stand on the pier opens, and I can eat donuts and drink coffee with the men while we talk about baseball, fish, and the weather. I like to listen while some of the younger men talk about women or tell jokes which I laugh at but often don't understand.

I need only to go to the cellar where the extra icebox holds my most important secret: worms. Not earthworms, but bloodworms from the rocky shores of Maine. They were purchased fresh yesterday, since no bait shop opens this early; they come in a white Chinese-food container filled with sea grass. A dozen worms, each with a head equipped with four nasty barbs not to be taken lightly.

Knapsack over my shoulder, I open the large front door with its ornate glass and step into the crisp sea air. There really is nothing quite like the first smell of morning at this hour. The salt blankets this Queen of Resorts like fairy dust. Breathing is easy; everything seems fresh and smells sweet like seaweed. I feel fortunate on mornings like this to live in Atlantic City, a place that never really sleeps. There is always a bar closing somewhere, tired women going home to wash off someone else's sweat, a drunk still conscious enough to wave down a jitney, those small buses that run up and down Pacific Avenue; miniature arks amidst the flood of too many people. I never feel alone.

I feel very much a man. Here I am up and going to work when other boys my age are sleeping. This is the hour for adults only, and I'm walking down New Hampshire Avenue to the jitney. I always consider myself lucky, especially as I pass the place where Luke and his father live. Luke was a high school football player who broke his back twelve years ago after being hit in the air while trying to catch a pass. I don't know exactly how it happened, but he hasn't been able to move a single part of his body ever since. He can sort of smile, and he blinks twice for "yes" and once for "no" when I ask him questions. I love to sit with him, opening and closing his fingers as he sits in his old wooden wheelchair, and I tell him stories about fishing. Sometimes other kids make fun of me for even touching Luke, but I don't care. He's my friend, and even though I don't even remember how I started spending time with him, I am his only friend. I wish that someday he would just open those fingers all by himself.

The ride on the jitney from the inlet to Arkansas (prounced are-CAN-zis in Atlantic City) Avenue is always short on these mornings. From my sack I take the white sailor's parka purchased for a dollar from a man who preferred wine to warmth. This marvelous sailcloth always makes me feel like a great fisherman who catches giant ocean fish. And as I walk the long block to the pier I imagine fishing from one of those boats built for angling; the ones with long noses in the front so men can walk out and harpoon sharks, tuna, or billfish. I am the man inching his way along the narrow gangplank waiting for just the right moment to throw the barb-headed weapon into the heart of the beautiful blue marlin, exhausted and side-up after its struggle with the hook still caught in its mouth. I, in my white sailcloth, am man enough to kill.

Finally I reach the boardwalk, its shops closed by iron shades and covered with a fog more mysterious than the rip-off auction houses, or the places that sell saltwater taffy, which doesn't contain salt water, or even the beach itself, where tourists tan themselves to colors they otherwise despise.

Directly across the boardwalk is the Million Dollar Pier. Built at the turn of the century by one Captain Young, whose magnificent house was once at the very entrance to the pier, it is now home to carnival booths, an Italian village, where I can get my fortune read for a quarter, and, at the very end, the fishing spot; a half mile of tar-coated pilings pounded deeply into the sand with a forest of planks nailed on top to make this a pier. I marvel at the sense of walking on water as I make my way to the net haul at the very end.

I'm usually the first to get there, and today's no exception. I open the locker, grab the fishing rod I made just last winter from a single piece of fiberglass, bait my line, and cast out. I loosen the drag and set the clicking device on my reel, then lean my pole against the railing. This way I can leave my rod alone and hear my line going out if a fish takes my bait, and at the same time go about my job of repairing the net. I imagine the pier from the sky looks like a big letter *J*, and the net hangs just below the surface of the water at the point where the letter curves on the inside.

I stand there in the quiet, watching some of the trapped fish search for a way out. They seem so tranquil even in their bewilderment, swimming easily to the surface and then down again. I wonder what they are thinking as one after another shows a quick glimpse of itself. When I look up I notice several of the regulars coming out to fish. It won't be until eight when the men from Barbera's Fish Market come out in their truck to pull the net, so I have some time to fish, repair my holes in the net with a large wooden needle and thick cotton thread, check the ropes for tangles, and talk with the other fishermen. During calm days like today there is little work to be done.

Fishing is slow today — a few kingfish caught closer to shore by Clarence, who seems always to know where the fish are. A skate is also brought up, and I watch its raylike wings being cut off for fish stew. I know it must be near eight because I hear the sound of the pickup truck's engine, and I look around to see the big Italian men driving too quickly toward me. The fish market's name on the side of the truck is still banged in from where a jitney slammed into it several years ago. They greet me with indifference, these hairy-chested men who are here to pull the net and then go back to bed. They know that I am well worth the small amount of money they pay to me to get here several hours before them to do the work Tony

Barbera wants done, but they are seldom in a good mood after a night of drinking, and they drink every night. I save them the trouble of getting up early or, God forbid, going to bed early.

Nine is the time to pull the net, and, since it is a real tourist attraction, many people have paid fifty cents to come and watch. I put on my oversized rubber hip boots and my rubber gloves with canvas palms and take my place in the center of the sorting pen, which is where the fish will be dumped and sorted after they are scooped up. Women, children, and men gather around me as if I were a circus announcer. I call the crowd to order and begin my speech. "Ladies and gentlemen, this is a pound net or trap net. There used to be many of these up and down the coast, but due to the scarcity of fish this is the only one left. Fish swimming up and down the coast in search of food strike the lead net, which you can see near the shore. Because of fear, they then head for deep water, following the net all the way. Finally, they pass through an opening, which faces the shore, in the large net below you. Once inside they never attempt ot escape by swimming toward shallow water. We will now pull the net, and I will be only too happy to answer any of your questions afterwards."

They never are really prepared for what comes up. This is a first-class appearing act. Materializing from below the waterline as we strain at the ropes threaded through the pullies are fifteen-foot sharks with their endless rows of teeth gnashing at the net, stingrays well over a hundred pounds and six feet across, flying fish, squid, stargazers, and edible fish by the ton. Back in the sorting pen, I am knee-deep in weakfish, flounders, kingfish, eels, rays, skates, and other fish of every size and shape.

Now my job is to identify the fish for the people who are standing a bit farther back than they had stood moments before. Mothers are holding their children tightly, and fathers are standing protectively in front of their families. The fish market men don't like talking to the crowd, and they are anxious to get the work done, so it is up to me to pull barbs from large rays to show danger or to lift an anglerfish and show how it fishes for other fish by dangling a wormlike piece of skin in the water above its ghastly mouth; or to describe how a squid swims backward by pushing water out from an opening in its head; or how a flying fish flies by spreading its pectoral fins like wings. The large sharks present the biggest problem for the onlookers. How could these creatures exist only a short distance from where people swim? I try to reassure them that sharks are timid creatures that avoid people, but they don't really believe me. All the time I'm talking, the men are sorting the fish into crates according to need. Some boxes will go to their fish market on Arctic Avenue, some will go to local restaurants willing to pay the high price to serve the freshest fish in town, and some will go to local farmers for fertilizer. The fish market men are concerned only with crating away the fish; names mean nothing to them, but I am the namer of fish, the fixer of nets, always saddened by the thought of these magnificent rays and sharks being plowed under the ground so that Jersey tomatoes and melons will grow larger and sweeter. After the last question is answered, I help finish the sorting and the loading of the crates onto the truck even as the tourists walk back toward the boardwalk, staring at the ocean, looking for sharks.

Two Atlantic City Poems

by Rochelle Ratner

1962

That's the year the flood was:
water resenting the fact
that water traps it.

My uncle stood out on the street
with a movie camera.
His car floated down the block.
Neighbors screamed from roofs.
The madman had it in his heart
to become a legend.

He grew helpless

as it flowed the wrong way:

a neighborhood

at the apex of transition.

Here it is this evening —

these same people scared to walk around.

A souvenir forever.

He clung to that damn machine

like it was his family.

His wife died eight years later.

He laughs about it even now,

how his camera caught her

in a tantrum, all the way up there.

Joe Jr.

Against the wind.
He feels it's right to be against
something.

No more schoolyard
set off from the traffic
where balls
were secure on the roof
till someone got them.

Still the same game.
Walking from Arctic Avenue
north:

the Negro section.

Each house

has at least one broken window,

half of them are torn down

or abandoned

what with the new condominiums

being promised.

On Baltic

the railroad tracks gone

warehouses

hold fort nightly,

their parking lots with fences

that divert him.

The Search for Marvin Gardens

by John McPhee

G o. I roll the dice — a six and a two. Through the air I move my token, the flatiron, to Vermont Avenue, where dog packs range.

❂

The dogs are moving (some are limping) through ruins, rubble, fire damage, open garbage. Doorways are gone. Lath is visible in the crumbling walls of the buildings. The street sparkles with shattered glass. I have never seen, anywhere, so many broken windows. A sign — "Slow, Children at Play" — has been bent backward by an automobile. At the lighthouse, the dogs turn up Pacific and disappear. George Meade, Army engineer, built the lighthouse — brick upon brick, six hundred thousand bricks, to reach up high enough to throw a beam twenty miles over the sea. Meade, seven years later, saved the Union at Gettysburg.

❂

I buy Vermont Avenue for $100. My opponent is a tall, shadowy figure, across from me, but I know him well, and I know his game like a favorite tune. If he can, he will always go for the quick kill. And when it is foolish to go for the quick kill he will be foolish. On the whole, though, he is a master assessor of percentages. It is a mistake to underestimate him. His eleven carries his top hat to St. Charles Place, which he buys for $140.

❂

The sidewalks of St. Charles Place have been cracked to shards by through-growing weeds. There are no buildings. Mansions, hotels once stood here. A few street lamps now drop cones of light on broken glass and vacant space behind a chain-link fence that some great machine has in places bent to the ground. Five plane trees — in full summer leaf, flecking the light — are all that live on St. Charles Place.

❂

Block upon block, gradually, we are cancelling each other out — in the blues, the lavenders, the oranges, the greens. My opponent follows a plan of his own devising. I use the Hornblower & Weeks opening and the Zuricher defense. The first game draws tight, will soon finish. In 1971, a group of people in Racine, Wisconsin, played for seven hundred and sixty-eight hours. A game begun a month later in Danville, California, lasted eight hundred and twenty hours. These are official records, and they stun us. We have been playing for eight minutes. It amazes us that Monopoly is thought of as a long game. It is possible to play to a complete, absolute, and final conclusion in less than fifteen minutes, all within the rules as written. My opponent and I have done so thousands of times. No wonder we are sitting across from each other now in this best-of-seven series for the international singles championship of the world.

❂

On Illinois Avenue, three men lean out from second-story windows. A girl is coming down the street. She wears dungarees and a bright-red shirt, has ample breasts and a Hadendoan Afro, a black halo, two feet in diameter. Ice rattles in the glasses in the hands of the men.

"Hey, sister!"

"Come on up!"

She looks up, looks from one to another to the other, looks them flat in the eye.

"What for?" she says, and she walks on.

❂

I buy Illinois for $240. It solidifies my chances, for I already own Kentucky and Indiana. My opponent pales. If he had landed first on Illinois, the game would have been over then and there, for he has houses built on Boardwalk and Park Place, we share the railroads equally, and we have cancelled each other everywhere else. We never trade.

☼

In 1852, R. B. Osborne, an immigrant Englishman, civil engineer, surveyed the route of a railroad line that would run from Camden to Absecon Island, in New Jersey, traversing the state from the Delaware River to the barrier beaches of the sea. He then sketched in the plan of a "bathing village" that would surround the eastern terminus of the line. His pen flew glibly, framing and naming spacious avenues parallel to the shore — Mediterranean, Baltic, Oriental, Ventnor — and narrower transsecting avenues: North Carolina, Pennsylvania, Vermont, Connecticut, States, Virginia, Tennessee, New York, Kentucky, Indiana, Illinois. The place as a whole had no name, so when he had completed the plan Osborne wrote in large letters over the ocean, "Atlantic City." No one ever challenged the name, or the names of Osborne's streets. Monopoly was invented in the early nineteen-thirties by Charles B. Darrow, but Darrow was only transliterating what Osborne had created. The railroads, crucial to any player, were the making of Atlantic City. After the rails were down, houses and hotels burgeoned from Mediterranean and Baltic to New York and Kentucky. Properties — building lots— sold for as little as six dollars apiece and as much as a thousand dollars. The original investors in the railroads and the real estate called themselves the Camden & Atlantic Land Company. Reverently, I repeat their names: Dwight Bell, William Coffin, John DaCosta, Daniel Deal, William Fleming, Andrew Hay, Joseph Porter, Jonathan Pitney, Samuel Richards — founders, fathers, forerunners, archetypical masters of the quick kill.

☼

My opponent and I are now in a deep situation of classical Monopoly. The torsion is almost perfect — Boardwalk and Park Place versus the brilliant reds. His cash position is weak, though, and if I escape him now he may fade. I land on Luxury Tax, contiguous to but in sanctuary from his power. I have four houses on Indiana. He lands there. He concedes.

☼

Indiana Avenue was the address of the Brighton Hotel, gone now. The Brighton was exclusive — a word that no longer has retail value in the city. If you arrived by automobile and tried to register at the Brighton, you were sent away. Brighton-class people came in private railroad cars. Brighton-class people had other private railroad cars for their horses — dawn rides on the firm sand at water's edge, skirts flying. Colonel Anthony J. Drexel Biddle — the sort of name that would constrict throats in Philadelphia — lived, much of the year, in the Brighton.

❂

Colonel Sanders' fried chicken is on Kentucky Avenue. So is Clifton's Club Harlem, with the Sepia Revue and the Sepia Follies, featuring the Honey Bees, the Fashions, and the Lords.

❂

My opponent and I, many years ago, played 2,428 games of Monopoly in a single season. He was then a recent graduate of the Harvard Law School, and he was working for a downtown firm, looking up law. Two people we knew — one from Chase Manhattan, the other from Morgan, Stanley — tried to get into the game, but after a few rounds we found that they were not in the conversation and we sent them home. Monopoly should always be *mano a mano* anyway. My opponent won 1,199 games, and so did I. Thirty were ties. He was called into the Army, and we stopped just there. Now, in Game 2 of the series, I go immediately to jail, and again to jail while my opponent seines property. He is dumbfoundingly lucky. He wins in twelve minutes.

❂

Visiting hours are daily, eleven to two; Sunday, eleven to one; evenings, six to nine. "NO MINORS, NO FOOD, Immediate Family Only Allowed in Jail." All this above a blue steel door in a blue cement wall in the windowless interior of the basement of the city hall. The desk sergeant sits opposite the door to the jail. In a cigar box in front of him are pills of every color, a banquet of fruit salad an inch and a half deep — leapers, co-pilots, footballs, truck drivers, peanuts, blue angels, yellow jackets, redbirds, rainbows. Near the desk are two soldiers, waiting to go through the blue door. They are about eighteen years old. One of them is trying hard to light a cigarette. His wrists are in steel cuffs. A military policeman waits, too. He is a year or so older than the soldiers, taller, studious in appearance, gentle, fat. On a bench against a wall sits a good-looking girl in slacks. The blue door rattles, swings heavily open. A turnkey stands in the doorway. "Don't you guys kill yourselves back there now," says the sergeant to the soldiers.

"One kid, he overdosed himself about ten and a half hours ago," says the M.P.

The M.P., the soldiers, the turnkey, and the girl on the bench are white. The sergeant is black. "If you take off the handcuffs, take off the belts," says the sergeant to the M.P. "I don't want them hanging themselves back there." The door shuts and its tumblers move. When it opens again, five minutes later, a young white man in sandals and dungarees and a blue polo shirt emerges. His hair is in a ponytail. He has no beard. He grins at the good-looking girl. She rises, joins him. The sergeant hands him a manila envelope. From it he removes his belt and a small notebook. He borrows a pencil, makes an entry in the notebook. He is out of jail, free. What did he do? He offended Atlantic City in some way. He spent a night in the jail. In the nineteen-thirties, men visiting Atlantic City went to jail, directly to jail, did not pass Go, for appearing in topless bathing suits on the beach. A city statute requiring all men to wear full-length bathing suits was not seriously challenged until 1937, and the first year in which a man could legally go bare-chested on the beach was 1940.

❂

Game 3. After seventeen minutes, I am ready to begin construction on overpriced and sluggish Pacific, North Carolina, and Pennsylvania. Nothing else being open, opponent concedes.

❂

The physical profile of streets perpendicular to the shore is something like a playground slide. It begins in the high skyline of Boardwalk hotels, plummets into warrens of "side-avenue" motels, crosses Pacific, slopes through church missions, convalescent homes, burlesque houses, rooming houses, and liquor stores, crosses Atlantic, and runs level through the bombed-out ghetto as far — Baltic, Mediterranean — as the eye can see. North Carolina Avenue, for example, is flanked at its beach end by the Chalfonte and the Haddon Hall (908 rooms, air-conditioned), where, according to one biographer, John Philip Sousa (1854-1932) first played when he was twenty-two, insisting, even then, that everyone call him by his entire name. Behind these big hotels, motels — Barbizon, Catalina — crouch. Between Pacific and Atlantic is an occasional house from 1910 — wooden porch, wooden mullions, old yellow paint — and two churches, a package store, a strip show, a dealer in fruits and vegetables. Then, beyond Atlantic Avenue, North Carolina moves on into the vast ghetto, the bulk of the city, and it looks like Metz in 1919, Cologne in 1944. Nothing has actually exploded. It is not bomb damage. It is deep and complex decay. Roofs are off. Bricks are scattered in the street. People sit on porches, six deep, at nine on a Monday morning. When they go off to wait in unemployment lines, they wait sometimes two hours. Between Mediterranean and Baltic runs a chain-link fence, enclosing rubble. A patrol car sits idling by the curb. In the back seat is a German shepherd. A sign on the fence says, "Beware of Bad Dogs."

Mediterranean and Baltic are the principal avenues of the ghetto. Dogs are everywhere. A pack of seven passes me. Block after block, there are three-story brick row houses. Whole segments of them are abandoned, a thousand broken windows. Some parts are intact, occupied. A mattress lies in the street, soaking in a pool of water. Wet stuffing is coming out of the mattress. A postman is having a rye and a beer in the Plantation Bar at nine-fifteen in the morning. I ask him idly if he knows where Marvin Gardens is. He does not. "HOOKED AND NEED HELP? CONTACT N.A.R.C.O." "REVIVAL NOW GOING ON, CONDUCTED BY REVEREND H. HENDERSON OF TEXAS." These are signboards on Mediterranean and Baltic. The second one is upside down and leans against a boarded-up window of the Faith Temple Church of God in Christ. There is an old peeling poster on a warehouse wall showing a figure in an electric chair. "The Black Panther Manifesto" is the title of the poster, and its message is, or was, that "the fascists have already decided in advance to murder Chairman Bobby Seale in the electric chair." I pass an old woman who carries a bucket. She wears blue sneakers, worn through. Her feet spill out. She wears red socks, rolled at the knees. A white handkerchief, spread over her head, is knotted at the corners. Does she know where Marvin Gardens is? "I sure don't know," she says, setting down the bucket. "I sure don't know. I've heard of it somewhere, but I just can't say where." I walk on, through a block of shattered glass. The glass crunches underfoot like coarse sand. I remember when I first came here — a long train ride from Trenton, long ago, games of poker in the train — to play basketball against Atlantic City. We were half black, they were all black. We scored forty points, they scored eighty, or something like it. What I remember most is that they had glass backboards —

glittering, pendent, expensive glass backboards, a rarity then in high schools, even in colleges, the only ones we played on all year.

I turn on Pennsylvania, and start back toward the sea. The windows of the Hotel Astoria, on Pennsylvania near Baltic, are boarded up. A sheet of unpainted plywood is the door, and in it is a triangular peephole that now frames an eye. The plywood door opens. A man answers my question. Rooms there are six, seven, and ten dollars a week. I thank him for the information and move on, emerging from the ghetto at the Catholic Daughters of America Women's Guest House, between Atlantic and Pacific. Between Pacific and the Boardwalk are the blinking vacancy signs of the Aristocrat and Colton Manor motels. Pennsylvania terminates at the Sheraton-Seaside — thirty-two dollars a day, ocean corner. I talk a walk on the Boardwalk and into the Holiday Inn (twenty-three stories). A guest is registering. "You reserved for Wednesday, and this is Monday," the clerk tells him. "But that's all right. We have *plenty* of rooms." The clerk is very young, female, and has soft brown hair that hangs below her waist. Her superior kicks her.

He is a middle-aged man with red spiderwebs in his face. He is jacketed and tied. He takes her aside. "Don't say 'plenty,' " he says. "Say 'You are fortunate, sir. We have rooms available.' "

The face of the young woman turns sour. "We have all the rooms you need," she says to the customer, and, to her superior, "How's that?"

✪

Game 4. My opponent's luck has become abrasive. He has Boardwalk and Park Place, and has sealed the board.

✪

Darrow was a plumber. He was, specifically, a radiator repairman who lived in Germantown, Pennsylvania. His first Monopoly board was a sheet of linoleum. On it he placed houses and hotels that he had carved from blocks of wood. The game he thus invented was brilliantly conceived, for it was an uncannily exact reflection of the business milieu at large. In its depth, range, and subtlety, in its luck-skill ratio, in its sense of infrastructure and socio-economic parameters, in its philosophical characteristics, it reached to the profundity of the financial community. It was as scientific as the stock market. It suggested the manner and means through which an underdeveloped world had been developed. It was chess at Wall Street level. "Advance token to the nearest Railroad and pay owner twice the rental to which he is otherwise entitled. If Railroad is unowned, you may buy it from the Bank. Get out of Jail, free. Advance token to nearest Utility. If unowned, you may buy it from Bank. If owned, throw dice and pay owner a total ten times the amount thrown. You are assessed for street repairs: $40 per house, $115 per hotel. Pay poor tax of $15. Go to Jail. Go directly to Jail. Do not pass Go. Do not collect $200."

✪

The turnkey opens the blue door. The turnkey is known to the inmates as Sidney K. Above his desk are ten closed-circuit-TV screens — assorted viewpoints of the jail. There are three cellblocks — men, women, juvenile boys. Six days is the average stay. Showers twice a week. The steel doors and the equipment that operates them were made in San Antonio. The prisoners sleep on bunks of butcher block. There are no mattresses. There are three prisoners to a cell. In winter, it is cold in here. Prisoners burn newspapers to keep warm. Cell corners are black with smudge. The jail is three years old. The men's block echoes with chatter. The man in the cell nearest Sidney K. is pacing. His shirt is covered with broad stains of blood. The block for juvenile boys is, by contrast, utterly silent — empty corridor, empty cells. There is only one prisoner. He is small and black and appears to be thirteen. He says he is sixteen and that he has been alone in here for three days.

"Why are you here? What did you do?"

"I hit a jitney driver."

✪

The series stands at three all. We have split the fifth and sixth games. We are scrambling for property. Around the board we fairly fly. We move so fast because we do our own banking and search our own deeds. My opponent grows tense.

✪

Ventnor Avenue, a street of delicatessens and doctors' offices, is leafy with plane trees and hydrangeas, the city flower. Water Works is on the mainland. The water comes over in submarine pipes. Electric Company gets power from across the state, on the Delaware River, in Deepwater. States Avenue, now a wasteland like St. Charles, once had gardens running down the middle of the street, a horse-drawn trolley, private homes. States Avenue was as exclusive as Brighton. Only an

apartment house, a small motel, and the All Wars Memorial Building —
monadnocks spaced widely apart — stand along States Avenue now. Pawnshops,
convalescent homes and the Paradise Soul Saving Station are on Virginia Avenue.
The soul-saving station is pink, orange, and yellow. In the windows flanking the
door of the Virginia Money Loan Office are Nikons, Polaroids, Yashicas, Sony TVs,
Underwood typewriters, Singer sewing machines, and pictures of Christ. On the
far side of town, beside a single track and locked up most of the time, is the new
railroad station, a small hut made of glazed firebrick, all that is left of the lines that
built the city. An authentic phrenologist works on New York Avenue close to
Frank's Extra Dry Bar and a church where the sermon today is "Death in the Pot."
The church is of pink brick, has blue and amber windows and two red doors. St.
James Place, narrow and twisting, is lined with boarding houses that have wooden
porches on each of three stories, suggesting a New Orleans made of salt-bleached
pine. In a vacant lot on Tennessee is a white Ford station wagon stripped to the
chassis. The windows are smashed. A plastic Clorox bottle sits on the driver's seat.
The wind has pressed newspaper against the chain-link fence around the lot.
Atlantic Avenue, the city's principal thoroughfare, could be seventeen American
Main Streets placed end to end — discount vitamins and Vienna Corset shops,
movie theatres, shoe stores, and funeral homes. The Boardwalk is made of yellow
pine and Douglas fir, soaked in pentachlorophenol. Downbeach, it reaches far
beyond the city. Signs everywhere — on windows, lampposts, trash baskets —
proclaim "Bienvenue Canadiens!" The salt air is full of Canadian French. In the
Claridge Hotel, on Park Place, I ask a clerk if she knows where Marvin Gardens is.
She says, "Is it a floral shop?" I ask a cabdriver, parked outside. He says, "Never
heard of it." Park Place is one block long, Pacific to Boardwalk. On the roof of the
Claridge is the Solarium, the highest point in town — panoramic view of the
ocean, the bay, the salt-water ghetto. I look down at the rooftops of the side-
avenue motels and into swimming pools. There are hundreds of people around the
rooftop pools, sunbathing, reading — many more people than are on the beach.
Walls, windows, and a block of sky are all that is visible from these pools — no
sand, no sea. The pools are craters, and with the people around them they are
countersunk into the motels.

❂

The seventh, and final, game is ten minutes old and I have hotels on Oriental,

Vermont, and Connecticut. I have Tennessee and St. James. I have North Carolina and Pacific. I have Boardwalk, Atlantic, Ventnor, Illinois, Indiana. My fingers are forming a "V." I have mortgaged most of these properties in order to pay for others, and I have mortgaged the others to pay for the hotels. I have seven dollars. I will pay off the mortgages and build my reserves with income from the three hotels. My cash position may be low, but I feel like a rocket in an underground silo. Meanwhile, if I could just go to jail for a time I could pause there, wait there, until my opponent, in his inescapable rounds, pays the rates of my hotels. Jail, at times, is the strategic place to be. I roll boxcars from the Reading and move the flatiron to Community Chest. "Go to Jail. Go directly to Jail."

○

The prisoners, of course, have no pens and no pencils. They take paper napkins, roll them tight as crayons, char the ends with matches, and write on the walls. The things they write are not entirely idiomatic; for example, "In God We Trust." All is in carbon. Time is required in the writing. "Only humanity could know of such pain." "God So Loved the World." "There is no greater pain than life itself." In the women's block now, there are six blacks, giggling, and a white asleep in red shoes. She is drunk. The others are pushers, prostitutes, an auto thief, a burglar caught with pistol in purse. A sixteen-year-old accused of murder was in here last week. These words are written on the wall of a now empty cell: "Laying here I see two bunks about six inches thick, not counting the one I'm laying on, which is hard as brick. No cushion for my back. No pillow for my head. Just a couple scratchy blankets which is best to use it's said. I wake up in the morning so shivery and cold, waiting and waiting till I am told the food is coming. It's on its way. It's not worth waiting for, but I eat it anyway. I know one thing when they set me free I'm gonna be good if it kills me."

○

How many years must a game be played to produce an Anthony J. Drexel Biddle and chestnut geldings on the beach? About half a century was the original answer, from the first railroad to Biddle at his peak. Biddle, at his peak, hit an Atlantic City streetcar conductor with his fist, laid him out with one punch. This increased Biddle's legend. He did not go to jail. While John Philip Sousa led his band along the Boardwalk playing "The Stars and Stripes Forever" and Jack Dempsey ran up and down in training for his fight with Gene Tunney, the city

crossed the high curve of its parabola. Al Capone held conventions here —
upstairs with his sleeves rolled, apportioning among his lieutenant governors the
states of the Eastern seaboard. The natural history of an American resort proceeds
from Indians to French Canadians via Biddles and Capones. French Canadians,
whatever they may be at home, are Visigoths here. Bienvenue Visigoths!

❂

My opponent plods along incredibly well. He has got his fourth railroad, and
patiently, unbelievably, he has picked up my potential winners until he has blocked
me everywhere but Marvin Gardens. He has avoided, in the fifty-dollar zoning, my
increasingly petty hotels. His cash flow swells. His railroads are costing me two
hundred dollars a minute. He is building hotels on States, Virginia, and St. Charles.
He has temporarily reversed the current. With the yellow monopolies and my blue
monopolies, I could probably defeat his lavenders and his railroads. I have Atlantic
and Ventnor. I need Marvin Gardens. My only hope is Marvin Gardens.

❂

There is a plaque at Boardwalk and Park Place, and on it in relief is the leonine
profile of a man who looks like an officer in a metropolitan bank — "Charles B.
Darrow, 1889-1967, inventor of the game of Monopoly." "Darrow," I address him
aloud. "Where is Marvin Gardens?" There is, of course, no answer. Bronze,
impassive, Darrow looks south down the Boardwalk. "Mr. Darrow, please, where is
Marvin Gardens?" Nothing. Not a sign. He just looks south down the Boardwalk.

❂

My opponent accepts the trophy with his natural ease, and I make, from notes,
remarks that are even less graceful than his.

❂

Marvin Gardens is the one color-block Monopoly property that is not in
Atlantic City. It is a suburb within a suburb, secluded. It is a planned compound of
seventy-two handsome houses set on curvilinear private streets under yews and
cedars, poplars and willows. The compound was built around 1920, in Margate,
New Jersey, and consists of solid buildings of stucco, brick, and wood, with slate
roofs, tile roofs, multi-mullioned porches, Giraldic towers, and Spanish grilles.
Marvin Gardens, the ultimate outwash of Monopoly, is a citadel and sanctuary of
the middle class. "We're heavily patrolled by police here. We don't take no

chances. Me? I'm living here nine years. I paid seventeen thousand dollars and I've been offered thirty. Number one, I don't want to move. Number two, I don't need the money. I have four bedrooms, two and a half baths, front den, back den. No basement. The Atlantic is down there. Six feet down and you float. A lot of people have a hard time finding this place. People that lived in Atlantic City all their life don't know how to find it. They don't know where the hell they're going. They just know it's south, down the Boardwalk."

Irregular Intervals

by Anndee Hochman

A fter his third night of work, Ivan Glatz figured out a way to wriggle into the peanut suit without asking his parents for help. He balanced the silk top hat on his head, held the monocle over his right eye, and looked in the mirror. Not bad. Not bad for a summer job at the shore — just 5-9 p.m. six nights a week. Minimum wage and a pound of free nuts every Friday.

"What happened to the last Mr. Peanut?" he'd asked in the job interview, after demonstrating his soft-shoe routine for the manager of Planter's Peanut World.

"We had to let him go. He was 72, he had arthritis, and I think he was stealing cashew clusters. You're no thief, are you, kid?"

Ivan tipped his hat. "Do I look like the kind of kid who'd steal cashew clusters?"

Arnie Greenwood shook his head. "No, you look like the kind of kid who'd sit up front and drive your teachers crazy. Go on out there and bring me some customers."

At 15, Ivan wasn't technically old enough for the job. But he was tall enough to fit into the peanut suit, and Greenwood was desperate. The north end of the Atlantic City boardwalk was rotting like a set of neglected teeth, and few people ventured down as far as Peanut World. Greenwood gave him a tattered manual, full of the kind of puns Ivan's father loved. "We serve all kinds of nuts — just take a look at our customers" was one suggested line. Or, "Don't be shy — come on out of your shell."

Ivan ignored the script. Instead, he made the boardwalk his personal vaudeville stage, improvising magic tricks and pratfalls, soft-shoe routines he'd learned from watching old movies. He twirled his cane and spun his hat, tap-danced on the creaky boards.

"Ma, come see Mr. Peanut," kids shouted, dragging their parents toward the store. Once they got close enough, the smell inevitably drew them in — a nutty, salty heat, part earth, part sea. The families trooped down aisles of nuts, shelled and unshelled, salted and dry-roasted, macadamias and almonds and walnuts, chocolates in the shape of baseball bats and American flags. Mr. Peanut banks and pennants and toothbrushes and paperweights and mugs.

"Can I be Mr. Peanut for Halloween?" one little girl whined. "Mom, can I pleeeaasse be Mr. Peanut?"

"We'll see," her mother said, juggling an armload of Mr. Peanut purchases. "Let's get through Labor Day first, okay?"

Ivan wasn't supposed to take tips — "Peanut World employees shall not accept gratuities," the book said — but Greenwood told him he could keep whatever he made, as long as he got people into the store. So Ivan left each evening with an envelope full of coins and a chocolate-covered pretzel for a snack.

Then he wandered slowly along the boardwalk. The Drift In & Sea Boutique had a window full of dusty paperweights and wind chimes made out of shells — "Close-Out Sale All 40 Percent Off," a hand-scrawled sign said. The saltwater taffy place was still there, but Spuds French Fry Corner had closed, plywood nailed haphazardly where the counter used to be. Paulie's Pretzels was long gone, and What a Bargain had lost some letters from its sign: Wha A Bar, it said now.

The only place that showed signs of life was Madame Zeta's fortune-telling shop. A curtain of purple beads swung in the doorway, and a plywood sheet propped in front said, "Palms read. Futures seen. Pasts revealed. Only $5." Sometimes Madame Zeta herself was visible through the dirty window, sitting at a table with a fringed cloth, her head wrapped in an orange turban, cigarette smoke threading itself over her face.

On the other side of the boardwalk, the beach side, there was one amusement pier left, but its lights seemed weaker than Ivan remembered from previous summers, as if the whole place were a flashlight whose batteries had run down. He walked along, testing himself at each cross-street: Pennsylvania Avenue was a green, along with North Carolina and Pacific. Tennessee was orange; so were New York and St. James. He could close his eyes and picture where each property was set on the Monopoly board.

There was a break in the row of shops, and the old Marlborough-Blenheim Hotel loomed over the boardwalk. The place had been empty for a few years; Ivan had heard it would be bulldozed this summer. There was something unsettling about the huge building, its cornices like smashed wedding cakes, its upper windows cracked, the landscaping a knot of overgrown shrubs.

Ivan forced himself to stop and stare at the building. There were a few lights in the third- and fourth-floor rooms. A couple of the old rolling chairs, their wicker seats dirty and broken, still sat along the boardwalk rails. Then a black flapping startled him. A seagull swooped down, snatched his chocolate-covered pretzel and flew off, with other birds squawking in protest.

The block after the hotel was the Catholic Children's Respite Home, where nuns pushed pale children in wheelchairs around the yard. Ivan's parents said the home dated back to the days when salt air was supposed to be curative and rich families sent their anemic children to grow robust by the seashore.

In the center of the hospital's yard, not far from the broken swingset, was a statue of the Virgin Mary, surrounded by a circle of flowers and a ring of tiny footlights. Ivan had seen the nuns out there weeding, their habits flapping in the ocean breeze. This time, he stopped. Someone had put a pair of hot-pink sunglasses on the statue's face and slipped a shirt over her concrete torso: "My Son Went to Atlantic City and All I Got Was This Lousy T-shirt."

Finally Ivan passed Park Place — one of the expensive dark-blues — and then Arkansas Avenue, his parents' beige Continental idling by the boardwalk ramp. He opened the back door and lay down; the costume made it difficult to sit. Ivan's father looked back with a grin. "Make good money tonight? Or was it just peanuts?"

"Dad, that's not funny. It wasn't funny the first 25 times you said it."

"Really?" his father said. "Okay, what do rich peanut-store managers wear on their feet? Cashews! Get it? Cash-shoes?"

From the back seat, Mr. Peanut groaned.

❂

Ivan was entertaining the early-bird crowd, mostly old people who shuffled along the boardwalk, leaning on four-footed canes and each other. He bent down to a woman in a wheelchair and plucked a bouquet of carnations from her ear. The woman broke into a toothy smile.

"What a nice young man," she said. "Handsome. And so talented. You should be in show business."

"Give me a break," said a voice. "I could do that trick when I was six."

Ivan looked up. The voice belonged to a girl in green shorts and a T-shirt, standing near a group of kids and nuns from the Catholic Children's Home. Some were in wheelchairs; a few even had IV bottles on little wheeled poles, and they looked white as sand, as if they hadn't been outdoors all summer. But this girl had skin the color of honey-roasted peanuts, and a long black braid. Ivan guessed she was ten or eleven.

"Oh, yeah? Well, I bet you couldn't do this." And he began the piece he usually saved for his finale, juggling a peanut, an apple, and a sneaker. He could feel her eyes, her I-dare-you stance. He tossed the sneaker too low, grabbed the apple awkwardly in his left hand, and watched the peanut drop between two slats of the boardwalk. "Shit," he said.

Two of the nuns in the front began whisking the children into a group. "Can we go to the pier?" said one boy. "Can we go on some rides? I want to ride the spider."

"Jeremy, you know you can't go on rides. Some of your little friends are too ill for that, and it wouldn't be fair if you went and they didn't."

"Well, what about some cotton candy, then?"

"No, the ones who are diabetic can't have it. Besides, we're taking you all back for dinner now."

"I hate that stupid hospital food," Jeremy sulked. "I want french fries."

"Come on, everybody," the one who seemed to be in charge was saying. "Come on," she said to Ivan's heckler.

"Hey, I was only kidding," the girl said to Ivan. "Really, you're a good magician.

I've watched you before." Her cheeks flushed a little, and Ivan decided to forgive her. He took a deep bow, lowering his hat and sweeping his arm until it touched the boardwalk.

"Merci, mademoiselle," he said, in the best French accent he could manage. But when he stood up again, she was gone. He watched the children's backs as they walked away from the store, the nuns on either side of them, like a community of small black tents. When they passed Madame Zeta's, his heckler drifted away from the others to peer through the beaded curtain.

"Sorcery. Pure sorcery," he heard a voice snap. A black-cloaked hand reached out for the girl's shoulder, and she vanished again into the group.

❁

Mondays were always slow, but tonight was awful. Between seven and eight, Peanut World had only two customers — one of them a homeless man who wandered up and down the aisles, sniffing at all the packaged nuts, and a nervous, tanned young woman who asked if they sold any low-calorie peanut butter.

The scene on the boardwalk was even duller. Ivan could have done nude backflips and not attracted anyone to the store. People ventured as far as the amusement pier, surveyed the empty storefronts, and turned around, trudging back to their hotels. At 8:15, Greenwood told Ivan to go on home.

His father wouldn't be at Arkansas Avenue for 45 minutes. Ivan wandered down the boardwalk, toward the amusement pier. Just a few years ago, he'd begged his parents for money to ride the Orient Express, the Tilt-a-Whirl, the Swings. Now the rides looked small. A series of empty carts circled the track of the Orient Express, clacking in and out of the faded red doors.

"Try your luck, three hits for a dollar," barked a man in a booth. Ivan had tried this one before. Players got three golf balls; the object was to knock down a foot-high clown doll that seemed to operate on some kind of hinge. Even if you hit it, the thing inevitably bounded back up. Only a complete knock-out qualified. Ivan had a dollar in change. "Here, I'll try," he said, and the carnival man burst into a wide grin.

"Step right up, Mr. Peanut, could be your lucky night." Ivan had almost forgotten he was still in his costume. "Knock 'em down and pick a prize for your sweetheart. You got a sweetheart?"

"No," Ivan said. His first toss hit the proscenium of the stand and dropped to the ground. The second glanced off the top of a clown's head; it wobbled but didn't fall. He gritted his teeth. Thwack! The ball smacked a clown in the solar plexus, hard; it tipped backward and stayed there. One second, two seconds, three.

"Looks like Mr. Peanut won himself a prize. Any one of these," the man said, pointing to a row of stuffed animals in pastel colors. Ivan looked up: a blue unicorn, a lavender koala bear, a pale yellow kangaroo, a light green monkey.

"Um … I don't know what kind she'd li—"

"Aha, so you do have a sweetheart. I thought so, big boardwalk celebrity like you. I bet all the girls want a date with Mr. Peanut. What's her name?"

Ivan was embarrassed to tell the man he had no idea, that in fact he was choosing a stuffed animal for a girl who lived in a hospital with nuns and might, for all he knew, have some terrible, incurable disease. "Do you have any in more animal-like colors?" Something told him this girl wasn't the lavender-koala type.

"Look, kid, who you givin' it to, the queen? What you see is what we got."

"Okay, I'll take the kangaroo," Ivan said.

Ten more minutes until his father or mother would come. Ivan walked past shut-down frozen custard stands and half-empty pizza parlors, the broken shells of stores and restaurants, Skee Ball parlors, arcades. Madame Zeta leaned in the doorway of her storefront, the beaded curtain falling over her like hair.

"You want to see future?" she said as he passed. Her voice was thick and husky, like layers of stiff fabric rubbing against each other. Cigarette smoke rose in a veil around her turbaned head. Ivan stopped for a second, close enough to see the charcoal-colored tattoos on the backs of Madame Zeta's hands. A pungent smell scraped his nostrils, and he felt a little dizzy.

"No, not tonight. Maybe some other time." And he kept going, fast, toward Arkansas Avenue. By the time he reached the Catholic Children's Respite Home, he was practically running. But he slowed down enough to see that all the lights were out in all the rooms, and that the Virgin Mary was no longer wearing her T-shirt. Probably the nuns made everyone go to bed early. Probably they only took the kids out once a month. He'd never even see her again, little smart-alecky what's-her-name.

It was his mother in the Continental tonight, and Ivan felt grateful for the big car, its familiar backseat. He stretched out, kicked off his shoes, then tossed the stuffed kangaroo into the front. "Here, I won you something. From me, Ivan the Terrible."

"Not Ivan the Terrible, Ivan the Wonderful." It was a joke they'd had since Ivan was old enough to talk. "Ivan the Thoughtful," his mother said. "Ivan the Terrific."

"Mmmph." In the back seat, Ivan closed his eyes, and was nearly asleep by the time his mother pulled into the driveway.

❁

On Sunday, Ivan's day off, he rode his bike past churches and clusters of people walking to and from them. He knew there must be synagogues at the shore, too, but his family never went to one. They were what his father called "three-times-a-year Jews."

Without planning it, Ivan suddenly found himself pedaling along the boardwalk, past the Catholic Children's Respite Home. As he rode by, a tower bell began to chime 10 o'clock, a set of double doors opened, and a few kids came running into the yard, followed by a priest and the nuns. Other kids followed, more slowly, on crutches or in chairs they pushed themselves, thin arms pumping at the wheels.

Ivan reached down and pulled off his left sneaker. He had an apple and some peanuts in the backpack, left from the night before. Tossing the sneaker first, he began to juggle them, sending high easy arcs into the air. Left, right, left; the trick was to think about throwing, not catching, and let the items fall into the cups of his waiting hands.

She saw him first. "Mr. Peanut?" she called, and started to run across to the boardwalk.

"Rosa, no running! Remember your lungs." So that was her name, Rosa. She didn't look like anything was the matter with her lungs.

"Hi," she said, and stopped to catch her breath. "So that's what you look like in normal clothes. I wondered."

"Oh," Ivan said. Then, in the pause while Rosa surveyed him, he said, "My name is Ivan. Ivan Glatz."

"Mine's Rosa."

"I know. I heard the nun call you. Do they always yell like that?"

"No, just when they're scared I might do something and have an attack. You know, I was going to come see you tonight — they're taking a group of kids on the boardwalk — but I'm grounded."

"What did you do?"

Rosa grinned. "Well, you know those T-shirts that say, 'My son, or parents, or whatever, went to Atlantic City and —'"

"That was you? And the sunglasses?" She nodded. "I thought that was hilarious."

"Well, Sister Marie didn't."

"Sister Marie? Is that the head nun?"

Rosa looked at him, her head tilted. "You're not Catholic, are you?"

"No, Jewish. Why?"

"Because if you were Catholic, you'd know we have a Mother Superior, not a head nun. And anyway, Sister Marie isn't. She's new here, actually. She asked the diocese for a transfer from Newark because she said she wanted to work with sick children, but it's really because she's in love with Sister Theresa."

"Really?" Ivan thought nuns weren't allowed to be in love with anybody. "How do you know?"

"Oh, it's obvious. The way they look at each other when one of them is going upstairs and the other one's on her way down. And I once saw Sister Theresa leave a red rose in Sister Marie's room. The Mother Superior doesn't like it. She's always talking about not having particular friendships."

"Particular friendships?"

"Uh-huh. You're not supposed to love one person especially, because God loves everyone the same, all the time."

"Oh."

"Of course, people don't. Love each other all the same, I mean." Rosa looked down for a minute, and one of the nuns began walking across the yard toward them.

"Listen, today's my night off from Peanut World. So you would have missed me even if you weren't grounded. Do they let you have visitors? Maybe I could come and — I don't know, bring ice cream or something."

"We can have visitors in the lounge until 7," Rosa said. "So come at 6."

"Okay." Then Ivan remembered the question he'd been wanting to ask. "Rosa, what do you have? I mean, why are you here?"

"Asthma," she said. "I breathe at irregular intervals." That sounded like something a doctor had told her; it was the way his parents talked when they got hospital calls late at night. "Really," she said, "my parents wanted to get rid of me for the summer, so they could fight as much as they want. They can't get a divorce 'cause they're Catholic, and they can't live together because they argue so much it gives me asthma. So they're stuck, and I'm here. What about you? Are your parents together?"

"Yeah," Ivan said. "They're both doctors in the same hospital. They actually met here, on the boardwalk. That's why we come every summer. We rent a house near Ventnor Avenue."

"Ventnor," she said. "One of the … yellows. Next to Marvin Gardens and Atlantic." Just then, Sister Marie — or was it Sister Theresa? — was at Rosa's side. She raised her brows at Ivan, then put a hand on Rosa's shoulder and gently steered her back to the building.

❂

Ivan tossed a pint of chocolate ice cream from one hand to the other as he waited for someone to answer the bell. A nun opened the door. "Yes?" she said.

"I'm here to see Rosa. We had a date — I mean, an appointment. Uh — she wanted me to come sit in the lounge at six."

"I see. Well, come this way. I'm Sister Marie." Ivan wondered what you had to do to become a nun. Was there a school? Did you have to pass a test? Rosa was already in the lounge, talking in Spanish to two other girls. She seemed to be telling them a joke; she gestured broadly in the air, and her voice rose higher and quicker, then finally delivered a rapid line, and all three broke into laughter.

"Rosa, you have a visitor," the nun said, and the two other girls began to giggle, then backed their wheelchairs into a corner near the television set.

Ivan held out his hand. "Sorry it's freezing — from holding the ice cream."

"It's okay," Rosa said, and put both her hands on either side of Ivan's, rubbing them briskly. "Better?"

"Yes," he told her. While Rosa spooned ice cream into two plastic bowls and hunted for napkins, Ivan said, "You know, I was thinking. My parents are both doctors, pediatric surgeons, actually. Maybe they could take a look at you and —"

"No more doctors!" Rosa spun around. "I'm sick of doctors. Every other one gives me a different medicine in a little inhaler, and the rest say there's nothing wrong with me, it's all in my head."

"What do they say here?"

"The hospital doctor gave me this," and she pulled a small blue inhaler out of one pocket, "but Sister Theresa gave me this." And she took a strand of beads from the other one.

"A necklace?"

"It's a rosary. You're supposed to say prayers — Hail Marys and stuff — while you hold it, but Sister Theresa says you can say anything, a poem or just some words you like a lot. She says it's the repetition and the beads, just touching them, that calms you down. Something regular that goes on and on. She said to use it when I feel like I can't breathe."

"Sometimes I feel like I can't breathe," Ivan said. "Like right before I take a test, or when I know I'm going to miss a shot in basketball, or when my mom's really mad at me. Maybe I should get a rosary."

"What do Jews have — I mean, instead?"

"You mean to calm down with?" Ivan laughed. "Jews don't calm down. We have prayers, I guess, but I don't really know them." He thought a minute. "I think we ask questions, tell jokes. It's kind of comforting. We tell stories about things that happened."

"Tell me a story," Rosa said, licking the last of her ice cream from the spoon.

"Um — okay. This is a true story. My parents met each other 18 years ago on the boardwalk. My dad was trying one of those carnival games, where you have to knock down tin cans with little rubber darts, and he kept missing. My mom was watching and asked if she could try his last dart, and he said okay. She knocked down the can. The man was all out of prizes, so he gave them a coupon for two soft ice creams. That was their first date."

"Then what?" Rosa said.

"Well, then they got soft ice cream. Oh, and later my dad borrowed money from his cousin to take my mom for a drink at the Marlborough-Blenheim Hotel. They said it was really beautiful and romantic then — red carpet in the lobbies, bellhops with hats, real rubber trees, marble counter. You'd never know it, now. In fact, they're going to wreck it on Tuesday morning.

"Really? We should go watch that," Rosa said. "It's a historic event — just think, if that hotel hadn't been there, your parents would have gone someplace else for their second date. Maybe it would have been awful, and they would never have gotten married, and then you wouldn't be here, either."

"The newspaper said they're going to start bulldozing at eight. Can I come get you?"

"Uh-huh. I can get a pass to go out for three hours. By then, I won't be grounded anymore. I think Sister Theresa put in a good word for me. I heard her giggling with Sister Marie about the T-shirt, and they even gave me back the sunglasses."

"Hey, one more thing. Rosa, how old are you?"

"Older than I look."

"Twenty-five?" he guessed.

"No, thirteen. I'm small for my age. And you?"

"Sixteen. Well, almost. My birthday's right after Labor Day." He looked up to see Sister Marie standing in the doorway. "Rosa, visiting hour is over. Please say goodbye to your guest." The nun stepped aside while Ivan scrambled into his jacket. She smiled as he backed out of the room. And then, maybe there was something in her eye, or maybe she was just nearsighted, but Ivan could have sworn he saw her glance at Rosa and wink.

❂

It was already hot, the packed wet heat of ocean summers, when Ivan and Rosa reached the crowd around the Marlborough-Blenheim. The hotel was surrounded by a plywood barrier, and people in hard hats milled around the site. One was shouting at the others through a megaphone. The crowd was mostly old people, but there were a few families, some parents with kids in strollers, a few people on skates or bikes who'd stopped to see what all the fuss was about.

"Here, we'll have a better view." Rosa climbed onto one of the benches facing toward the hotel, and reached for Ivan's hand to help him up. One of the ice-cream men, who usually trudged the beach with freezers slung over their shoulders, had come up on the boardwalk instead.

"Getcher pop-sicles, getcher fudgie-wudgies here. Ice cream sandwiches, getcher nice ice cream."

"Dad?" said a little boy near them, looking hopefully at his father as the ice-cream man passed. "No way," the man replied. "No fudgie-wudgies for breakfast."

"When my parents fight and I get sick," Rosa said, "they let me eat anything I want. One time I had chocolate-covered graham crackers and a strawberry milkshake for breakfast and banana pancakes for dinner."

"When my parents get mad at each other, and then they make up, we always order pizza. With extra garlic. My mom says the cheese glues them back together and the garlic makes sure no one else will interfere."

"That's great," Rosa said. "I love garlic pizza. Maybe my parents should try that. Except they never make up."

BRRRRACCCCKK! The wrecking ball swung back and hit the Marlborough-Blenheim's giant rotunda. It crumbled like a child's block tower, chunks of wood, plaster, and stone hailing to the ground. BRRRACCCCKK! The ball swung a second time, biting out a big piece of the upper stories. There were terrible creaks as beams broke against the grain, metal pipes twisted and clanged.

Near Rosa and Ivan, an old man started to cry, dabbing his eyes with a tissue he'd pulled from his sleeve. A young woman came through the crowd holding up a T-shirt with a picture of the hotel and the slogan, "I outlived the Marlborough-Blenheim." The ice-cream man kept up his pitch between swings of the wrecking ball: "Getcher fudgie-wudgies, getcher nice ice cream here."

BRRAACCCKKK!! The noise pounded against their ears, louder than the surf, louder than the voices of people watching and the man shouting through the megaphone, louder than Ivan's own heart batting his rib cage. It was the sound of a million dishes shattering to bits, glass to smithereens, whole rooms to toothpicks, an endless, endless noise of collapse.

Suddenly Rosa was tugging at his hand. "I — can't — breathe," she gasped, and her eyes were wide and wet. Her chest rose and fell with a weird syncopation — two rapid hiccups, then a tremble, then a rest, then a wheeze.

"Are you okay? Rosa, hang on, I'll get someone, I'll do something. Shit. Don't stop breathing, okay?" Rosa shook her head no, her whole frame straining to get air. Ivan squinted toward the Catholic Children's Home — only a block, but a long one. Could he carry Rosa there? Then he spotted one of the old wicker rolling chairs. He jumped down from the bench, pushed the chair over and said, "Get in." The wheels were a little rusty, but it worked.

"Excuse me, excuse me," he yelled, maneuvering Rosa through the crowd. BBRRRAAACCCKKK! The wrecking ball swung again, and the entire left side of the Marlborough-Blenheim folded over, like a person dropping to her knees.

"You're gonna be okay. I'll get you home. Keep breathing, Rosa, please keep breathing." Ivan pushed through the edge of the throng, past a bench and into a sudden fog of cigarette smoke. Rosa began to cough. It was Madame Zeta, surrounded by five shopping bags stuffed with clothes, books, blankets, candles, a pillow. Ivan could see the top of a whiskey bottle poking from one bag.

Madame Zeta's turban was on crooked, and her face was stained with tears. "You want to see future?" she said to them. "There — that is the future." The wrecking ball reared back, Rosa took a long wheezy breath, and Ivan pushed hard, bumping the rolling chair over the rotting boards.

❂

"Kid, what's the matter with you tonight? I seen you out there, juggling things and dropping them all over. You look like who did it and ran."

"I'm kind of in a crisis," Ivan said. "I don't want to talk about it."

"Crisis?" Greenwood said. "What, like some girl won't let you touch her whatchamacallit? Or your folks don't give you enough allowance? I'll tell you crisis. There's enough red ink in my books, it looks like a murder scene. Even with the extra customers you bring in, we're still losing money. This is gonna be our last season."

"I'm sorry business is so bad," Ivan said.

"Ah, it's not your fault. It's just — the way things are. Things get better, things get worse. Boardwalk used to be busy, now everybody wants to take vacation in Jamaica or some such. You'll see, it'll come up again. I just won't be around to see it."

"Mr. Greenwood, do you think I could leave a little early tonight?"

"Yeah, sure. You got problems, go take care of them. Maybe I'll stand here and sing, that'll bring the crowds down. Nah, probably they'd call the cops on me first. Go, go see your little friend. She hasn't been around in a while — she doing okay?" Ivan turned back, startled.

"You think because you wear that monocle, you're the only one who sees what's what?" Greenwood asked. "Wait a minute." He ducked into the store, then came out with a large flat box. "Here, take her this." It was a miniature Monopoly board, made entirely out of milk chocolate.

Sister Theresa answered the door with one hand over her mouth, stifling a laugh. Ivan realized then he was still in his Mr. Peanut suit. "Can I see Rosa? I brought her something."

"No, I'm afraid not. She's in an oxygen tent. We don't allow visitors. I'd be happy to give her your gift, though." Ivan handed over the box.

"Okay. She'll know it's from me.... Listen, Sister Theresa. Is Rosa going to die?"

"I don't know. I hope not. But it's not really up to us, you know. I pray for her every night."

"I don't want her to die," he blurted.

"I know that," said Sister Theresa, and looked at him for a long moment. "I'll give Rosa this chocolate as soon as she can eat." Then she started to shut the door.

"Oh — wait. One more thing. Which way does Rosa's room face?" Ivan asked.

"Let me think," the nun said. "The courtyard, the ocean. Yes, I believe she has an ocean view."

"Thanks. I just wondered. Thanks. 'Bye."

Ivan strolled across the yard as if he wanted to admire the flowers, check out the statue in the center ring. Etched into the concrete at the Madonna's feet was this message: "Queen assumed into heaven, pray for us." Ivan wondered what people said when they prayed. Did they ask for things or just talk? Jews didn't have statues in their temples, but once, when he visited a very old synagogue with his parents, Ivan felt like God was there, in the puzzle of the mosaic ceiling, in the books that had been used so long their pages were soft as flannel.

He glanced around to make sure no one was watching, then stepped over the footlights and the flowers and balanced his top hat on the Virgin Mary's head.

Then he started walking back in the direction of Peanut World. The light was on at Madame Zeta's, but she wasn't leaning in the doorway or sitting at the table inside. Ivan parted the beaded curtain and peered in. The place was a mess — clothes and books scattered around the room, a half-empty bottle of Jack Daniel's on the floor.

Madame Zeta was asleep on the couch with all her clothes on, her turban untwisted and her gray hair loose. Near her was some stationery with "Marlborough-Blenheim Hotel, Atlantic City" printed across the top. A cigarette butt smoldered in a small plate on the table, and Ivan squashed it out before leaving through the beaded doorway.

It was dusk, scarves of pink and yellow falling over the ocean, the sky the color of washed jeans. At the pier, a few lights blinked on and off, and Ivan could hear the thin beep of the kiddie rides, the whoosh of empty chairs as the Swings spun with no riders. Suddenly he was at the foot of the Ferris wheel, digging coins out of his pocket.

"Hey, I hear you work for peanuts," the ride man said. "Hah, hah. Pick any cart — not like there's much of a fight for 'em."

"I'll take a red one," Ivan said, and the man slowed the wheel until a faded red cart swung to a stop at the head of a short ramp. Ivan climbed in, feeling the chicken wire inside his suit crunch as he sat. The motor creaked, and Ivan's cart began to lift slowly over the pier. As it climbed, the beeps and rattles of the other rides grew softer. The cart rocked gently in the indigo sky.

Ivan's stomach took a dip as the cart rounded the top of the wheel and descended again. He could see a paper cone on the ground, still sticky with blue cotton candy, a stuffed animal that had been dropped and trampled, the sweat on the ride man's upper lip as he went by. Then the wheel turned, the cart rose, a breeze prickled the back of his neck.

Ivan imagined Rosa asleep in her oxygen tent. When she woke up, she would look out the window and see the Virgin Mary and laugh without having to catch her breath. His cart swayed, the wheel turned on its axis, around, around, and from the top Ivan could see everything: the dirty crater where the Marlborough-Blenheim had been, the top hat tilted rakishly on the Madonna's head, the tired pool of light from Madame Zeta's doorway, the ocean moving in and out, in and out in regular intervals, waving like a flag.

Razing the Tenements in Atlantic City

by Barbara Helfgott Hyett

1

The stairwell is all darkness, banisters mangled,
boards nailed up like coffin lids across the doors.
Stair risers ascend alone, their treads winding
strangely resolute toward the skylight
on the topmost landing. An open doorway,
number three: this is where I used to live.

Sunshine pouring in, a filthy curtain
in shreds through fractured glass,
the window frames that shaped a room
around a double bed, sun parlor, seven windows,
the sea rising on all sides.

The French doors are here, but the porch
has been lopped off, two pillars dangling.

Everywhere, violence:
of glass and shattered wood, of paint bitten
from paper, layers, stripped to a geometry.

Sun slants through the archway of the living
room, down the hall to the thin kitchen.
Where the stove was, debris, moldings,
jagged linoleum rotted in a cardboard box.
In the bathroom, a mass of pipes, rusting,
the ripped-out toilet's underside.
My brother's door is closed.

Finally, right-angled to his, my room.
I stand at the splintered threshold.
Coats carpet the floor; suede coats
matted with sand, wool coats, coats
with hoods, a pyramid of coats.
My youngest son climbs the nest, finds
the thin, abandoned book, sea-musty, blue,
A Short History of Freemasonry.

2

The whack of thunder.
A steel ball is pounding at the tenements,
door jambs cracking,
bricks splitting apart.
Shards of window glass explode.

Through the space that was two windows
I find my view: familiar rooftops,
a landscape, trapezoids of tar.
I stare past the roofs to the sea,
read the cuneiform of waves.

Across the street, the odd-numbered side
of Dewey Place leveled houseless, lot by lot
of sand and gravel, squares for a casino.
The next street over, Oriental Avenue, flattened.
New Hampshire Avenue, then Vermont, Connecticut,
down. At the tip of this sinking island
the lighthouse, unencumbered now,
stands finally visible.

Ziggurat, a city drowns beneath you.
Mediterranean, Baltic, my neighborhood,
past *Go* on the Monopoly board, is lost,
falling with the toss of someone else's dice.

Atlantic City

by Lisa Walker

Note from a young woman we know:

Recently, my friend Jane was given a free night for two at a hotel in
Atlantic City, along with complimentary tickets to a show, and because my
birthday was coming up she invited me along. When my other friends
called to see what I was doing for my birthday, I said, "Going to Atlantic City." All
of them except my friend Cathy responded exactly the same way. They said,
"Hmm. Well, everyone should go there at least once." Cathy said, "Too bad."

On Saturday morning, I met Jane at the Port Authority to catch the bus to
Atlantic City. The ride took over two hours, and on the way I listened to Guns N'
Roses twice on my headphones, we talked about Alan King, whose show we would
be seeing, and Jane primed me for the Boardwalk. She described Atlantic City as a
place where everything was red. She said that there was a really good mall in
Atlantic City, that we would be the youngest people there, and that we wouldn't
see one good-looking guy for two days.

Jane and I walk along the Boardwalk to our hotel. The day is hazy and
unseasonably hot, and people are carrying their coats over their shoulders like
pickaxes. The first thing I notice is the overwhelming smell of popcorn. You can't
smell the ocean, or even the grease from all the fast-food joints. All you can smell
is buttered popcorn. The entire Boardwalk smells like the inside of a movie house.

In the hotel elevator, loaded down with our stuff, we meet two these-boots-mean-I'm-a-cowboy-type guys, who wink at us and say, "What kind of girls bring books to Atlantic City?" They laugh as if that were the funniest thing they've ever said in their lives. Our books are a *Vogue* and a *Rolling Stone*. Our hotel room is not red but peach. We have a pretty view of the ocean and of something that looks like a Greek ruin.

Next, we go to a hotel casino, with eleven dollars in quarters. People are carrying around big plastic soda cups filled with change, and the sound of the coins clinking makes me think of treasure chests. I put a quarter in a machine and pull the handle. Jane tells me to put in six quarters — that I'll have a better chance of winning that way. I can't grasp this concept; it seems to me the more money I play, the more I'll lose. Jane tries to explain the mathematics of it, but I give her the look I gave so many teachers in high school. Jane gets mad, just the way they did, and everyone turns and looks. "The fun part for me is just pulling the arm," I say. Jane says we should leave.

We're carried on a conveyor belt through the Miss America tube, which has pictures of past Miss Americas in it and an oral history piped through invisible speakers. We hear from Bert Parks and Gary Collins, and Mary Ann Mobley and other, even less memorable Miss Americas. Then we go to the mall, and I buy a couple of T-shirts, a thousand-piece heavy-metal puzzle for my nephew, and a Magic 8 Ball. I ask the 8 Ball "Is this like Lake Tahoe?" and when I turn it over to see the answer, "Without a doubt" floats to the window.

Finally, it's Alan King time. We're seated at a small banquet table with three older couples. The women are all wearing big diamonds, and so are the men. The man next to me keeps telling us Rodney Dangerfield jokes as though he had made them up. The man sitting across from me drinks a lot of double Margaritas and his wife drinks a lot of double vodka-and-Perriers. She has the skin of a woman who divides her time between Florida and the Bloomingdale's makeup counters. She doesn't think that the Rodney Dangerfield man is funny when he says, "Gee, you look around forty, you better get your eyes checked." She fiddles with her contacts the rest of the evening. Alan King tells a lot of jokes and anecdotes about his family, and the audience is definitely relating. They're all saying, between sniffles and smiles, "That's just like my family."

After the show, we cruise through one more casino before bed, to see if a casino feels any different that late. I put three quarters in a slot machine and win seven dollars. Next morning, we oversleep, and, in a panic, run eight blocks to catch the bus for New York. We make it just in time, and thank everything in the world we can think of for our good luck. After a while, highway hypnosis sets in. I'm staring out the window at the trees and listening to "Welcome to the Jungle" for the fifth time in a row. Jane tugs on my headphone cord and, smiling like an actor in a bad horror movie, says, "Well, that was fun. Did you have fun? Was it a nice birthday for you?"

"Yeah, Jane, it was great," I answer. "As a matter of fact, I think this is the first birthday where I feel like I've actually aged."

Voice from the Ocean

by Joel A. Ensana

"I know, I know," Myron exclaimed angrily, "but I did it and that's that!"

"Here, I'll loan you the money," his mother said, searching in the large, black bag with the expandable pockets that he had sent her for Christmas, while she watched out of the corner of her eye for a jackpot on either of the two slot machines she was playing.

"Look, I brought only so much to gamble with and I will not throw good money after bad. I will not live beyond my means!"

"So, who are you saving it for? Listen, you're on vacation, so enjoy yourself while you're young," and then noticing the pained look on his face, she quickly added, "All right, all right, do as you want. I'm tired of talking and I'm also changing machines. These aren't paying off," and then she hurried off, disappearing into the crowd of other senior citizens. Watching her tiny, stooped figure and her lack of energy, Myron almost regretted that he was so hard on her, especially since he visited so seldom. Still, it had always been that way, her always having to have her way, like forcing him to take this trip to Atlantic City, for instance. He had told her he didn't want to go with her senior citizens' group on a special discount trip that included a free cocktail, but no, she had bought the tickets despite all his protesting, saying he'd enjoy it and that it was something to do besides watch television and relive past arguments between her and his late father.

So, reluctantly, head lowered, face red with anger, he had followed her onto the bus where she had been greeted by all her friends from the senior center, and he could see that she was in all her glory, wearing that same beautiful smile that had never changed, causing him to conclude that smiles never aged. It also proved that perhaps his mother wasn't having illusions when she said that men were still trying to make her because she had the cutest smile — men such as her dentist and the barber on Hiram Street.

On the bus, he was again sorry he had made such a scene, but of course, he couldn't give her the satisfaction, not yet anyway. Of course, if he had won a great deal of money or really had a good time, then he would say, "Yes, yes, I'm glad I came," and they would hug and kiss, with her saying, "You see, always listen to your mother. It pays off." Of course, since he had lost all his money immediately, she would not get any apologies; in fact, he would have her feeling very guilty that she had had her way about this trip as she had had her way about everything else — good or bad.

Myron shoved a path out of the noisy casino and found himself on the almost deserted boardwalk. The salt air and the vastness of the ocean and sky gave him a much better feeling about himself, as lately he had been disgusted with his life and with the person he had been, was, and would be stuck with for the rest of his life. As for changes, he thought, well, changing anything was so difficult for him, and there were so many things one could never change. Of course, there were some things one *could* change, temporarily or when necessary, and he had. But doing it, sticking to it, had not been easy, and he wondered if it was all worth it. He was always so relieved when he could arrive home, lock the door, and just be himself.

Now, looking out to sea, hearing the waves and seeing the sky sparkling with thousands of star, the noisy, smoke-filled casino behind him disappeared and he smiled as he saw two shadowy male figures disappear beneath the boardwalk, their voices covered by the sound of the waves. That one night, years ago, came back to him, when as a teenager he came to Atlantic City with friends from school and, unable to find a room in one of the many old boarding houses that had huge wrap-around porches with rocking chairs scattered about them and bamboo shades, he and his best friend, John David, who many people in their hometown thought was his brother, had slept underneath the boardwalk.

Then he recalled how his parents had fought to keep him from taking his first trip away from home without them.

"I'm fourteen and all the others are going, so I'm going."

"I don't know about that," his father had said, peering over his newspaper. "And who's driving?"

"Ray Hunt."

Then there had been much whispering between his parents. "I like him," he could hear. "His family lives near the park and he's on the basketball team."

"And who else?" his mother had questioned.

"The Arky twins."

"One I like, the other one's a real devil. Like day and night."

"Is that John David going?"

"Yes."

Then there was a long silence as his parents looked at one another, making faces that said, "Oh, no, him again." Finally they had given in, his mother saying, "Alright, you can go, but I'm warning you...."

Looking back he realized that his mother was always ending whatever she said to him with a warning, which made him wonder now what it was she was so afraid of, warning him about getting married, about choosing his friends, about staying away from certain places such as the Edison Diner. Later that night he had heard them saying something about John David and how he was also very attached to his mother.

John David and he had been inseparable right up into their thirties, until the usual reason for breaking up of friendships occurred — money loaned for an antique shop and never repaid until threats were made. But of course, looking back at those two young, small-town boys who drove to Atlantic City with friends from such a great distance of time, he found himself looking at strangers.

Behind him the sound of another tour bus pulling up to the entrance of one of the casinos and disgorging another load of hyper, hopeful seniors could be heard. But Myron didn't turn to watch as he was deep in reflection, thinking about how it was all gone, the rides, the old hotels with their gargantuan lobbies, the movie palaces with stars that twinkled in their ceilings. Then looking into the sea, somehow they all still existed. Of course, nothing could change the ocean, day or night, the awesome ocean, now lit by a full moon — that same moon that had shone that night when so much about himself had been exposed by the confessions of his best friend.

Then the youthful laughter beneath his feet began, light and carefree voices, but only one voice was feminine, whereas back then — and suddenly he heard it — a voice from the ocean, like that of a Lorelei singing — just like that voice on a record he had made for twenty-five cents — a record of voices giggling, two young, high-pitched voices, which had been made during that first trip away from home alone.

He and John David had been walking up and down the boardwalk, stomachs full of Taylor's pork roll sandwiches and french fries drenched in vinegar, teeth black from pieces of licorice saltwater taffy, their steps wobbly from all the rides, feeling dizzy from the merry-go-round and sometimes hiccupping from all the uncontrollable, silly laughter. They were exhilarated by the freedom of being able to carry on without someone always watching, as their parents knew or were distantly related to everyone in town. But here they could be themselves and so they ran from one stand to the other, one ride to the other, singing "On the Boardwalk in Atlantic City" until darkness came and they were almost at the end of the pier where they entered yet another arcade filled with wax figures of gypsies that told fortunes, penny games with tiny cranes that if you were lucky picked up souvenirs strewn among the stale jelly beans, and several booths — the ones that took photos they didn't bother to enter as there was one just like it back home in the five-and-dime.

But then they saw a booth where they could record their voices and take their records home. They screamed as they quickly squeezed into the booth. Then they had discussed what they would say or sing within the short time allowed them, and also decided that they would make separate records. Myron had first given his name, some background information; then he did a few impressions of guests, such as Senor Wences, on the Ed Sullivan show, then sang the number one song on the Lucky Strike hit parade, "Mr. Sandman, send me a dream, make his complexion like peaches and cream," with John David joining in at the very end until they both began to laugh hysterically. Then they sat, quivering with anticipation, fingers to lips, as the machine played back their recordings, and both were shocked to hear their voices for the very first time, just as people must have been when they had first seen pictures of themselves. But something about his voice had repulsed and depressed Myron, while John David had merely laughed, saying, "Well, there go our careers with Decca Records." Myron had cringed, frightened by the sound of his voice — that high-pitched, off-key, monotonous voice — and because he knew it was his forever. "I hate it," he recalled saying, "I hate it and I never want to hear it again!"

"Well," John David had said, "you're no Frankie Sinatra, but it's not that bad. Mine, I'm keeping forever."

"Well, I'm not," he had said, now holding the record that had slipped down a tube and into a metal basket. Then he ran from the arcade and down to the beach as John David followed, calling, "Myron, what are you doing?" Posing like a discus thrower, he had tossed the record as far as he could, and they watched it sink as John David tried to say something smart and witty, while Myron just kept repeating, "I'm glad no one heard. I hated it!" Moments later, the ocean had tossed it, mockingly, back at his feet, as though it hated it too. He had retrieved it and then waited until a large wave came in, and once again he fed it to the ocean; this time it did not return his offering. He had pictured it entangled in a mass of sunken ships and the bones of shipwrecked sailors.

That night they had slept under the boardwalk because all the rooms in the low-priced boarding houses were taken. But they had barely slept, just talked and ate hamburgers from the all-night White Castle, and that was how he had discovered what type of person he was and how John David had known for several years, but had been afraid to tell him. He had told Myron about how he would go to New York by himself, telling his parents he was going to see plays with classmates but actually going to certain places in Greenwich Village where others like themselves gathered. "You see, Myron, we both like men." Confused and frightened, Myron had kept on denying it, "I'm not different," while John David kept saying, "Wanna bet? Think about it, why do you always want to see Errol Flynn movies, and how you're always staring at Ray Hunt...."

Thinking back, Myron recalled how before hearing his voice — really hearing his voice — he had been satisfied with it even though at family affairs relatives would smile and his parents would say, "He's just a child. Some boys go through puberty later than others." And he had wondered what puberty was as he kept on singing "On the Good Ship Lollipop," his grandfather saying one day, "Look, he dances like a *kleine madchen*," and even though he couldn't understand German, he had been overcome by shame and had stopped dancing about the room as his mother had defended him. "He's just a child. And now look, you've hurt his feelings. Children know. But just wait until next year, you'll see, he'll be playing baseball." Myron had never played baseball, but he was still dancing about his apartment alone, after a few drinks.

When he had returned home from Atlantic City, he had practiced changing his voice until he had sounded like a truck driver or his cigar-smoking Uncle Phil, causing his parents to take pleasure in the fact that his voice had finally matured. "Maybe it was the salt air. Now, if only he could change his walk." Upon hearing that he did, forcing himself to take long strides, hands at side and no swiveling of the hips, causing his mother to say with relief, "You see, all that worrying, it was just what the school nurse called puberty." But it was all an act and at first never easy, and the only time he could relax was with John David and his newly acquired friends. They were a small circle in that small town — meeting to do homework and, when finished, dancing singly or together and putting on silly, impromptu fashion shows. From then on it was all an act — at college, in the service, at work, at the barns and even in bed — always trying to appear macho and never being able to really change that voice he had flung into the ocean.

Now, like listening to a seashell, Myron could hear his voice coming from the ocean as it was recorded so many years ago — the nervous giggling, the innocuous words of that insipid song. And Myron smiled as he pictured the record he had tossed into the Atlantic being played — the movement of the water acting like a stereo needle, with the waves, like giant speakers, causing the sound to rise until caught by the wind, which carried it this way and that, so that his recording was played over and over like a "Golden Oldie" brought back by popular demand. Then, after noticing that the boardwalk was deserted, Myron sang along with the recording in his true voice, which had never changed.

When he stopped singing, he wondered if he would have been happier just being himself twenty-four hours a day for all those years and just how successful his act had been, recalling that recently when he had gone to work with a cut from shaving too close, his coworkers had asked, "What is it? The plague?" And if he sneezed or appeared tired, relatives would warn, "Myron, with so much going on,

I hope you're being careful." So, when wasn't I being careful, he thought, as the wind died down, causing the voice from the ocean to hover like a star above the waves until it was silenced, momentarily, by his mother shouting through the darkness, "Myron, what are you doing out there? The action's all in here now. And I've found a real good machine. It's showing nothing but cherries. And Mrs. Katz is holding it for me."

"I like it out here," Myron shouted back. "I'm listening to the waves!"

"The waves? They all sound alike. Believe me, if you've heard one, you've heard them all...."

That's not true, Myron thought; each wave hits the shore differently, following the currents, pushed by changing winds, pulled by brighter moonbeams. No, everything is different, he decided, especially when examined closely, like snowflakes, for instance. Then he heard laughter from below and wondered if, perhaps, they too could hear that high-pitched voice from beneath the ocean and were laughing at it just as his relatives had done.

Myron turned, the sound of their laughter following him as he hurried toward his mother, carefully taking long, masculine strides and calling out in a voice that wasn't his, "Alright, alright, I'm coming!" and wishing that one day he might have the guts to just be himself. But not now, he decided, no. After all, his mother was in her seventies, so why hurt her. Why not make her old age as pleasant as possible, just as he had tried to make her as happy as possible all her life. He also questioned whether she would love him as much if he still used that voice in the ocean. Then something unexplainable — perhaps it was the full moon — caused him to sing along in his natural voice with the voice from the ocean, "Mister Sandman, send me a dream, make his complexion like peaches and cream," and hating to waste the beat of the music, he playfully danced over toward his mother.

She stood, stunned. Then, smiling that ageless smile, his mother said, "Now that's the way I like to see you, like the little boy I loved so much and living beyond your means," which made Myron laugh aloud at his mother's little joke and from the joy of finally being able to be himself in her presence as she drew him away from the deserted boardwalk and into the crowded casino.

Atlantic City

by Michael Baytoff

When Jerry Loves Jenny

by Elayne Clift

A single-engine airplane floats across the Atlantic City sky, silent and small at first. Then humming its way along the stretch of white sandy beach, it rouses us, and catches our collective Labor Day attention. Like a monarch butterfly flirting with the ocean spray, it dips its wing to the sea, shiny with sun-dappled sapphire and diamond baguettes, and turns to repeat its message which flutters gracefully behind.

"JENNY, WILL YOU MARRY ME? LOVE, JERRY."

Sun worshippers raise themselves up from striped towels and smile. Readers lay Danielle Steele face down in their laps. Volleyball teams stop mid-stream and players shield their eyes with upheld hands ready for the return. Young mothers watch their toddlers, then sigh with memory. Men glance nervously at each other.

"Oooh, how romantic!" one starry-eyed teenager squeals to another.

"God, I sure hope Jenny's out here," her friend prays.

"So do I," says her pragmatic father. "You know what one of those things costs? Man, they go by the quarter hour!"

"Oh, Harry," says his wife, who watches wistfully as the banner flaps in the breeze when the plane makes another sweep past.

"JENNY, WILL YOU MARRY ME? LOVE, JERRY."

Most of us are with her, and Harry be damned. Here, after all, is a guy ready to go down on his proverbial knee, not just before the father of the woman he loves, but in front of all of us, hundreds, maybe even thousands of strangers, sprawled before him with bated breath and suppressed cheers.

Maybe that's what it took to get his courage up, or to convince Jenny that he was serious: Public commitment and a potful of pennies.

Maybe he's an impulsive so-and-so, and Jenny should be careful.

Maybe Jenny can't stand him and he should get out of her face.

But that's an option we don't want to consider, at least not the females now fantasizing about this little drama. We prefer to believe that Jerry is a dreamer, a living doll who worked out all the details so that Jenny would be leaning on the railing of her condo at just the right moment to see his message and swoon. And Jenny, of course, is a real sweetie-pie in her own right, clever enough to have thought of this sort of thing herself, and wise enough never to let on that she suspected something like this might happen on this very holiday weekend.

After fifteen minutes (Harry was right), the little plane that may well have sealed Jerry and Jenny's future makes one final swoop and then disappears into the horizon toward Margate, its message trailing behind like an afterthought. People return to their sun worship, their reading, their volleyball, their children, their memories and daydreams.

How many of them, later that evening, I wonder, raised their glass in a toast to Jenny and Jerry (as I did)? What was Jenny's answer? If she said yes, will they still be happy by Labor Day next year?

No matter, really, for the spectators. Because to us, Jerry will always be a hero, a reminder that chivalry and romance still reside in the hearts and souls of men. Jenny will always be a heroine in the drama of daily life. And romance will always flourish, the Harrys of the world — God love them — notwithstanding.

So here's looking at you, Jerry and Jenny. May the wind be ever at your back, may your problems be no greater than an ocean mist, and may your days be filled with a banner of Yes!

Margie and Herb

by Jane Elkington Wohl

Nobody knew how it started except Margie, and she never let on that there was anything odd about her friendship with Herb, almost twice her age and long retired. No one even knew anymore how long they had been having breakfast together at the Busy Bee. Margie had been there longer than anyone else, and when Joe and his wife bought the place 10 years ago, Margie and Herb were already a fixture. He'd come in and follow her to the same table, the same chair every day, the table by the window which looked out on Atlantic Avenue and where you could see Lucy the old elephant-shaped hotel with its little cupola across the street. He'd some in every day about 10:00 and she'd say, "Hi, Herb, you sleep good last night?" and he'd say, "Yeah, Toots, pretty good." Then she'd call out to Joe, "Takin' a break, Joe," and hang her apron on the hook behind the cash register and sit down at the table across from Herb. They didn't even have to order. It was the same thing every day, and even a new waitress caught on fast; 2 coffees, 2 orange juices, 2 orders of scrambled eggs, and 2 orders of wheat toast. Margie always handed Herb the catsup, and he would put a small puddle on the side of his plate and carefully dip each bit of eggs into it. They'd talk quietly while they ate. Sometimes he'd show her pictures of his granddaughter, her pictures from Girl Scouts, her prom pictures, her graduation from high school, and college, and a few years later her wedding pictures. Sometimes he told her about his wife who had been dead for twenty years and his daughter who lived in Los Angeles, and sometimes he told her about his work as head of maintenance at the Convention Center and how he had worked his way up from peanut vendor on the boardwalk. After about half an hour, they'd get up, Herb would pay the bill and Margie'd put her apron back on. Early on she'd tried to pay for her own breakfast but Herb wouldn't let her, and she'd quickly seen that it was somehow important to him and had let it go. Sometimes Herb would go visit his granddaughter, and then Margie would work straight through the morning. She only took the 10:00 break if Herb came in.

Once last year, Herb was ill and when he was in the hospital, Margie went after work to see him. She was the one who picked him up and took him home when he was well enough to leave, and she told me later it was the only time she'd ever been in his house, a small house on Fontenac Street with a tiny patch of grass in front. He'd let her carry her things to the front room but then he'd said, "OK, Toots, I can take it from here and I'm going to lie down a bit before I unpack, so you run along now, Toots."

"Are you sure you're OK, Herb?" she'd asked, but he had walked her slowly to the door.

"I'll be in for breakfast tomorrow, you'll see," and she'd found herself on the porch as he shut the door. And there he was the next day at the Busy Bee, telling her, "Yeah, Toots, I slept pretty good."

Then one day he didn't come in, and Margie told Joe that Herb was visiting his granddaughter in Philadelphia. She'd come down to the shore to get him and had taken him back with her for two weeks. So Margie continued to wait tables and ring up checks like she always did and sometimes she went to the movies with Harry, an old friend from high school who, after being in the service, had come back to work as a carpenter at one of the casinos. But when two weeks stretched to three you could see Margie getting nervous. Every day at 10:00 she'd look up and then untie and retie her apron, but Herb didn't walk through the glass doors of the Busy Bee. Finally on the fourth Saturday, Margie took a walk before work and found herself on Fontenac Street as if she'd planned it all along. She walked up the front steps and knocked. The house looked different. The blinds were up and Margie recognized the young woman who came to the door. "Yes?" the woman asked, looking at Margie with slight interest.

"I'm Margie and I'm looking for Herb," Margie said tentatively. The granddaughter invited her in and then explained that Herb had died suddenly while he'd been at her house in Philadelphia, and "I just now have finally had a chance to come down here and begin to sort things out. Mother's in California and she and Grandpa didn't get on too well anyway... but you wouldn't know who Grandpa had breakfast with every day, would you? He talked about his friend, the one he called 'Toots,' the one he saw every day, the one who took him home from the hospital, but he never used a name."

So Margie told her how every day he'd come in and every day they'd have the same things to eat — she didn't even know if he really knew her name was Margie. But it started before that, she said. Herb and she had had breakfast for 15 years, but before that he used to come in with this other fellow, Manny. Herb and Manny came in every day. She thought that Herb and Manny had had breakfast together since high school, but when she started working at the Busy Bee 25 years ago they were coming in. As they got older, they'd joke. Manny had one bad ear and Herb would say, "I can't sit on that side of him. I talked too much and ruined his ear. Have to sit on this side and ruin the other one." Every day Herb would order for both of them. "The usual, Toots," he'd say, and she knew he meant 2 coffees, 2 orange juices, 2 scrambled eggs, and 2 orders of wheat toast. Eventually she didn't even have to total it. It was always the same, until they raised the sales tax, and even then it was always the same. Herb always paid for both of them, and it wasn't until much later that he told her that Manny's family had taken him in and let him live with them during the Depression when he was unemployed, and he'd never forgotten. But then one day Herb came in alone and sat at the usual place and stared out the window at old Lucy the elephant-shaped hotel, at the tourists taking pictures of her. She asked him if Manny was coming in and he turned and said, "Not today, Toots. Manny passed away, Toots," and he looked so sad staring out the window at the run-down old elephant-shaped hotel and beyond that at the grey November ocean that she walked into the office and told the boss she was taking a break to have breakfast with Herb.

"And so," she said, looking at the young woman whose pictures Herb had been showing her for the last fifteen years, "I'm the friend. He called me Toots. You can too," and she stood up. "Gotta get to work. Stop by for breakfast sometime. It'll be my treat."

The Elephant, Margate

by John Grey

Moonlight breaks over
your broad back.
Not expecting you,
it eases down
your wooden withers.

It hasn't the heart
to treat you as a post-card joke
or boardwalk irreverence,
paints your eye,
floods your mouth,
spills down your trunk
before losing itself in shadows.

My imagination

stomps all over your wooden guts

during the day,

echoing inside you

loud as the Atlantic

and its tourist brood.

But, by night,

it follows the trek

of the light,

an irreverent breeze

way up in your victorious headquarters,

blowing through your frame

so hard, so eager,

you almost trumpet.

from **Unto the Sons**

by Gay Talese

T he beach in winter was dank and desolate, and the island dampened by the frigid spray of the ocean waves pounding relentlessly against the beachfront bulkheads, and the seaweed-covered beams beneath the white houses on the dunes creaked as quietly as the crabs crawling nearby.

The boardwalk that in summer was a festive promenade of suntanned couples and children's balloons, of carousel tunes and colored lights spinning at night from the Ferris wheel, was occupied in winter by hundreds of sea gulls perched on the iron railings facing into the wind. When not resting they strutted outside the locked doors of vacated shops, or circled high in the sky, holding clams in their beaks that they soon dropped upon the boardwalk with a splattering *cluck*. Then they zoomed down and pounced on the exposed meat, pecking and pulling until there was nothing left but the jagged, salty white chips of empty shells.

By midwinter the shell-strewn promenade was a vast cemetery of clams, and from a distance the long elevated flat deck of the boardwalk resembled a stranded aircraft carrier being attacked by dive bombers — and oddly juxtaposed in the fog behind the dunes loomed the rusting remains of a once sleek four-masted vessel that during a gale in the winter of 1901 had run aground on this small island in southern New Jersey called Ocean City.

The steel-hulled ship, flying a British flag and flaunting hundred-fifty-foot masts, had been sailing north along the New Jersey coast toward New York City, where it was scheduled to deliver one million dollars' worth of Christmas cargo it had picked up five months before in Kobe, Japan. But during the middle of the night, while a number of crewmen drank rum and beer in a premature toast to the long journey's end, a fierce storm rose and destroyed the ship's sails, snapped its masts, and drove it into a sandbar within one hundred yards of the Ocean City boardwalk.

Awakened by the distress signals that flared in the night, the alarmed residents of Ocean City — a conservative community founded in 1879 by Methodist ministers and other Prohibitionists who wished to establish an island of abstinence and propriety — hastened to help the sailors, who were soon discovered to be battered but unharmed and smelling of sweat, salt water, and liquor.

After the entire thirty-three-man crew had been escorted to shore, they were sheltered and fed for days under the auspices of the town's teetotaling elders and ministers' wives; and while the sailors expressed gratitude for such hospitality they privately cursed their fate in being shipwrecked on an island so sedate and sober. But soon they were relocated by British nautical authorities, and the salvageable cargo was barged to New York to be sold at reduced prices. And the town returned to the tedium of winter.

The big ship, however, remained forever lodged in the soft white sand — unmovable, slowly sinking, a sight that served Ocean City's pious guardians as a daily reminder of the grim consequences of intemperate guidance. But as I grew up in the late 1930s, more than three decades after the shipwreck — when the visible remnants at low tide consisted only of the barnacle-bitten ridge of the upper deck, the corroded brown rudder post and tiller, and a single lopsided mast — I viewed the vessel as a symbol of adventure and risk; and during my boyhood wanderings along the beach I became enchanted with exotic fantasies of nights in foreign ports, of braving the waves and wind with wayward men, and of escaping the rigid confines of this island on which I was born but never believed I belonged.

I saw myself always as an alien, an outsider, a drifter who, like the shipwrecked sailors, had arrived by accident. I felt different from my young friends in almost every way, different in the cut of my clothes, the food in my lunch box, the music I heard at home on the record player, the ideas and inner thoughts I revealed on those rare occasions when I was open and honest.

I was olive-skinned in a freckle-faced town, and I felt unrelated even to my parents, especially my father, who was indeed a foreigner — an unusual man in dress and manner, to whom I bore no physical resemblance and with whom I could never identify. Trim and elegant, with wavy dark hair and a small rust-colored moustache, he spoke English with an accent and received letters bearing strange-looking stamps.

Those letters sometimes contained snapshots of soldiers, wearing uniforms with insignia and epaulets unlike any I had seen on the recruitment posters displayed throughout the island. They were my uncles and cousins, my father explained to me quietly one day early in World War II, when I was ten; they were fighting in the Italian army, and — it was unnecessary for him to add — their enemy included the government of the United States.

I became increasingly sensitive to this fact when I sat through the newsreels each week at the local cinema; next to my unknowing classmates, I watched with private horror the destruction by Allied bombers of mountain villages and towns in southern Italy to which I was ancestrally linked through a historically ill-timed relationship with my Italian father. At any moment I half expected to see up on the screen, gazing down at me from a dust-covered United States Army truck filled with disheveled Italian prisoners being guarded at gunpoint, a sad face that I could identify from one of my father's snapshots.

My father, on the other hand, seemed to share none of my confused sense of patriotism during the war years. He joined a citizens' committee of shore patrolmen who kept watch along the waterfront at night, standing with binoculars on the boardwalk under the stanchioned lights that on the ocean side were painted black as a precaution against discovery by enemy submarines.

He made headlines in the local newspaper after a popular speech to the Rotary Club in which he reaffirmed his loyalty to the Allied cause, declaring that were he not too old for the draft (he was thirty-nine) he would proudly join the American troops at the front, in a uniform devotedly cut and stitched with his own hands.

Trained as an apprentice tailor in his native village, and later an assistant cutter in a prominent shop in Paris that employed an older Italian cousin, my father arrived in Ocean City circuitously and impulsively at the age of eighteen in 1922 with very little money, an extensive wardrobe, and the outward appearance of a man who knew exactly where he was going, when in fact nothing was further from the truth. He knew no one in town, barely knew the language, and yet, with a self-assurance that has always mystified me, he adjusted to this unusual island as readily as he could cut cloth to fit any size and shape.

Having noticed a "For Sale" sign in the window of a tailor shop in the center of town, my father approached the asthmatic owner, who was desperate to leave the island for the drier climate of Arizona. After a brief negotiation, my father acquired the business and thus began a lengthy, spirited campaign to bring the rakish fashion of the Continental boulevardier to the comparatively continent men of the south Jersey shore.

But after decorating his windows with lantern-jawed mannequins holding cigarettes and wearing Borsalino hats, and draping his counters with bolts of fine imported fabrics — and displaying on his walls such presumably persuasive regalia as his French master tailor's diploma bordered by cherubim and a Greek goddess — my father made so few sales during his first year that he was finally forced to introduce into his shop a somewhat undignified gimmick called the Suit Club.

At the cost of one dollar per week, Suit Club members would print their names and addresses on small white cards and, after placing the cards in unmarked envelopes, would deposit them into a large opaque vase placed prominently atop a velvet-covered table next to a fashion photograph of a dapper man and woman posing with a greyhound on the greensward of an ornate country manor.

Each Friday evening just prior to closing time, my father would invite one of the assembled Suit Club members to close his eyes and pick from the vase a single envelope, which would reveal the name of the fortunate winner of a free suit, to be made from fabric selected by that individual; after two fittings, it would be ready for wearing within a week.

Since as many as three or four hundred people were soon paying a dollar each week to partake in this raffle, my father was earning on each free suit a profit perhaps three times the average cost of a custom-made suit in those days — to say nothing of the additional money he earned when he enticed a male winner into purchasing an extra pair of matching trousers.

But my father's bonanza was abruptly terminated one day in 1928, when an anonymous complaint sent to City Hall, possibly by a rival tailor, charged that the

Suit Club was a form of gambling clearly outlawed under the town charter; thus ended for all time my father's full-time commitment to the reputable but precarious life of an artist with a needle and thread. My father did *not* climb down from an impoverished mountain in southern Italy and forsake the glorious lights of Paris and sail thousands of miles to the more opportunistic shores of America to end up as a poor tailor in Ocean City, New Jersey.

So he diversified. Advertising himself as a ladies' furrier who could alter or remodel old coats as well as provide resplendent new ones (which he obtained on consignment from a Russian Jewish immigrant who resided in nearby Atlantic City), my father expanded his store to accommodate a refrigerated fur storage vault and extended the rear of the building to include a dry-cleaning plant overseen by a black Baptist deacon who during Prohibition operated a small side business in bootlegging. Later, in the 1930s, my father added a ladies' dress boutique, having as partner and wife a well-tailored woman who once worked as a buyer in a large department store in Brooklyn.

He met her while attending an Italian wedding in that borough in December 1927. She was a bridesmaid, a graceful and slender woman of twenty with dark eyes and fair complexion and a style my father immediately recognized as both feminine and prepossessing. After a few dances at the reception under the scrutiny of her parents, and the frowns of the saxophone player in the band with whom she had recently gone out on a discreet double date, my father decided to delay his departure from Brooklyn for a day or two so that he might ingratiate himself with her. This he did with such panache that they were engaged within a year, and married six months later, after buying a small white house near the Ocean City beach, where, in the winter of 1932, I was born and awoke each morning to the smell of espresso and the roaring sound of the waves.

My first recollection of my mother was of a fashionable, solitary figure on the breezy boardwalk pushing a baby carriage with one hand while with the other stabilizing on her head a modish feathered hat at an unwavering angle against the will of the wind.

As I grew older I learned that she cared greatly about exactness in appearance, preciseness in fit, straightness in seams; and, except when positioned on a pedestal in the store as my father measured her for a new suit, she seemed to prefer standing at a distance from other people, conversing with customers over a counter, communicating with her friends via telephone rather than in person. On those infrequent occasions when her relatives from Brooklyn would visit us in Ocean City, I noticed how quickly she backed away from their touch after offering her cheek for a kiss of greeting. Once, during my preschool days as I accompanied her on an errand, I tried to hold on to her, to put my hand inside the pocket of her coat not only for the warmth but for a closer feeling with her presence. But when I tried this I felt her hand, gently but firmly, remove my own.

It was as if she were incapable of intimate contact with anyone but my father, whom she plainly adored to the exclusion of everyone else; and the impression persisted throughout my youth that I was a kind of orphan in the custody of a compatible couple whose way of life was strange and baffling.

One night at the dinner table when I casually picked up a loaf of Italian bread and placed it upside down in the basket, my father became furious and, without further explanation, turned the loaf right side up and demanded that I never repeat what I had done. Whenever we attended the cinema as a family we left before the end, possibly because of my parents' inability or unwillingness to relate to the film's content, be it drama or comedy. And although my parents spent their entire married life living along the sea, I never saw them go sailing, fishing, or swimming, and rarely did they even venture onto the beach itself.

In my mother's case I suspect her avoidance of the beach was due to her desire to prevent the sun from scorching and darkening her fair skin. But I believe my father's aversion to the sea was based on something deeper, more complex, somehow related to his boyhood in southern Italy. I suggest this because I often heard him refer to his region's coastline as foreboding and malarial, a place of piracy and invasion; and as an avid reader of Greek mythology — his birthplace is not far from the renowned rock of Scylla, where the Homeric sea monster devoured sailors who had escaped the whirlpool of Charybdis — my father was prone to attaching chimerical significance to certain bizarre or inexplicable events that occurred during his youth along the streams and lakes below his village.

I remember overhearing, when I was eleven or twelve, my father complaining to my mother that he had just experienced a sleepless night during which he had been disturbed by beachfront sounds resembling howling wolves, distant but distinct, and reminiscent of a frightful night back in 1914 when his entire village had been stirred by such sounds; when the villagers awoke they discovered that the azure water of their lake had turned a murky red.

It was a mournful precursor of things to come, my father explained to my mother: his own father would soon die unexpectedly of an undiagnosed ailment, and a bloody world war would destroy the lives of so many of his young countrymen, including his older brother.

I, too, had sometimes heard in Ocean City at night what sounded like wolves echoing above the sand dunes; but I knew they were really stray dogs, part of the large population of underfed pets and watchdogs abandoned each fall by summer merchants and vacationers during the peak years of the Depression, when the local animal shelter was inadequately staffed or closed entirely.

Even in summertime the dogs roamed freely on the boardwalk during the Depression, mingling with the reduced number of tourists who strolled casually up and down the promenade, passing the restaurants of mostly unoccupied tables, the soundless bandstand outside the music pavilion, and the carousel's riderless wooden horses.

My mother loathed the sight and smell of these dogs; and as if her disapproval provoked their spiteful nature, they followed her everywhere. Moments after she had emerged from the house to escort me to school before her mile walk along deserted streets to join my father at the store, the dogs would appear from behind fences and high-weeded yards and trail her by several paces in a quiet trot, softly whimpering and whining, or growling or panting with their tongues extended.

While there were a few pointers and terriers, spaniels and beagles, they were mostly mongrels of every breed and color, and *all* of them seemed unintimidated by my mother, even after she abruptly turned and glared at them and tried to drive them away with a sweeping gesture of her right arm in the air. They never attacked her or advanced close enough to nip at her high heels; it was mainly a game of territorial imperative that they played each morning with her. By the winter of 1940, the dogs had definitely won.

At this time my mother was caring for her second and final child, a daughter four years my junior; and I think that the daily responsibility of rearing two children, assisting in the store, and being followed, even when we children accompanied her, by the ragged retinue of dogs — a few of which often paused to copulate in the street as my sister and I watched in startled wonderment — drove my mother to ask my father to sell our house on the isolated north end of the island and move us into the more populated center of town.

This he unhesitatingly did, although in the depressed real estate market of that time he was forced to sell at an unfavorable price. But he also benefitted from these conditions by obtaining at a bargain on the main street of Ocean City a large brick building that had been the offices of a weekly newspaper lately absorbed in a merger. The spacious first floor of the building, with its high ceiling and balcony, its thick walls and deep interior, its annex and parking lot, provided more than enough room for my father's various enterprises — his dress shop and dry-cleaning service, his fur storage vaults and tailoring trade.

More important to my mother, however, was the empty floor of the building, an open area as large as a dance hall that would be converted into an apartment offering her both a convenient closeness to my father and the option of distance from everyone else when she so desired. Since she also decorated this space in accord with her dictum that living quarters should be designed less to be lived in than to be looked at and admired, my sister and I soon found ourselves residing in an abode that was essentially an extended showroom. It was aglow with crystal chandeliers and sculpted candles in silver holders, and it had several bronze claw-footed marbled-topped coffee tables surrounded by velvet sofas and chairs that bespoke comfort and taste but nonetheless conveyed the message that should we children ever take the liberty of reclining on their cushions and pillows, we should, upon rising, be certain we did not leave them rumpled or scattered or even at angles asymmetrical to the armrests.

Not only did my father not object to this fastidiously decorative ambiance, he accentuated it by installing in the apartment several large mirrors that doubled the impression of almost everything in view, and also concealed in the rear of the apartment the existence of three ersatz bedrooms that for some reason my parents preferred not to acknowledge.

Each bed was separately enclosed within an L-shaped ten-foot-high partition that on the inside was backed by shelves and closets and on the outside was covered entirely with mirror. Whatever was gained by this arrangement was lost whenever a visitor bumped into a mirror. And while I never remember at night being an unwitting monitor of my parents' intimacy, I do know that otherwise in this domestic hall of mirrors we as a family hardly ever lost sight of one another.

Most embarrassing to me were those moments when, on entering the apartment unannounced after school, I saw reflected in a mirror, opposite a small alcove, the bowed head of my father as he knelt on the red velvet of a prie-dieu in front of a wall portrait of a bearded, brown-robed medieval monk. The monk's face was emaciated, his lips seemed dry, and as he stood on a rock in sandals balancing a crosier in his right arm, his dark, somber eyes looked skyward as if seeking heavenly relief from the sins that surrounded him.

Ever since my earliest youth I had heard again and again my father's astonishing tales about this fifteenth-century southern Italian miracle worker, Saint Francis of Paola. He had cured the crippled and revived the dead, he had multiplied food and levitated and with his hands stopped mountain boulders from rolling down upon villages; and one day in his hermitage, after an alluring young woman had tempted his celibacy, he had hastily retreated and leaped into an icy river to extinguish his passion.

The denial of pleasure, the rejection of worldly beauty and values, dominated the entire life of Saint Francis, my father had emphasized, adding that Francis as a boy had slept on stones in a cave near my father's own village, had fasted and prayed and flagellated himself, and had finally established a credo of punishing piety and devotion that endures in southern Italy to this day, almost six hundred years after the birth of the saint.

I myself had seen other portraits of Saint Francis in the Philadelphia homes of some of my father's Italian friends whom we occasionally visited on Sunday afternoons; and while I never openly doubted the veracity of Francis's achievements, I never felt comfortable after I had climbed the many steps of the private staircase leading to the apartment and opened the living room door to see my father kneeling in prayer before this almost grotesque oil painting of a holy figure whose aura suggested agony and despair.

Prayer for me was either a private act witnessed exclusively by God or a public act carried out by the congregation or by me and my classmates in parochial school. It was not an act to be on exhibition in a family parlor in which I, as a nonparticipating observer, felt suddenly like an interloper, a trapped intruder in spiritual space, an awkward youth who dared not disturb my father's meditation by announcing my presence. And yet I could not unobtrusively retreat from the room, or remain unaffected or even unafraid as I stood there, stifled against the wall, overhearing during these war years of the 1940s my father's whispered words as he sought from Saint Francis nothing less than a miracle.

Throughout the winter of 1944, Joseph prayed several times each day in the living room of his home, kneeling on the red velvet of the prie-dieu under the portrait of the saint, ignoring the store bell below and leaving the operation of his business largely to his wife. He did this at Catherine's suggestion, for he had been hospitalized after Christmas holidays with appendicitis, and after returning to work he had become so uncharacteristically curt with the customers that he realized the business would be better served by his absence. A high percentage of the clientele now were American servicemen on shore leave, young men demanding quick service, often insisting that their uniforms be pressed or their newly earned chevrons be sewn on while they waited; and among such customers, many of whom had returned from triumphant tours in Sicily and Italy, Joseph could not always conceal the humiliation and divided loyalty he felt as an emotional double agent.

He had dutifully attended the memorial service for the town's first war victim — Lieutenant Edgar Ferguson, a customer's son who had died in Italy (Joseph had hesitated only briefly before approaching the victim's family to express his condolences) — and Joseph had punctually participated in his daily shore patrol assignments along the boardwalk, on the lookout for German submarines with his fellow Rotarians, until his hospitalization had interfered; but since his release from the hospital in early February 1944, he had tried to isolate himself from his friends and business associates on this island that had become increasingly jingoistic as the war's end seemed to be nearing and victory for the Allies seemed inevitable. He had stopped having lunch as usual at the corner restaurant near his shop because he was weary of the war talk at the counter, and tired of hearing such tunes on the jukebox as "Praise the Lord and Pass the Ammunition." He ceased attending the ten-fifteen Mass on Sunday mornings and went instead to an earlier one, at seven, which was less crowded and fifteen minutes shorter; it came without the sermon, which tended to be patriotic, and without the priest's public prayers that singled out for blessing only the servicemen of the Allies.

Joseph continued to keep up with the war news in the daily press, but now he bought the papers at a newsstand beyond the business district, a six-block trip instead of the short walk to the corner cigar store, because he wanted to avoid the neighborhood merchants and his other acquaintances who lingered there and might try to draw him into their discussions about the war in Italy. The last time he had gone there, during the summer before his illness, Mussolini had dominated the headlines (he had just been imprisoned by the Italian king) and as Joseph left with his papers underarm, he heard a familiar voice calling out from the rear of the store: "Hey, Joe, what's gonna happen to your friend now?"

Joseph glared at the men gathered around the soft-drink stand, and spotted his questioner — a thin, elderly man named Pat Malloy, who wore a white shirt and black bow tie and had worked for years behind the counter of the corner restaurant.

"He's no friend of mine!" Joseph shouted, feeling his anger rise as he stepped down to the sidewalk and went quickly up the avenue with his papers folded inward so that the headlines and the photographs of the jowly-faced interned dictator were covered. Joseph did not make eye contact with the soldiers and sailors he saw among the strollers, although he could hardly avoid the American flags that flapped across the sidewalk in front of every shop on Asbury Avenue, including his own; and it was never possible at night to forget the ongoing war: the town was completely blacked out — all the streetlamps were painted black; lowered shades and drawn curtains hid the lighted rooms within houses; and few people drove their automobiles after dark, not only because there was a gas shortage but also because the required black paint on their headlights induced automobile accidents and collisions with pedestrians and wandering dogs.

Although there had been no new German submarine attacks in the area since an American tanker had been torpedoed ten miles south of Ocean City a year before, the island's continuing blackout had introduced new problems: gangs of hoodlums from the mainland regularly ransacked vacant summer homes during the winter months; they also operated a flourishing trade in pilfered cars, having an abundance of parked vehicles to choose from during the nocturnal hours, when it was more difficult to drive cars than to steal them.

Joseph secured his dry-cleaning trucks each night in a garage, and he chained the bumper of his 1941 Buick to a stone wall in the lot behind his shop. Before driving it he often had to hammer the ice off the lock, but he accepted such delays as by-products of the war and the blackout — a blackout which, in his case, extended well beyond the boundaries of his island. He had been cut off from communication with his family in Italy, and his cousin in Paris, for many months. Antonio's last letter, received in the spring of 1943, before the Allies had attacked Sicily, described the Maida relatives as sustaining themselves but expecting the worst, and added that the POW husband of Joseph's sister (captured by the British in North Africa) might have been shot while trying to escape; in any case, no official word of his whereabouts had been received. Whether Joseph's brother Domenico was dead or alive was also questionable; he had not been heard from in more than a year. Antonio had passed on the report that Domenico was possibly with a German-led Italian infantry division near the Russian front — Antonio had received this information from a contact in the Italian Foreign Ministry — but he had emphasized to Joseph that the report was unsubstantiated. Since the arrival of Antonio's last letter, the Allied invasion of southern Italy had begun; Mussolini had been rescued from prison by Germans to serve as Hitler's puppet; and Joseph was now trying to recuperate on this island where he had lived compatibly for almost twenty-two years but on which he currently felt estranged as never before.

While his withdrawal was voluntary, having not been prompted by flagrant personal slights or expressions of ostracism toward his business, Joseph felt powerless to free himself from his remoteness and the hostile emotion that too often erupted within him after such remarks as Pat Malloy's. It was possible that Malloy's referring to Mussolini as Joseph's "friend" was a casual remark, made without ill intent. Joseph was, after all, the town's most prominent Italian-born resident, one who had delivered lectures on Italian history and politics to community groups on the island and the mainland; and there had also been no derisive tone in Pat Malloy's voice, to say nothing of the cordial informality he had always shown toward Joseph in the restaurant. Furthermore, to be linked with Mussolini in Ocean City was not necessarily insulting, for the anti-union, Communist-baiting policies of the Duce had long been popular among the staunch Republicans who governed the island; and even in recent years, as the Fascist and Nazi regimes had closed ranks, Mussolini gained from whatever *was* to be gained in the United States by being identified as less odious and murderous than Hitler.

Still, during this winter, Joseph dwelled in a state of exile, adrift between the currents of two warring countries; he would read the newspapers at the breakfast table until nearly ten a.m., his children having already left for school and his wife gone down into the shop, and would then exit down the side stairwell of the building and out the back door, wearing his overcoat and homburg and with a heavy woolen scarf wrapped around his neck, and proceed across the lot to the railroad tracks, and then onward through the black ghetto toward the bay — in the opposite direction from the ocean and his binoculared submarine-searching friends and acquaintances who were lined up with their feet on the lowest railings of the boardwalk and their eyes squinting toward the sea. The bayfront district was the most desolate section of town during the winter months; a few black men and women ambled through the bungalow- and shack-lined streets and the weedy fields cluttered with rusting car parts and other rubble, but there was no other sign of human life back here, save for the motorists driving along Bay Avenue, and the white workmen who sometimes scraped the bottoms of overturned dinghies and sloops in the boatyards, and repaired the docks in front of the vacated yacht club. There were hardly any sea gulls around the bay, where the scavenging possibilities could not compare with those offered by the ocean; and never during Joseph's excursions did he meet pedestrians whom he knew well enough to feel obligated to pause and converse with, and explain why he was off by himself traipsing about on the broken concrete sidewalks and frosty fields of this black, backwater part of town. His doctor had not suggested that daily walks would be beneficial to the restoration of his health, although Joseph had said so in explaining to his employees his comings and goings from the store; and it also became the excuse his wife gave to those regular customers who inquired, as some did, why he was constantly out of the shop and spotted frequently by them as they motored along Bay Avenue. Joseph had full confidence in Catherine's ability to make whatever he did seem plausible and proper, and meanwhile to carry on the business without him. She was assisted of course by her saleswomen, and by the old retired tailor from Philadelphia, who now worked a six-day week on the island; and she was supported as well by the reliable Mister Bossum, the black deacon and bootlegger who supervised the dry-cleaning plant and had taken over the responsibilities for the punctuality of the irresponsible pressers, especially the one presser everybody called Jet, the flat-footed, carbuncled ex–jazz musician who even on snowy days arrived for work wearing sandals and short-sleeved silk Hawaiian shirts.

Joseph passed close to Jet's boardinghouse each morning en route to the bayfront, and he was sometimes tempted to stop in and see if Jet had left for work yet; but Joseph resisted, having more urgent concerns. His mother was rarely out of his thoughts during his walks, although he found himself chiding her as much as praying for her. If only she had followed his father to America, Joseph told himself again and again, all the family would now be better off. They would be living with Joseph, or near him, somewhere in America, sparing him his present anxieties about their welfare, and his nagging suspicion that he had somehow abandoned them. If only he had some confirmation that his mother and the rest of his family were alive, that the Allied troops had skirted Maida and left the village undestroyed, he believed, he would no longer be the reclusive and petulant man he had become.

But the war news from southern Italy was scant and inconclusive as far as Maida was concerned. From the Philadelphia and Atlantic City papers he purchased each morning, and from *The New York Times* he received each afternoon in the mail, sometimes two days late, he knew only that the Allies were pushing back the Germans from several locations in the general vicinity of Naples. But Maida was too small, or too insignificant militarily, to warrant mention in the reports; and whatever damage had occurred there, or was occurring now, was left to Joseph's ever-darkening imagination.

When he returned from his walk, by noon if not sooner, he would unlock the rear door on the north side of the building and ascend to the apartment by the walled-in staircase without being seen by anyone in the shop. He would then press once on the wall buzzer near the living room door, signaling to his wife at her desk downstairs that he was home; and usually within seconds she would acknowledge his message with a return signal, and would press twice if she wanted him to pick up the phone extension to discuss something she thought he should know before she closed the shop at five-thirty and came up for the evening. Only on rare occasions did Catherine press twice, however, for there was hardly anything about the business that she could not handle at least as well as he could — a fact that they were both aware of, but that neither discussed. Catherine felt herself sensitive to his every mood and vulnerability, particularly at this point in the war, and in the aftermath of his illness. Having lived under the same roof with him virtually every hour of their almost fifteen years of marriage, except for the recent fortnight of his hospitalization, she thought she knew his strengths, his weaknesses, and his daily routine perhaps better than she knew her own. She knew that when he returned from the bayfront walk, he would first hang up his coat and hat in their bedroom closet in the rear of the apartment, then walk through the corridor back into the living room to kneel briefly at the prie-dieu. A quick lunch would follow in the kitchen, invariably consisting of a plain omelet with crisp unbuttered toast, and a cup of reheated coffee left over from breakfast. He ate little during the day and preferred eating alone. He washed and dried his dishes, but never put them away, leaving this chore for his daughter, Marian, when she came home from school.

Catherine did not leave the shop at lunchtime; instead she had the saleswomen who had their lunches at the nearby five-and-ten soda fountain bring back a milk shake for her. If it was relatively quiet in the shop at midday, as it nearly always was in wintertime, Catherine could hear her husband walking through the corridor after lunch to the mahogany Stromberg-Carlson console in the far corner of the living room, near his record collection. By this time she had already turned off the two particular neon lights in the front of the shop that caused most of the static upstairs on the radio; and if she did not hear him pacing the floor as he listened to the war news, she assumed Joseph was seated in the faded velvet armchair next to the set, leaning forward while twirling his steel-rimmed glasses. He would usually switch stations every three or four minutes, turning the console's large brown asbestos knob slowly and cautiously, as if fearing what the next broadcast might bring. At night she had often observed the intensity with which he listened to the news, awaiting each battlefront bulletin with his face so close to the set that his soulful expression varied in color as the console's green "eye" fluttered in and out of frequency. The children were asleep at this time, these nightly reports often being broadcast well beyond midnight; Catherine herself usually retired shortly after closing the children's bedroom doors, having earlier helped them with their homework. But for hours afterward she lay awake restlessly, not because of the softly tuned radio that continued to absorb her husband's attentions in the living room, not because of the pink light from the corridor torchère that was reflected forty feet away on the ceiling above the L-shaped ten-foot-high mirror-faced divider that masked the marital bedroom. She was disturbed instead by her husband's pacing back and forth in the living room *after* he had turned off the set, pacing that continued sometimes until dawn, to end only when he had fallen asleep

on the sofa, fully clothed. In the morning, hoping not to wake him, Catherine
would whisper as she alerted the children for school; but he was always up before
they had finished breakfast, and before shaving he would come into the kitchen in
his rumpled suit to greet the children formally and then address his wife more
gently, usually speaking to her in Italian so the children would not understand.

Except when disciplining them, Joseph paid a minimum of attention to the
children during this troublesome winter. Each had been assigned daily chores, both
in the apartment and in the store. Even when the chores were performed
punctually and competently, Joseph regularly found things to criticize. His
complaints were expressed as assertively to eight-year-old Marian as to twelve-
year-old Gay. Of the two, only Marian was bold enough to defend herself against
his accusations; she alone had the nerve to defy him. While she agreeably carried
her mother's shopping list to the neighborhood grocery store, where the family
had a charge account — it was actually a barter arrangement dating back to the
Depression, when her father and the grocer began exchanging goods and services,
making up the difference with gifts at Christmastime after the annual tallying —
Marian was far less cooperative in her parents' store. She dusted the glass cases
carelessly, swept the floors of the fitting rooms grudgingly when she did so at all,
and reacted to her father's reprimands sometimes by dropping the broom or
dustpan and stomping out of the shop, ignoring her father's promises of
punishment.

"You're more stubborn than my mother," he once shouted at Marian, whom he
had named in honor of his mother, although physically she clearly favored his wife's
side of the family. Marian had her mother's fair complexion and the red hair of her
mother's father, Rosso. She did not appear to be the sibling of her olive-skinned,
dark-haired brother, who, while more tractable and less defiant than she, was also
more capable of remaining out of their father's sight. Only during his father's
illness and self-imposed exile from the shop did Gay enter it without feeling tense
and apprehensive — and return to it after school without fear of being late, for his
mother was not a clock-watcher; and thus in the winter of 1944 he began taking a
more leisurely route home each afternoon, stopping first at the Russell Bakery
Shop on Asbury Avenue, where a friend, the baker's grandson, could be counted
on to bring a few éclairs out to the alley for a delicious, hastily consumed treat,
and then play catch for a few minutes with the rubber ball that Gay always carried

in his schoolbag.

Later, in the pressing room, after delivering to Jet and the other presser, Al, enough hangers-with-guards to fulfill their needs for at least a half-hour, Gay had the option of exiting through the back door via the steam screen provided by the pressers, and practicing his pitching form in the lot behind the shop — hurling the rubber ball against the brick wall of the neighboring hardware store's annex, and at times letting it carom off the roof of his father's chained Buick before catching it. He was secure in the knowledge that his father spent the afternoons up in the apartment on his knees, or sitting in the living room listening to operas or news broadcasts, and so he was stunned one afternoon to hear the thumping sounds of his ball punctuated by the urgent rapping of his father's knuckles against the rear window that overlooked the lot.

Gay ran back into the safety of the pressers' steam and quickly resumed the task of affixing guards to hangers, and also sandpapering and unbending those rusty and crooked hangers that customers had provided in response to the store's advertised appeal, and its promise to pay half a penny for each wire hanger, because of the wartime metal shortage. As he worked, he feared the appearance of his father and some form of retribution that might well be overdue. In recent weeks, he had received a failing report card after the midterm examinations; and he had been warned repeatedly by his father to discontinue making his prized model airplanes, for the glue used in sealing their parts cast a hypnotic and possibly toxic odor throughout the apartment. His father had furthermore charged that the glue was most likely the cause of his son's daydreaming and general dimwittedness in school, the lack of scholarship that had been noted, in kinder terms, by the Mother Superior on the bottom of the recently received report card.

Gay anxiously worked at the hangers, still awaiting his father's arrival in the workroom, knowing that he could expect no protection from Mister Bossom, or Jet, or Al, or the old tailor. But as the minutes continued to register on the misty-faced clock that hung on the workroom wall, and he sandpapered one hanger after another without interruption, he lost track of the time until he saw in front of him his mother's high-heeled shoes and heard her consoling voice suggesting that he was working too hard. It was also closing time, she said, as she extended a hand to help him up from his crouched position.

He was surprised to see that the tailor and the pressers had already left; now only slight sizzling sounds rose from the valves of the machines. Marian also stood waiting, holding a light bundle of groceries in the cloth sack their mother had made because of the paper scarcity. Gay walked up the interior staircase behind his mother and sister, then entered the living room and saw his father seated near the console with his back turned, leaning forward with his head in his hands. The radio was off. He could hear his father softly crying.

His sister, who seemed unaware of it, headed toward the kitchen with the groceries. Gay followed her. Catherine hastened toward her husband and placed a hand on his shoulder. For several minutes they could be heard speaking quietly in Italian. Then she left him and went into the kitchen to prepare the children's dinner; she explained to them that their father was feeling worse than usual, and added that after they had finished dinner they were to go to their rooms and close their doors, and, as long as they kept down the volume, they could listen to their radios. There was no homework to worry about. It was Friday night. Tomorrow a more leisurely day was in the offing, the always welcomed Saturday that brought no school bus or any chores in the shop until after ten a.m.

Joseph spent Friday night on the sofa, having hardly touched the dinner on the tray Catherine had placed on the coffee table in front of him. She had remained in the living room with him until midnight, continuing to speak in Italian. English was heard only when Catherine went to warn Marian that her radio was too loud, and to remind her that she should soon turn off the bed lamp because the following morning she would be picked up by the parents of one of her classmates, with whom she would be attending a birthday party on the mainland.

On Saturday morning after nine, when Gay got up, he saw that his sister had already left. Her door was open, her bed unmade. His parents' bedroom door was shut, as usual, but he knew his mother was downstairs, opening the store for the busy Saturday trade. He could hear the bell downstairs as customers opened and closed the shop's main door on Asbury Avenue. It was a sound he associated with Saturdays, as he always found the tones reassuring, signals of his family's financial stability. In the kitchen, as he poured himself some orange juice, he noticed that there were newspapers on the table that had not been there the night before. Returning to the front of the apartment, he saw no sign of his father. He found it odd to be in the apartment by himself and uniquely exhilarating to be able to walk around freely and privately, answerable to no one. As he approached the console, he noticed that its usual gleaming mahogany exterior was now smudgy with fingerprints. He then saw his father's bathrobe lying on the floor behind the sofa, and the ashtray filled with cigarette butts, and sections of newspapers that had been crumpled up and hurled in the other corner, and had come to rest near the piano. Since his father had always been the family's enforcer of tidiness and order, Gay could not even venture a guess as to the cause of this laxity.

Back in the kitchen, sitting in front of a bowl of dry cereal that his mother had left for him, he looked at the headlines and photographs on the front pages of the newspapers. One was an Italian-language paper that he of course could not read; another was *The New York Times*, which he refused to read because it did not have comics. But on this day he was drawn to the front pages of these and other papers because most of them displayed pictures of the devastation left after recent air raids — smoke was rising out of a large hilltop building that American bombers had attacked in Italy, and had completely destroyed. The headlines identified the ruins as the Abbey of Monte Cassino, located in southern Italy, northwest of Naples. The articles described the abbey as very old, dating back to the sixth century. They called it a cradle of learning throughout the Dark Ages, a scholarly center for Benedictine monks, who had occupied it for fourteen centuries; it was built on a hill that Nazi soldiers had taken over during the winter of 1943-1944. The raid on February 15, 1944, had involved more than a hundred forty of America's heaviest bombers, the B-17 Flying Fortresses; these, together with the medium-sized bombers that followed, released nearly six hundred tons of bombs on the abbey and its grounds. It was the first time the Allies had deliberately made a target of a religious building.

After breakfast, while brushing his teeth in the bathroom, dressed and ready to go down to the store, Gay heard strange noises in the apartment, a pounding on the walls and the cursing of an angry male voice. When he opened the door, he saw his father, in overcoat and hat, swatting down the model airplanes suspended from Gay's bedroom ceiling by almost invisible threads.

"Stop it, they're mine!" Gay screamed, horrified at the sight of his carefully crafted American bombers and fighter planes, framed with balsa wood and covered with crisp paper, being smashed into smithereens by his father. *"Stop, stop, stop — they're mine, get out of my room, get out!"* Joseph did not seem to hear, but kept swinging

wildly with both hands until he had knocked out of the air and crushed with his feet every single plane that his son had for more than a year taken countless evening hours to make. They were two dozen in number — exact replicas of the United States' most famous fighter planes and bombers — the B-17 Flying Fortress, the B-26 Marauder, the B-25 Mitchell, the Bell P-39 Airacobra fighter plane, the P-38 Lockheed Lightning, the P-40 Kittyhawk; Britain's renowned Spitfire, Hurricane, Lancaster; and other Allied models that until this moment had been the proudest achievement of Gay's boyhood.

"I hate you, I hate you," he cried at his father before running out of the apartment, and then down the side staircase to the first landing, where he grabbed his roller skates. "I hate you!" he yelled again, looking up toward the living room door, but seeing no sign of his father. Crying, he continued to the bottom of the staircase and out onto the avenue, then thrust his skates around his shoe tops without bothering to tighten them; and as quickly as he could, he headed up Asbury Avenue, thrashing his arms through the cold wind and sobbing as he sped between several bewildered people who suddenly stepped aside. As he passed the Russell Bakery Shop, he lost his balance and swerved toward the plate-glass window. People were lined up in front of the pastry counter, and two women screamed as they saw the boy, his hands outstretched, crash into the window and then fall bleeding with glass cascading down on his head.

Unconscious until the ambulance arrived, and then embarrassed by the crowds staring silently behind the ropes that the police held in front of the bakery's broken window, he turned toward his father, who was embracing him in bloody towels, crying and saying something in Italian that the boy did not understand.

"*Non ti spagnare,*" Joseph said, over and over — don't be afraid — using the old dialect of southern Italians who had lived in fear of the Spanish monarchy. "*Non ti spagnare,*" Joseph went on, cradling his son's head with his bloody hands, and closing his eyes as he heard his son repeating, tearfully, "I hate you."

Joseph then became silent, watching the ambulance crew arrive with a stretcher as the police ordered the people in the crowd to keep their distance. When Joseph next spoke, he did so in English, although his son found him no less bewildering than before, even as Joseph repeated: "Those who love you, make you cry...."

Killing Time

by Therése Halscheid

Ocean City, New Jersey

The beach is empty in autumn
and all along the boardwalk

the shops are closing one by one
with barricades

with signs: GOING OUT OF BUSINESS
BUY NOW! I stop,

eat pizza by the slice then move on
into an arcade

where electric games cave in
around me, sucking me

onto airstrips and racetracks
the battlefields, the loud sounds

of guns shooting
are in the distance, coming closer

and I am lost. No,
I am only entering a world

I am not used to —
missing the flowers in the forest

missing the forest —
I place a sweaty hand

on the palm reading machine
which does not work

does not need to work
I know how to use the quarter it takes

to fly away on the pink horse
with the snow white mane.

Love

by Claude F. Koch

I

In his mordant moods, Warden referred to his memory as "the morgue" — an old newspaperman's legitimate pun. Warden ceased to be newspaperman and became journalist upon his employment by *Pry* magazine. It was a term that covered a multitude of sins — or uncovered them, depending on one's point of view. Warden had almost ceased to have a point of view. He was the first to admit it, though he was not quite so candid in all matters; this, he would say candidly, was because words were a large part of his survival kit, and he used them as need be.

He fancied himself as master of two languages: through one he communicated with the editors and readers of *Pry*; by the other, he communed with himself. Sometimes he suffered a slight panic, like that impelled by a slip upon hidden ice, imagining they both had become one.

But this winter day, with a mean wind across the Hudson belting the South Jersey bus along, he burrowed in a rear seat in the tacky overcoat that an unwise but hopeful interest in lotteries and horses, and an overdue alimony, allowed him; and, in his own voice, sorted certain facts concerning the poet Ruthven Lewes (lately deceased) that made this journey necessary.

The elderly Jewish lady in mink who boarded at Hackensack, declaring at large "The bus is good. Who would travel alone?" and whose publicly announced goal was to take the warm salt baths at the Marlborough-Blenheim at Atlantic City, interrupted his concentration.

"You have children?" she said. "They're trouble. My son — he asked me if I wanted a blue coffin; and there I was sick."

Warden had no children. "But you understand," she said, paying not the least attention, so thoroughly did her being bend to her motherly concern; "my only son. The army taught him to drink. His wife, now — a good woman. She said: 'I'll get a lawyer.'" Then: "I came to America with the clothes on my back — now my son gets $135,000 when I die. God can do anything."

It was one of those dun November days when anything is given back as from a flawed marble surface. Warden saw his face sliding along the glass store fronts of chilled little Jersey towns like graffiti that someone else had recorded, implying complaints and aspirations and defeats he no longer recognized.

"My son is fifty-eight," the little woman said into her mink. "What do you do to live?"

Warden explained with a straight face that he was an investigative reporter. "It's a blessing to pour out one's heart to a total stranger," the lady said. It was Atlantic City, and Warden helped her with her suitcase. "A fine ride," she said. Perhaps. Warden, who was chary of sentiment, saw it rather as an interruption in the business of survival. But there had really been only two bad moments (the ice again): he had misread the sign at Sea Girt as "Sea Girl," and by a lonely sandy road an arrow seemed to have pointed to "Misty Isles." After the first shock, he realized it as only Mystic Islands. About certain failings he'd joke, because he did have a quirky self-deprecating armor, but the possibility of the word failing him made him uncomfortable.

The bus got underway again. He waved to the mother where she waited for her jitney, wrapped in her mink and thoughts of her son. He had seen her before, in depots and railways stations, pilgrim of love, hopeful of the jitney that would bundle her to some uncomplicated consummation and rest. He recognized the purple prose of *Pry* in that, and returned to Ruthven Lewes and negotiable facts.

Ahead were Sea Isle and Townsend's Inlet and Avalon, the marshes and inland waterway, and the empty summer homes of his childhood, toward which, at one time, long trains moved over the wetlands in amphibrachs. It had taken a foreigner to bring him back after forty years.

I I

The facts were that Ruthven Lewes, literary London's chronic expatriate and elusive philanderer, had died at Townsend's Inlet near Sea Isle City, in what he slandered as "the Colonies." Scarcely had he been commemorated by memorial stone in the chancel of Magnus Martyr at London Bridge and his body ceremoniously translated to a bleak churchyard in the mists of Wales than the exploitation of his remains began. There was cause enough, even had he not aspired to the Laureateship; and, as for that, after Auden's refusal only John Betjeman stood in his way. But then, alas, Ruthven was unexpectedly visited by that Sir Death whom he had celebrated, more than once, in his erotic and enigmatic poems.

It was considered no little thing to have been his intimate, and he would have been blasphemous but unsurprised at the number laying claim to such impropriety. It was a fact that he who had been good copy in the turbulence of his life was proving better copy dead, though this seemed to Warden simply a way of saying that, in this most likely of all probable worlds, fiction seldom defers to the fact.

Mr. Warden pursued fact with the avid unscrupulousness of a master of fiction. It was a habit he'd found necessary, then fascinating. Now, concerning Ruthven Lewes, he asked himself: Why — with New York's loveliest and most inaccessible at his feet — had this wild Welshman betaken himself to a fisherman's shack at Townsend's Inlet, where Great Egg Harbor Bay absorbs the tides of the Atlantic, and the channeled whelk marks the incursions of the sea? Warden had ceased to ask himself unqualified questions. *Pry* was paying for such exotic elaboration, and by the word.

It was a question to be put to Sylvia, if she could be found.

"Who is Sylvia, what is she?" The beaches he had ranged as a near-sighted child, anticipating treasure in the wrack of the sea, appeared and disappeared between the gaunt and neglected houses at the ends of deserted streets, and the bus moved not at all with Ruthven Lewes' rhythms but like that "wounded snake that drags its slow length along." It was almost empty now, and as the coast road veered across the marshes the few travelers might have been pilgrims crossing Acheron, so self-absorbed were they. Warden found his line changing: "Who is Warden, what is he?"

III

Sylvia Fern-Lofton had served as Lewes' secretary for the final five unsettling years among, as he took malicious pleasure in saying, "the alien corn." She was an odd and fragile woman, teetering on middle age — small featured, small breasted, with the damask complexion celebrated in certain sonnets — who, like the inconspicuous jingle shells spun up by the Atlantic tides, became prettier the closer one got. Lewes called her "Ruth." When his obsequies were done, she returned unobtrusively to the shanty that rose tentatively on pilings over the bay, a continent away from that wanderer's resting place; and it was there that Warden expected to find her, on the kind of desperate hunch that barely kept him in pocket money. It was ten o'clock when the bus rocked into Sea Isle — though who could know it from the way the sun sulked under layers of cloud? As though by common consent the streets were empty, and the boys that Warden half-expected to see, wordless and solitary and happy, in knickers from which all elastic had gone and disreputable sneakers cut open at the toes, had disappeared past houses whose windows opened wide as the eyes of a child, and down those beaches, forty years ago. He got off at the Coast Guard station, into a dwindling morning light that seemed lonelier for his recollections.

IV

He tracked her down, literally, on the winter beach, following her footsteps toward Townsend's Inlet as the tide wrinkled out. It was a discovery not unlike Robinson Crusoe's at this time of year — but that was another story, incompatible with *Pry*.

"You mean," he was inconsolable (it was a matter of food and drink to him, and the trip had been tedious), "you mean that you worked with that man cheek by jowl for five years and there was nothing between you? Come on. His reputation …?"

All in all she had not been difficult to find. In a widow's veil at Magnus Martyr while the High Anglican service unfolded majestically and Ruthven's coffin was incensed, she had not wept, but she had been noticed. Ruthven's wife had snubbed her; his mistresses (those resident in England at the time) were conspicuous — two were already under contract to one of the more sensational London dailies. Then she dropped out of sight. It was a quality, after all, that Warden was aware he had in common with Lewes that led him to the South Jersey shore. He too would have cut his wife off without a penny — though for Ruthven there were few pennies, only the fisherman's shanty, the typewriter, and bills, the reverse of which he used for his notes. Even the most trendy of poets could hardly claim royalties.

"But to come back here…?" Warden dismissed the empty winter beach and the low horizon with one deflating gesture.

Sylvia wore a runner's hooded sweatshirt. She tucked her chin into her shoulder like a sandpiper against the wind, and shoved her hands into the pockets of her jeans. "It was his … he gave it to me." Then she raised her eyes to the level of Warden's shoulders, but no higher, and said: "I don't like you, you know. I wish you'd go away."

"That's the story of my life," Warden said, "but even mothers have confided in me." He was a scruffy little man whose unhappiness did not arise from such rebuffs. "It doesn't make any difference whether you like me or not. You've got to live; I've got to live. If you've got a story, I've got a contract." He was not unkind: he spoke so softly that the wind carried his voice away: "We both have to live."

"What?" Sylvia said. "What?"

"Live," Warden said apologetically. Then, stridently, because she bent close, and he thought it was her hearing: "Live! Live!"

"He said that." She raised her eyes to his, in surprise, as though at the discovery that he existed. Her eyes were the powdery grey of the wintry sea, as sullen and remote; the sea flowed into them, and withdrew toward the same low horizon.

He looked through her at the desolate and pewter sky where not a gull stirred; and when she pulled her slight shoulders up against the wind, for the moment he hardly realized she had gone.

Then he thrust his chin into his scarf and followed after. The fringes of the scarf were wet where it unwound and dragged underfoot while he thought of other things. Scarves are made for bigger or at least more self-regarding men. Past Townsend's Inlet, across the channel, beyond the misty dwellings of Avalon, perhaps the world was different. In winter, one forlorn South Jersey resort was like another, and an opalescence hugged the skyline of that little distant town.

A wind was at his back, but the dream of hope was his weakness and he knew it — though what hope lay in the diminished and vulnerable figure already out of the sound of his voice down the beach was a question that defied elaboration. Warden resigned himself to optimism in the sense that he kept his feet moving.

The distance increased between them. Sylvia was lighter and the wind was strong. There was a dun, brutal astringency to the beach that chilled him more than the wind: the comfortable, slovenly human litter of summer gone, it was the end of the earth now — barebones jetty and piling, no place for flesh. It occurred to Warden then, and not for the first time, that he had no home, that perhaps mankind had no home. And a verse of Ruthven Lewes' roared, bawdy like Ruthven's public voice, with the wind:

> *Between the mountain's knees there is no peace;*
> *Death cuckolds me and all the land is Death's.*
> *For God's sake give me rest in some reprise —*
> *A Dance not Death's between some human knees.*

No one was ever in Lewes' poems but Lewes, and Warden, who had just stepped up to his ankle in a tidal pool, could almost understand. One reached that point where words spoke only of the insular heart — if only to hide it. He gasped while the icy water filled both his shoes. What the hell had brought him here? The end of his credit? Delinquent alimony? Kidney trouble? Because the place was there? He looked up from his chilled feet to find himself crying.

Down the beach, Sylvia had halted too and turned back toward him. She did not beckon, and yet there she waited, and he could not believe it. He held out his hand. Still she did not move. Perhaps she could not even see the gesture; she was remote and singular as a child.

There was no point in going back; there was little to return to. In sheer willfulness, Warden stamped on through the tidal pool. At one point it rose above his ankles. Driftwood, partially submerged, cut his leg. When he reached Sylvia, his teeth clicked incontinently; he was blue with cold. He was quite willing to believe that it was the end of more than the island.

A curtain lifted ever so lightly over the drawbridge beyond Avalon on a pendant of opal sky. That, too, was in her eyes — they were a window upon it. "God," he said, "I'm cold." That she had waited was invitation enough. He followed her across the dunes, and they climbed the chancy wooden steps to Ruthven Lewes' last shelter.

V

If a fisherman had ever lived there he left no trace. It was more like an abandoned doll's house where some child had played — something hammered together with love and no experience at all by a parent who had no occasion to give his work a second thought. It was, in space, a bit like his own life in time: jerry-built, a temporary shelter.

When his teeth subsided and his eyes ceased to water, Warden could stretch his hands to the potbellied stove and almost touch the far wall of the room. Intimacy was unavoidable, but Sylvia had nothing to say. She sat him down in the one easy chair, brought him an afghan from an even smaller room beyond, settled it around his shoulders, and knelt to untie his shoelaces. He made half-hearted, sniffling grunts of protest, but she ignored them.

"Ruthven Lewes lived *here?*" Then he sneezed, and she shook her head with the tolerant disgust that one scarcely shows to strangers. "You're kind," he said. He leaned over her shoulders and spread his fingers to the stove. "You don't have a drink, for God's sake?" Perhaps she did not hear him.

"It was the only place he lived."

She sat back on her heels with her hands on her knees and seemed to diminish still further before him. "He lived here and died here." Then, concerning something beyond him, no higher than his shoulder: "He didn't live out there." *Out there* was Warden's country — he didn't have to be told.

"And you?" It was sheer politeness; his thoughts were on the clear possibility of pneumonia.

"Yes, I lived." Sylvia pressed her hands to her knees; even when she stood, she was not much taller than his head. "I lived for five years." Warden had the impression that she identified him as an offending party, as a straggler, wandered in from the years before — or the years to come. There was that mild contempt in her posture, in the distaste with which she draped his socks over the one remaining chair dragged before the stove. He was not surprised except that she bothered at all. His wife had successfully convinced him, in the final days, that his appeal to womankind was radically limited. The tough skin that *Pry* had grafted served him then.

But Sylvia turned back from poking at the cannel coal in the firebed of the stove. Her eyes that had been the sea and the sky's grey were amethyst. What days, he wondered, were reflected now? A contemptible part of him said, apologetically: "I can't get warm. I need a drink, for God's sake."

"You won't like what I have. It's *Rock and Rye*. It's for what ails you."

"Oh my God," Warden said, "you'll be offering me a mustard footbath next." Yet it was comforting; it took him back.

The cabinet was under a misted window, tilting in its frame. Sylvia poured into a coffee cup: "I don't care what they write about him. Out there's where he ran when he was afraid; that's where he hid — and in his poems." She sipped the drink, then handed the cup to him. She sat on the floor between Warden and the stove. He could see the line of her shoulder blades as she bent over her hands, head bowed to the palms as though they had a message for her. If his drink were scotch and he had his usual portion, those could be wings folded under her bodice. Certainly the advantage of drinking religiously was that it made for a better world.

Her voice was so low that he thought at first she was humming — or keening: "When he was here he sat on the steps in the sun. He listened to the gulls and watched the sea. He knew the plants that grow wild back beyond the dunes, yarrow and sea lavender; he knew all the terns and all kinds of sandpipers." The recitation was guileless, almost academic. "And he told me about the clouds, cumulus, cirrus ... I never knew so many." She lifted her hands to her cheeks: "He said he could see the gods beyond the horizon, like Poussin...."

Her mouth was small, the lips pursed like a maiden's in a Book of Hours. It was piety he feared, more than pity, so he said: "But you *slept* in there." She lifted her head, not comprehending, and he could not sustain the cruelty: "*You*, I mean."

Whatever he had meant made no difference. "I never knew the names of things until I met him; he taught me the names of things. I wasn't anything at all." She spread her hands. He pulled his arms against his sides and shivered: "It's the cold," he said. "I can't get warm."

She rose to pour him another drink. Something outside the window held her there. "The first time I saw him I was sitting on that jetty," she said. "It was March; it was raining. He brought out a poncho. I didn't know who he was. He was very quiet and happy." Sylvia put the glass in his hand, and sat as though to disguise a shyness: "He said I looked ... I looked like a peri. I didn't know what he meant. That's what I remember best about him...."

Warden tried again: "The state of others was hardly a Lewes theme, was it?" He quoted gently:

> "Let Adam die by inches or by yard,
>
> Prodigious the performance or inept,
>
> Yet praise the randy insolence that swept
>
> Under Time's rug the nonsense by the way
>
> Up to the grand rest of the Seventh Day,
>
> And bed for Heloise and Abelard...."

"Oh," she propped her chin on her elbow, "that's only his poetry. He never read me that." She looked at Warden with her silly, untutored innocence: "He needed me."

Warden was annoyed: "People can make fools of themselves, thinking of others."

"I don't know...."

"But you *were* his 'secretary'?"

"I lived with him, and he helped me to see." Her knuckles were white, and just for a moment the fire that burned in the open grate was in her eyes; then it was out, and the stubborn, unwilling tears startled him. "He gave me his secrets, he said. That's why he called me his secretary. He said nothing else would matter."

Warden fumbled with the afghan to find his handkerchief. He knelt before her and drew her head in against the rough weave. He felt hopeless and incompetent, and the little, odd comforting sounds he made were strange even to his ears.

VI

It was only for a moment. She did not indulge herself, but Warden was put in mind of the inconsolable griefs of childhood that seem to exist only to evoke tenderness in others, else why would they linger, without origin and without redemption?

"Don't," he said, "for Christ's sake...."

She pulled back to the limit of his arms, and they knelt, undone and helpless in the possession of such knowledge as they had of each other. Even as he struggled to speak again, and at last said in little better than a whisper "Can I stay?" and berated himself for a fool, Warden saw himself drowning in the unbearable compassion of her eyes. For hadn't he served *Pry* all these years under the impression that it was truth that could scarcely be endured? No matter — she would hardly forgive him for comforting her, and of course she did not. She shook her head.

There was nothing for it but to leave.

Sylvia was regretful and withdrawn. But she struggled with a suitcase shoved under a cot in a corner, and it did Warden no good to protest. She hauled it forth, elegant leather and expensively monogrammed *RL* in regal gold capitals. The bizarre turtleneck sweater she pressed upon him had last been worn by Ruthven Lewes in that heated reading at the New York YMHA that had stood the world of poetry on its ears. It hung from his shoulders like a shroud, but it was warm. So, shortly, in his own overcoat and shoes, but in Lewes' scarf, sweater, and socks, he stood at the bus stop by the ramp of the bridge to Avalon, feeling peculiarly transformed, at least on the face of things. The last bus inland reared over the center span and butted down the ramp. It was the way — past pilgrims of Hackensack to the Hudson shore. Sylvia was still on the steps of the shanty where he had left her, her face hooded against the cutting wind. She seemd like a caryatid in that uncertain light; and he thought that she had watched Ruthven Lewes so, when he prepared for his flight inland on such days as this. Wet sand blew in his eyes, the Almost-Laureate of England waited for a South Jersey bus, a horn hooted — and one gesture of her hand would have released him. Could it be that Lewes, tutoring her in the names of things, and had neglected the common "Farewell"? Warden watched the taillight of the bus recede up the empty road.

There was one thing to do: he could cross the drawbridge to Avalon, and deliver her from where she stood to retire into a little warmth with whatever mysteries she had of Lewes. It was ten cents to use the pedestrian lane — not an expensive charity.

At the center of the span he saw that Avalon was an illusion — the skies had not cleared at all. And back on the Inlet side, no longer erect but huddled against the steps of the shanty like a shape cast up by the sea, Sylvia. He knew he could go back — if he dared.

But he could not stand, irresolute, on the bridge. A Coast Guard cutter, its horn wailing, rounded the point of the Inlet toward the open sea. Warden was still a professional. In spite of other matters, the first florid sentence of an article shaped itself to his mind:

> When Ruthven Lewes fled from his mistresses and his
> poems to the Jersey shore, what rescue awaited him?
> What treasure did the wild Welshman seek in the shadow of Avalon?

Pry would like that.

But then, while a chill bit at his writing fingers, it came to him that he could not answer his own question — except by appealing to something stranger than fiction that would bring no delight to *Pry* at all. The machinery of the bridge rumbled even as he stood on it, and the guard gesticulated from his shack. Warden looked back, almost timidly. Fallen angel, sea wrack — whatever she was — it was his heart that was foundering, and this time he could not help himself. Within him a voice long subdued struggled to raise what seemed to be a question of some import. Alas, it was shouted down by the guard who stormed from his shack and, like a beached and land-locked Charon, shooed him across the bridge toward Avalon.

The Southern Shore

Top: Wildwood by Michael Baytoff
Bottom: Ocean City by Donna Connor

Ocean City by Donna Connor

Cape May by Michael Baytoff (both pages)

Ocean City by Donna Connor

Ashes to Ashes

by Karen de Balbian Verster

A man, when he burns, leaves only a handful of ashes. No woman can hold him.

Tennessee Williams

C liff touches my shoulder and softly says my name. Although tired, I'm instantly awake. In the gray stillness, I quietly get dressed, not bothering to brush my teeth or wash my face since I know in a short time I'll be back in bed. I hear Cliff enter his mother's room, her sharp intake of breath, his murmured communication. I'm waiting in the living room when he emerges. I catch his eye and he shrugs his shoulders, before donning a jacket. At six o'clock in the morning it will be cold on the beach.

"Come on," he says. "Let's go."

As we walk the short distance to the beach, I ask Cliff about his mother's response.

"She didn't want to come," he says.

"Was she really upset?"

"No, she just shook her head and went back to sleep."

By now we've reached the dunes and are following the path to the beach.

I always have the same reaction each time I reach the crest of the dune and see the ocean for the first time, especially early in the morning when the sun is just rising. My chest expands to take in the enormous vista spread before me and my body suddenly relaxes. This morning it's a little overcast and the sun shining on the ocean creates a Jacob's ladder of light. I look in both directions and there is not another soul on the beach.

It takes us a while to reach the ocean because it's low tide and this is the widest part of the Avalon beach, the feature that made Bea and Jack prize it so, plus the nearby wildlife preserve which gives minimal access to shoobies, those unfortunates who only come for the day. The beach narrows again in both directions, intensifying the density of its population — to the south because of all the hotels, and to the north because of the boardwalk and group rentals. We've come to think of the Sixty-fourth Street section as our own since we've spent so many summers there. After we got married, Cliff's parents let us have the Avalon house to ourselves for a week and it started a tradition.

We stand at the water's edge, letting our feet get accustomed to the cold as the waves fan out. Cliff opens a small cardboard box and takes out a handful of his father's ashes. He gently tosses them in a wide arc, looking like Millet's *The Sower* as he does so.

I watch him, trying to dredge up some fond memories of Jack, but my emotions are as frozen as my toes. The only thing I can muster is a faint feeling of disapproval since Cliff has already distributed most of the ashes at other locations, and all this spreading around of Jack's ashes makes me nervous. Somehow, I feel they should be kept together, as though his soul will dissipate or be homeless, if not. The Pennsylvania authorities must agree, for Cliff had to verbally pledge that he was taking them for burial in a cemetery or piece of family property. At the time he took them, he thought he would be burying them on his uncle's farm, which had been designated a historical landmark, thereby ensuring that they would never be disturbed by future developers. But then Cliff decided there wasn't enough significance to that location since this uncle, his mother's brother, had only recently moved there.

I hold out my cupped hand for some ashes and examine them carefully. They are not at all what I expected, certainly not like ashes from a wood fire, which are chalky and thin as moth's wings. These look more like gravel or lava. They're hard and rocklike, pitted, about the size of pebbles, in various shades of grey. As I look into my hands, I have to remind myself that these came from Jack's body, they are his remains. More than ever, I get a shaky feeling that I'm breaking some ancient taboo, that it's immoral to separate the parts of a man's body. Yet, it's clear that the handfuls Cliff is tossing will not remain together, that in a very short time they will be ground to a powder finer than sand, indistinguishable to any beachcomber or deep sea diver.

I think about the ashes of my own father, which I never saw nor held since his second wife so hastily stashed him in the ground. Desirous of honoring my father with a memorial that we thought was closer to his heart, my mother and I planted a tree on the Vanderbilt campus near the science center where he did research and taught for seven years. Then we invited all of Dad's friends and stood around the tree swapping stories. I was amazed to hear how popular he was, how much of an impression he'd made on people. For all his flaws, my father was one of a kind, and I relished being among those who had revered him in life and missed him in death.

I take a breath and prepare to throw my handful of ashes. I'd like to say something profound about Jack, something that Cliff will always remember and associate with this day, but I can't. It horrifies me to realize that I never really knew Jack. I knew his shell — the person who wore a hideous blue plaid jacket to my wedding, who liked to read about birds, who liked to tinker with the magic set we gave him, who played tennis like a pro, who was always mixing a drink.

Six hours later we are again at the beach, Bea and I on those little legless chairs, Cliff on a towel. It amazes me how differently Cliff and I behave at the beach. I can lie there all day, immersed in my book, donning sunscreen, T-shirt, and hat as needed to prolong my stay. Cliff is only good for short bursts. He comes down in the morning, lies face down on his towel, refusing suntan lotion because he wants to get tan, and remains inert as a time bomb until a fly lands on the back of his leg. He smacks it a few times and then gets up with a cranky I-knew-this-wasn't-going-to-work attitude. He stomps off to the water and returns even more grumpy because it's too cold or too flat or too riddled with jellyfish. Then he puts his tennis shoes on over his bare sandy feet, which always makes me grit my teeth, and heads back to the house to watch some tennis on TV and take a snooze. He usually reappears around three o'clock, much less fretful, like a baby refreshed by its nap.

When Cliff leaves, Bea and I gratefully resume reading our books. We can sit like this for hours unless Bea happens to be reading a less than enthralling book, in which case she'll talk to me about something Cliff or his sister, Dana, has done that is presently mystifying her. On this particular day the topic on her mind is Jack's ashes, although she starts off by telling me about the death of the husband of a good friend of hers. "I said, 'Jean, you've crossed through that magic doorway. Now you belong to my club.'"

I silently consider this, knowing the club she's referring to is widowhood. When she says nothing further, I resume my reading.

"Did you do what you said you were going to do?" she asks.

"Why don't you let Cliff explain it to you when he comes back," I say, anxious to refrain from acting as arbiter between Bea and her son.

She seems dissatisfied with my answer, but picks up her book and goes back to reading.

❁

From the start, Bea did not want to know anything about the disposal of Jack's ashes. When Cliff and I visited his mother several weeks previously, it was ostensibly to take her car in for an inspection, but Cliff was also there to retrieve his father's ashes from his friend Phil, who had been storing them in his house. Although Phil would never admit it, they were giving him the creeps. All of this had to be carried out in a very hush-hush manner because Bea got hysterical at the very mention of the word "ashes."

Before taking the car in for inspection, we dropped Bea off at work because, at the age of sixty-four, she'd never learned to drive. Jack had always gotten her wherever she needed to be, which she was now beginning to see had its disadvantages. Then we drove over to Arborlea, the tennis club Cliff's father had presided over as president for fifteen years. When we got there, no one was around so Cliff climbed over the chain link fence and dropped down on the other side. He planned to distribute the bulk of the ashes around the courts, which were in a secluded, wooded area.

Cliff followed the periphery of the clay courts, careful to avoid getting any of the ashes on the courts themselves, which had just been swept that morning, since he knew his father would disapprove of his disturbing their smooth finish. When he was done, he stood still and looked up at the dome of the sky visible through the tops of the trees. "Dear Dad," he said. "I hope you'll be happy here. This is where I knew you best." He remembered playing on these courts with his father, remembered how his father would snake his way up into what's called no man's land and finish off his opponents with wierdly angled shots. He'd never seen anyone else play the game like that. "Dear God, take care of him please," he added. "I know he could use some help. He tried hard to be a good father and I love him. Amen." Then he climbed back over the fence and we headed for home.

Some days later, Cliff put a handful of ashes into a porcelain egg we'd received as a wedding present. Then he put a pinch into a small wooden box he'd gotten for his sister, Dana, and mailed them out to her along with her birthday present. He put a note on the box saying, "Read the card before you open this," but Dana failed to do so. She opened the box and did not know what to make of the contents.

Her boyfriend said, "Honey, it looks like ashes to me. Maybe it's your father."

At which point Dana shrieked and nearly fainted. Then she called her mother. Bea, taking on Dana's hysteria like an Olympic torchbearer, called Cliff to let him know how much his thoughtlessness had injured his sister. Cliff immediately called Dana to apologize. But Dana didn't know what Cliff was talking about. She wasn't upset.

The last of the ashes Cliff saved for the shore.

✪

Right on schedule, Cliff comes traipsing across the sand, carrying a cooler of cold, clear sodas and some fruit. Three o'clock is about the time I start wishing the day would last forever. Most of the locals conform to a set routine — early morning walk from seven to nine, breakfast on the pier or Bill's Pancake House, set up camp by ten (the beach is never crowded), go home for lunch at one (you can leave all your stuff on the beach unguarded), then at four people shake their towels, fold their chairs, and head home for showers and cocktails. By five, the beach is sparsely populated, by six, deserted. Six to eight is my favorite time on the beach, but I only get to stay that late when Cliff and I are there alone.

"Did you have a good nap?" Bea asks.

"Fine," says Cliff.

There's a pause and then Bea whispers something to Cliff.

"We did it right here at Sixty-fourth Street," he says.

"You did?" She does this shooing motion with her hand, while shaking her head, as though trying to fling the tears from her eyes. It takes a moment for the constriction to leave her throat. "I wish I could have been here somehow, but it was just too much for me."

"That's okay, Mom. You were here in spirit," Cliff says.

"Remember last time we were here, last summer, and we saw those dolphins?" I say.

We all turn and look out to sea.

"Look," Cliff says. He's pointing at two dark shapes about fifteen yards from shore, two dark shapes that are diving and cavorting in the water.

"Oh, my God," I say, "I can't believe they're here right after I said that."

"It's Dad sending you a sign, Mom, a sign that he's okay," Cliff says.

Bea's eyes fill with tears. I put my arm around her and so does Cliff. We stand at the edge of the water, watching the dolphins frolic in the sparkling waves, and have our memorial after all.

Senior Week

by Jason Wilson

"Rumor around town says you might be thinkin' about goin' down to the Shore."

"Uh, yeah. I think I'm going to go down to the Shore."

"What're you gonna do down there?"

"Oh, I don't know. Play some video games. Buy some Def Leppard T-shirts."

— from "Bitchin' Camaro" by the Dead Milkmen

"I'm *gonna stab you and throw you off the porch!"*

That was a joke. We told jokes like that when we drank at our parents' summer homes in Ocean City, New Jersey. It usually went something like this:

"If you break that pitcher, I'm gonna stab you and throw you off the porch!"

"If she yaks in my bathroom, I'm gonna stab you and throw you off the porch!"

"Use a coaster! If you leave a water mark on that table, I'm gonna stab you and throw you off the porch!"

And everybody laughed and the keg of Natural Light flowed outside on the porch and the only thing that got tossed over were about 9,000 cigarette butts, a few dozen red plastic cups, and the rare green bottle, shattered against rocks to startle half-naked boys and girls hooking up on the beach. *"Anybody busts another bottle and I'm gonna stab them and throw them off the porch!"*

Inside the house was like this: People played Vegetable Thumper, pounding the table screaming vegetable names, "Asparagus! Asparagus! Pea! Pea!" and so on, until someone couldn't say it anymore and had to finish a full lukewarm beer. At the kitchen counter was a game of Anchor Man and quarters plopped into a giant flower vase full of beer. First team to sink three quarters made the other one drink. Someone at the table named Game Girl would be yelling, "This game sucks! You don't drink enough! Let's play Circle of Death!" Another someone would decide it's a fine idea to pass around shots of tequila. In the living room, people watched the video jukebox and dialed the 1-900 number to request "Cycle Sluts from Hell," which only cost $2.50 a pop, but they would do it about a dozen times because it's funny.

"Is that Game Girl throwing up in the bathroom?"

"Probably."

People made runs. Runs at four a.m. to buy cheese dogs at Wawa. Runs to the boardwalk to see if we could get thrown off by the summer cops for not wearing any shoes — a violation of city ordinance. Runs over the bridge and into the next town simply to buy more beer — Ocean City calls itself "America's Greatest Family Resort" and the virtuous, Methodist town fathers make damn sure booze is unavailable.

In the morning, we'd make breakfast for Game Girl, who had passed out on the couch. We'd lend her a thick college sweatshirt. We'd drive her to work, where she served Italian water ice to people at the beach. "Later," she'd say.

The scene repeated itself. Monday. Tuesday. Wednesday. Thursday.

But not on Friday. No, definitely not on Friday.

That's because in "America's Greatest Family Resort," Fridays mean *parents are on their way*. Down the Shore they come. Quick, mop that bathroom! Air out the house! Your parents are driving at full speed on the Atlantic City Expressway this very minute! Moms and Dads trying to escape their muggy, suburban neighborhoods around Philadelphia, where they spend the week sweating in cars and cutting lawns and dream about eating blue crabs and mussels at sunset and caramel popcorn on the boardwalk. Moms and Dads who want their beach houses clean with cool ocean breezes and no bottle caps stuck in their garbage disposal.

Moms and Dads who don't want their beaches littered with broken glass or their trash cans filled with Milwaukee's Best or their liquor cabinets curiously absent of Chivas Regal. Then, for two days, all is family barbecues and mini-golf and feeding seagulls — until Sunday night when the parents all go back to the suburbs and their kids take over once again.

This is the weekly cycle: a compromise, almost a wink and nudge from Mom and Dad. And all the kids have to do is make sure nothing in the house is broken or damaged and no police come. Thus, the threat is invented — *If you trip over that couch one more time, I'm gonna stab you and throw you off the porch!* — to make sure your friends don't get out of hand. And that threat, of course, becomes a joke.

This is Ocean City and it's a beautiful way to pass the summer when you're 16 or 18 or maybe even 20 years old.

❂

But I want to tell you about a particular summer when I was 22 and had just graduated from college and was too old to be living at my family's house in Ocean City. Too old to be playing Vegetable Thumper and Anchor Man until 4 a.m. or driving 16-year-old girls to work at the Italian water ice stand or cleaning up the bathroom and kitchen every Friday morning. Yet that's exactly what I was doing.

I should have realized by then that the Jersey Shore is really just for high school and college kids. It hadn't yet dawned on me that most of the people I hung out with still drank on fake IDs and still figured a 12-pack for their night's drinking would "about do it." All of the people I knew took tickets at mini-golf or cut fruit salads and shucked corn at the produce market or sold fudge and salt water taffy or checked beachgoers to make sure they'd purchased beach badges. They would all be going back to school before Labor Day rolled around.

My job that summer was quite different. On those days when I dropped Game Girl off to scoop water ice, I drove to work at *The Press of Atlantic City* — where my job entailed writing stories for a daily newspaper that 100,000 people read and many accepted as the gospel truth. I was an intern, a cub reporter, and covered four other Shore towns — Wildwood, North Wildwood, West Wildwood, and Wildwood Crest — located on a five-mile island 30 minutes south of Ocean City. The four town names are irrelevant to anyone who doesn't live there and most people simply call the whole island Wildwood. Unless you happened to summer in

"America's Greatest Family Resort" like we did. In that case, you'd refer to Wildwood as "Childwood" or "Vilewood" and scrunch up your nose when speaking of it, as if you were holding a dirty diaper.

My friends laughed about my job over drinking games and called me "Scoop," especially those weekday evenings when I found myself working late, stuck in Childwood, a half-hour away from our nightly party.

✪

In a shop on the boardwalk in Wildwood — next to the place that pierces your eyebrow or tongue or nipple — hung a purple T-shirt that read: "Good Girls Go To Heaven, Bad Girls Go To Wildwood."

I noted this detail during my first week as a reporter for *The Press of Atlantic City* as I watched three high school girls in hot pink thong bikinis, hair lacquered to the sky with Aqua Net, cigarettes dangling, flash middle fingers to a group of hooting, tank-topped high school boys with Super Soaker squirt guns.

Bad girls go to Wildwood. A nugget of truth, I believed. It was obvious to see the bad girls come to town every weekend. And how did they get here? They caught rides with the bad boys, the ones you saw driving down from Philadelphia in electric blue bitchin' Camaros that nearly bottomed out because they were so laden with beer. And where did the bad boys and girls stay? They piled themselves 20 to a room in cheesy motels and rooming houses where they inevitably dumped the deck furniture in the pool and threw beer bottles at passing cars. They got in each others' faces in front of the video arcade and shouted, "What the fuck you lookin' at?" They urinated on buildings, in the street, under the boardwalk. Every Friday. Every Saturday. Every Sunday. No parents. No laws against parading around the boardwalk in thongs or bare feet. Bars stayed open until 5 a.m. and several seemed to serve anyone over the age of 14.

By Sunday, all the boys and girls were sunburnt and hung over. The boys sported new neon tank tops with slogans: "Zero to Horny in 2.5 Beers"; "Ten Reasons Why Beer Is Better than a Woman"; "People say all I do is sit around all day and drink beer. Sometimes not true. I throw up." Over their bikinis, the girls wore halter tops with computer scanned photos of their best friend or airbrushed portraits of Jon Bon Jovi.

On this particular Sunday afternoon I was on assignment, following around the tank-topped boys with Super Soakers. This was the summer Super Soakers became a national crisis. Too many kids had drenched too many adults. Kids were shooting Super Soakers into the windows of cars. And some really nasty kids were filling them with gasoline and Clorox and acid. People believed the toy guns were breaking down America's moral fiber — barbarians were at civilization's gate and they were armed with Super Soakers. Wildwood had threatened to ban the guns on the boardwalk and I had to write a story.

After the boys got tired of squirting the bikini-clad girls, they turned their attention to spraying unsuspecting tourists riding the boardwalk tram cars. Old men and women shouted "The federal government, they ought to ban those things!" The teenaged tram-car attendants just chuckled.

"Watch the tram car, please," intoned the mechanical tram voice.

"This is all part of summer," said one of the boys. "I don't think this is dangerous. It's just fun."

The editors at *The Press* liked this quote. I had access to young people in a way the older reporters didn't, they said. They let me write more Wildwood news. I wrote about a bungee jumping accident at an amusement pier. A woman had broken her neck because the operators fitted her with the wrong size cord and it didn't snap back in time. I covered another accident at another bungee jumping site. The crane had toppled over the pier and crashed onto the beach. The editors let me do investigative news: two dozen syringes washed up on the beach and I had the story. Soon, they let me do features. I wrote about the abundance of fake palm trees growing around Wildwood's many 1950s Tahitian-style hotels, ones with names like The Rio, The Aquarius, The LuFran, and The Kona Kai. "If you built a hotel in Wildwood, you had to have a palm tree," I was told.

But all of these stories were just a preamble to what was supposed to be my main focus while covering a summer in Wildwood.

Senior Week was coming, the editors said. Graduates from Philadelphia high schools would be flocking to Wildwood by the hundreds. That meant an entire week, not just a weekend, of bad boys and girls. There's always action during Senior Week, the editors said, and nearly licked their lips.

Local residents said Senior Week was actually two weeks in June and spoke of it as if Armageddon were near.

✪

Meanwhile, the parties in Ocean City continued. We got bored of our old drinking games and started to play new ones. Chase quarters: "Okay, you have to sink your quarter in the glass before the other people catch you or you have to drink." Dice games: "If you roll seven, 11, or doubles, you make somebody drink." Categories: "Everybody has to come up with a "Dukes of Hazard" episode or they have to drink." Game Girl was in her glory.

A guy called Blinky nearly knocked over a shell lamp. "If you break my mother's lamp…"

"I'm gonna stab you and throw you off the porch!" everyone yelled.

"We should all go down to Wildwood one of these nights," someone said. "I heard it's so easy to get into bars. You don't even need an ID."

"Senior Week's coming to Wildwood this week," I said. "The editors keep telling me there's sure to be a big story."

That cracked everyone up. "Scoop!" they shouted. "I can see the headline, 'Kid Drinks Beer in Wildwood.'"

A pony-tailed girl said kids at her high school did Senior Week in Childwood every year. "But the news makes like such a big deal out of the whole thing," she said. "It's just kids drinking and having a good time."

When we ran out of beer, everyone was too tired or drunk to drive for more. They drifted outside, onto the deck in the cool ocean air. Several of us quietly watched the moon.

The pony-tailed girl and I decided to see the sun rise. "God," she said. "I've got to be at work by noon tomorrow and I have to work all weekend long." She was employed by a boardwalk shop that sold sand pails and shovels and beach chairs and overpriced sweatshirts and T-shirts that read, of course, "America's Greatest Family Resort."

I fell asleep in a chair before dawn and when I awoke she was gone.

✪

Senior Week erupted and Wildwood's residents coined a new term — "animal house." That's what they called the apartments and motels that specialized in stuffing a dozen graduating seniors into rooms meant for four. People shouted about shutting down animal houses, passing laws against animal house landlords, and sending police into animal houses "like the gestapo" to clear out rowdy teenagers.

Nowhere were the animal houses worse than on Wildwood's East Maple Avenue. Residents on that block were sandwiched between the Maple Leaf Motel and Fitzpatrick's Apartments, both teeming with high school kids. On trash day at those places, you could count more than 20 huge cans full of beer bottles and beer boxes and beer balls, and that was just what wasn't lying smashed in the street. During the second and third weeks in June, more than 70 boys and girls had been arrested on East Maple Avenue for everything from underage drinking, public indecency, and public urination to assaults, with or without a weapon. Police were investigating several rapes. This, I guessed, was the story my editors were drooling over. So I met with a group of people who lived on East Maple Avenue, which mostly consisted of old, weather-beaten vacation homes standing about a block from the boardwalk.

Uncle Lou, the owner of Uncle Lou's Pancake House on the corner, ranted for an hour. For two weeks, high school kids had been heaving bottles from the balcony of the Maple Leaf Motel into his restaurant parking lot, aiming at windshields. Some of the kids had even tried to pee onto his customers' heads. Uncle Lou had threatened the kids with police and then physical harm, and they'd laughed at him. Now, he'd had to close down his parking lot. "I may as well close the restaurant, too!" he shouted.

An old woman named Adele said the kids had already chucked her patio furniture into the street. "Animals! What can you do?" she asked. Adele counted 300 kids milling around on some nights, some armed with baseball bats, and she couldn't sleep. She was afraid just to walk to the post office in the middle of the afternoon. Worse, poor Adele had been trying to sell her home and get off this godforsaken block and she'd even found a potential buyer. But when the buyer came to inspect the house, a couch — thrown from the Maple Leaf Motel — crashed onto the sidewalk a few yards away. Not surprisingly, the buyer lost interest.

A man named Matty, who rented vacation condominiums on East Maple, said he'd had two "nice, respectable families" pack up and leave because so many drunk kids had been running through his property, fighting, relieving themselves in his bushes. "They've chased all the families out of Wildwood," he said.

I wrote all this down and bit my tongue hard at times to keep from chuckling as I pictured the kids' exploits. "You're a young guy," Uncle Lou said to me. "Is this something you would have done? Of course not! Know why? 'Cause you were raised right!" I nodded and kept scribbling in my notebook.

The guy who owned the Maple Leaf Motel just laughed when I interviewed him. "I'm the one who started Senior Week 40 years ago!" he belched. "These kids drop more money in one week than the adults do in one month."

I wrote my story. ANGER MOUNTS OVER SENIOR-WEEK WILDNESS.

Good stuff, strong reporting, the editors said, but we want more from the kids' perspective. *We want more.*

"What else is there to say?" I asked. "You let a bunch of kids run free and they're going to get drunk and do crazy things."

"Just watch," they said. "Something always happens during Senior Week."

❂

Stabbings happened. Two high school seniors stabbed in North Wildwood, one right in the butt. Neither died, only wounded. Suddenly distinctions between the island's towns were made. Wildwood police — and businessmen — were careful to point out that the stabbings happened on the streets of *North* Wildwood. Kids on East Maple Avenue might be bad, they implied, but at least nobody got stabbed. Just a few rotten eggs giving everybody else a bad name, said the town fathers in North Wildwood.

Then, one sunny Wednesday morning, *The Press* received an anonymous phone call about a murder: High school kids; North Wildwood; late last night. The police reporter was away on vacation, and after some deliberation, it was decided the story would be mine. Do a good job, I was told, and this could end up on page A1.

The details went like this: A group of kids, including 18-year-old Stephen Freeman, were partying in a house they'd rented on East 17th Street for Senior Week — they were celebrating their graduation from a suburban Philadelphia high school. During the night, another group of boys from the same high school, including a 17-year-old named Michael Amoroso, crashed the party and a big fight began. Several of the boys knocked Freeman to the floor. Freeman then rose, grabbed a steak knife, and stabbed Amoroso in the chest. The boy died two hours later. Beyond that, all the police would say was there had already been friction between the two groups back home.

I ran red lights to get to the crime scene, but the police had already done their business by the time I arrived. East 17th Street was quiet. Unlike East Maple Avenue, the street had no motels with porches full of drunk, screaming kids. There were no beer bottles strewn down the sidewalks. Instead, this North Wildwood neighborhood — one I'd never visited before as a reporter — consisted of rows of duplexes, most with lawns and driveways and barbecues on the patios. Some of the duplexes had been rented out to high school seniors, others occupied by families.

I'd never covered a murder before and didn't know the first thing to do, so I just sort of wandered across the street, looking for anyone who might add what my editors would call "color." Through a sliding glass door I saw four boys, maybe 16 or 17, sitting around tossing quarters into a pitcher of beer. I tapped the window and asked if they'd talk to me. Sure, the boys said, chugging their beers before opening the door.

Yeah, they were down in North Wildwood for Senior Week, too. Yeah, they'd seen the commotion across the street last night. Nah, they didn't really know any of the kids involved. Yeah, some kids just tried to crash the party and a fight started. It pretty much happened like that. Why? Who knew why? "It's crazy," said one of them. "I'm down here to have fun. I don't want to stab anyone."

At the house where the stabbing took place, I could see a group of four sunburnt kids packing up a car. I ran over to them, too excitedly, and began asking questions. Two of them scurried inside, but one boy stood by his car and answered in whispers. They'd been evicted by their landlord, he said. Their parents called and wanted them home immediately. A classmate had been killed. Another classmate had done the killing. "I don't know what else you want to know," he said.

An 18-year-old girl from a different high school would speak with me further. She'd been renting the house next door. She'd met Stephen Freeman earlier in the week and thought he was loud. She said the fight had started on the porch of her duplex and moved next door. She said she was shocked by the whole thing. "Are you really a reporter?" she asked. "You look so young."

"Yeah, I'm a real reporter. I just graduated from college," I said, and continued questioning. "Senior Week is supposed be a celebration, a vacation. What does it feel like for the week to end like this?"

The boy and girl glared and I believed they would unleash all their grief and anger upon me. But they were unable, and instead I watched the four saddest eyes I have ever seen. The kids struggled for a moment to say something about what had happened. "Please," said the girl, and tears welled up. "Would you please not quote me? Please?"

After observing Stephen Freeman bawl uncontrollably at his arraignment later that day, I took all my facts and my quotes and my color back to the office and wrote: *Senior Week has ended in tragedy...*

I did a little dance later when I got the call from my editors telling me the story would appear the next morning on A1, right below the main story — the one about Charles Barkley, my favorite basketball player, being traded away from Philadelphia to Phoenix.

Yet, even in all the excitement of my first A1 story, the beginning of my entire career, I could not get out of my head the eyes of the boy and the girl I did not quote. How could you ever quote such sadness? Instead, other people got the last word on Senior Week, such as one Wildwood shopkeeper who summed up the stabbing this way: "It's just a wonder it didn't happen before this."

❂

I'd like to tell you I came to a great epiphany that day. That I drove home to Ocean City and didn't go out to a party. That I didn't get involved in a three-hour game of chase quarters. That I didn't laugh out loud when the late news came on and someone shouted at the television, "He stabbed him, but at least he didn't throw him off the porch!" Or that I finally decided I had to leave the Shore.

But nothing like that happened. I would end up getting hired full time at *The Press* and stay around for two more summers. One of my best stories would be a feature on fake IDs in which I interviewed all of my friends. Wildwood would never pass any new laws against animal houses and Senior Week would go on as usual. Stephen Freeman would be acquitted two years later, having proved the stabbing was in self-defense. The Maple Leaf Motel would be victimized by a suspicious, fatal fire. Two 16-year-olds in Wildwood would light a man on fire one evening as he slept on his front porch — and people would blame it on "Beavis and Butt-head."

The night of my big A1 story, Game Girl and I clinked quarters into glasses and downed beer after beer. We laughed at the pony-tailed girl who smoked cigarettes and cried because she wasn't as beautiful as her best friend from home. "You think you'd let your kids live alone at the Shore?" Game Girl asked me.

"I guess so," I said. "Drink your beer."

Breakfast at the Wildwood Motel, 1996

by Peter E. Murphy

Last night when I entered this city without reservations
I got lost in its wailing as fire trucks crawled
along Ocean Avenue for the Halloween Parade.
I was caught between engines and couldn't turn
as children jumped in the street to gather candy
tossed by goblins driving the huge rigs.
At a convenience store, Satan the clerk gave me
directions and I followed them. It's always open,
he said, even when no one is there.

I sit in a booth by a window. My dirty plate screams
of gluttony — smeared yolks, crust of rye toast,
home fries, resonance of ketchup.
A blind man taps into the coffee shop, sits
at the counter. Waitress sings, Good Morning, Doctor!
Brings him a horseradish omelette.

Rubber bats float from a slow ceiling fan.

In the window, Santa's elves retooled with axes

hack at the head of a Barbie doll. On the soundtrack —

Guns 'N' Roses warble "O Holy Night."

The blind man stabs his fork into his breakfast.

The waitress returns with coffee.

Outside the ocean churns.

Small ghosts dressed like children

knock at the motel door, beg for sweets, beg for someone

to let them in, each of them opening and closing his hands.

from Pride

by William Wharton

We ate the dinner Mom cooked on our little cooker off dishes Mom had brought with us. The salt-water taffy was delicious. My favorite kinds were the one with peanut butter inside and one that tasted like strawberries. The kind Dad likes were too strong, like his horseradish. But Laurel liked those kind, the same as Dad, so it worked out fine. I don't remember ever having had salt-water taffy before.

Mom washed the dishes in the little hand sink while Laurel and I got to dry them. It was like playing house. Then, afterward, I crawled under my bed and played with Cannibal. We played at fighting, that's the game she likes most. I try to fool her and reach in so I can touch her nose without her being able to hit my hand with her paw. She doesn't scratch me any more except by accident. I saved part of my hot dog and gave it to her, and I think under that bed was the first time I ever heard her try to purr. It sounded almost like something inside was broken and couldn't get started. She purred the way Mickey Saunders talks, and he stutters so he can hardly answer any questions in class. I had my feet sticking out from under the bed and then felt Dad's hand on my ankle. He softly tugged me out.

"What do you think of that, Dickie? How'd you like going back up on the boardwalk to see what's going on this late in the evening?"

I reach out fast, catch Cannibal, and put her in her box. I squiggle out from under the bed till I can look up at Dad. He's stretched out on the bed on his stomach with his head hanging down so he looks upside down to me looking up.

"Gee, Dad. That sounds great!"

I look around and Mom and Laurel are already in their sweaters and standing at the door. I scramble to my feet with Cannibal under my arm as Dad gets off the other side of the bed and swings his coat over his shoulder. I think my dad carries a coat jacket that way — one finger hooked under the neck part through the little loop for hanging a coat, that coat hanging down his back — more than he ever wears it. I think he only carries it along in case he might get cold, but he never seems to. My dad's hands and feet are always warm. Mom says that's what makes him one of the nicest people in the world to sleep with.

I pull on my sweater, push down my hair, turn up the sleeves and the waist part.

"Is it all right if I take Cannibal along? I want her to see that lion again."

Dad puts his hand on my shoulder, the hand he isn't using to hold his coat.

The other thing is my dad never wears a hat. He has curly, dark hair, really wavy not curls, and he hardly ever has to comb it. If I could have hair like that I'd never wear a hat either.

"Sure, Dickie. But maybe the lion will be asleep now or they'll be using him in that Wall of Death act."

"That's O.K. She'll love to see the lights and the merry-go-round."

So we start off. It isn't cold at all. It was much colder in Stonehurst Hills when we left, really beginning to feel like Halloween coming. But here it's warm. The air feels full of water, soft, but it's warm.

The first thing Dad does is buy more salt-water taffy. We know now what we like so he gets some of everybody's favorites. Mom is holding on to Dad's arm and leaning into him. They look like some of the high-school kids getting off the school bus. It's nice to see them that way; maybe they're that way a lot but I've never noticed it before. Dad's always working or tired and Mom's so worried and busy with the house they don't have much time just to be people.

We pass the merry-go-round and show them the animals we were riding on. It's more crowded now, with someone on almost all the outside animals. We watch and they only get about fifteen times around; I think we must have gone around thirty or more times.

"Do you kids want to take another turn?"

I look at Laurel and she shakes her head no, points down the boardwalk. We smile at each other. "Gee, Dad. There's another merry-go-round farther down the boardwalk, one we haven't tried yet. Could we go on that one?"

"Sure, kids, whatever you say."

We walk along some more. There are good smells. There's all the smells of the places selling candy, popcorn, hot dogs, salt-water taffy; but there's more: the smell of ocean, of sand and wood in the boardwalk. It all blends together.

We're getting near the Wall of Death when I begin hearing the motorcycles warming up, and then there's actually a roar from the lion. I look over at Dad. He runs his hand through my hair.

"I must say, Dickie, that sounds pretty impressive. We'll have to take a look at that, all right."

We start hurrying and there's a crowd around the little stage. By the time we get there, the older man is on his motorcycle, and he's standing up on the seat with his hands outstretched, balancing. The younger one is sitting back on his bike cleaning his teeth with his little fingernail. The lady is still talking about "the most amazing act in show business." Mom doesn't want us getting too close; she's afraid the man will fall, or that motorcycle will just go flying out into the audience; but we get up close anyway. I can tell Dad likes it as much as we do.

But more than anything I want to go over to visit the lion again. When the motorcycles roar, he roars back. He roars then growls and coughs. They have a light in the back of his cage so you can see him and he's pacing back and forth as if he's nervous. I'd sure be nervous if anybody put me in a motorcycle sidecar and hung me on the side of a wall like in those pictures.

It turns out the Wall of Death is the big round thing behind the lion cage and this little stage. It looks like the gas tank down at Long Lane and Marshall Road, only not as big, and it's made out of wood. There's a staircase like a fire escape up the side and people who buy tickets from the lady with the microphone walk up there. We can see others up at the top walking around a little platform, where I guess they can see right down in.

I take Dad's hand and pull him over to see the lion while he's still out there. They're pushing the motorcycles back down the ramp and inside now. The lady stays out, selling tickets. Pretty soon, I guess, the lion will be gone inside.

We all go over and stand in front of the lion's cage. Mom holds on to Dad with one arm and on to Laurel's hand with the other. I open Cannibal's cage a little bit so she can see, the same as last time, and she does the same thing, just sticks the top of her head out, her eyes peering over the edge of the box. That lion, pacing back and forth, is even more scary than he was sitting down. I never knew a lion was so long, that its tail was so thick. Dad's leaning forward looking hard.

"I think that poor creature's practically starving, Dickie. See his ribs and look how the skin's hanging under his stomach. I'll bet he needs about ten pounds of meat a day and these people probably don't make enough money to feed him properly."

I look and see Dad's right, the lion is hungry. I wonder if he knows we'd be good to eat.

Dad backs off a step, looks at the board with all the pictures, at the lady alone, nobody buying any more tickets. "Well, who wants to go in and see this with me? I know twenty-five cents is a lot of money, but this looks like something special, the kind of thing we'll remember all our lives."

"Oh no, Dick! You aren't really going up there and watch them do this, are you? Somebody's liable to get killed."

"Oh, come on, Laura. They've been doing it all summer long and nobody's gotten killed. They know what they're doing, and I'll bet it's a great act. Besides, a little money from us might help fill that poor lion's stomach some."

It turns out I'm the only one who will go with him. I think for a minute Laurel wants to go, too, but then she decides to stay and keep Mom company. I leave Cannibal in her cage with the top closed and hand it to Laurel. Dad just catches the lady with the tickets before she goes inside. He gives her the fifty cents.

"Hurry up, mister. They're about to begin the show."

Inside we can hear the motorcycles being started. We take the tickets and dash up the stairs. There's plenty of space up top when we go around to the other side.

I don't know what I expected but I'm really surprised when I look over the edge down into the Wall of Death.

There are lights over the top hanging down and it's all bright in the bottom. We look right straight down on two motorcycles. The men are on them but only one has his motor running. The sides of the Wall of Death are black with splintered boards and skid marks from tires and what I guess is black from the motors. In a strange way, there's something about this "Wall of Death" reminds me of our alley, or maybe it's the garages with the deep spots of oil from drippings out of cars. It smells something like a garage, too, damp and the smell of motors. The smell of the car gas Mr. Harding killed himself with, the smell of old wood from the porches, a slight smell of rotting garbage, too, and the smell of the lion is almost like alley-cat smell.

Just as we get settled against the wall, leaning over, one motorcycle starts off running along the bottom in a circle fast, then up the side of the wall, going faster and faster till it's right out sideways, going around the inside of the round wall, making everything rattle. Sometimes he comes so close to the top edge where we are I can't stop myself from ducking. I look over and Dad's ducking, too.

He leans close to me and cups his hand around my ear.

"Now, this is what I really call *something*."

He smiles and we both stick our heads up carefully. The man riding the motorcycle is standing on the seat now, the way he did outside, but he keeps hold of the handlebars. If he lets go, then he'd sure as the devil fall all the way to the bottom and be killed. It's the young one with the slicked-back hair who's up on the wall. His hair just stays in place without getting mussed up, even though he's going fast, so he must have some Wildroot Cream Oil or Vaseline, or some other kind of stickum on it. Mom tries to make my cowlick stay down for church sometimes by combing my hair with stuff, and when it drips off the comb into my eyes, it stings and stinks. She always used to do this when I served mass but I don't have to worry about that any more. When you have stuff like that in your hair and it dries, then your hair feels like broom bristles, not like hair at all. It feels as if, when you bend it, it'll break.

Now he's up on the handlebars bending at the waist, with his feet sticking out in space. He's doing a handstand on those motorcycle handlebars sideways! I can't figure what keeps any of it up on the wall. I keep looking but I don't *see* any tracks and he goes all different angles so there *can't* be that many tracks.

Now, the older man, thicker, slower-moving, takes off his cap, and I can see he only has thin blond hair like fuzz on his head. He puts on a helmet and climbs onto his motorcycle, then starts it with a hard kick. The young one is sitting back on his motorcycle as he rides and twice goes right across the bottom and up the other side; you'd swear he'd fly clear off that wall; then he turns and gets going fast as the wind again. He's shouting down at the older man. We can just hear him as he shouts over the sound of the two motorcycles.

"Come on, old man! I'll race you twenty-five turns."

The other motorcycle comes up the wall fast, almost to the top, then they start crossing back and forth over and under each other. The whole wall is practically rocking now, so I'm afraid the boards will break or maybe the wall will just lift up and turn over. The little walkway we're on is shaking and wobbling.

They're racing around those walls and everybody starts counting as they go around: nine, ten, eleven, twelve. Dad and I are counting, too. Everybody's doing it, and it gets louder and louder. At first the older guy gets a good lead so he's almost half a length around the wall in front of the young one. Then gradually as we get close to twenty the young guy starts gaining. Then, just as we're counting the twenty-fifth turn, he passes the older guy and goes up into his handstand, crossing his legs in the air. He comes down and sits straight on the seat with his hands out and goes around a few extra times, no-handed, while the older guy goes down to the bottom and parks his motorcycle. The young one comes down and rolls his bike outside through the door. Everybody applauds. The lady from the stage comes in with a megaphone in her hand and the two men push in a sidecar. They start attaching it to the older guy's motorcycle.

The lady is shouting up at us through the megaphone. She turns around as she talks so we can all hear:

"Now, ladies and gentlemen. You are about to see the only full-grown male lion who can ride on the Wall of Death in a sidecar. Let me introduce Satan, the Dare-Devil Lion!"

She points over at the side with her hand and I see another door, one I didn't even notice before. It opens and there's a barred door that the older guy pulls up.

He has a whip in his hand and snaps it a few times on the floor, making it really pop. The lady takes a jacket and helmet from the young one and puts them on. It looks as if *she's* going to ride that lion around the wall because she climbs on the motorcycle.

She only has those bare legs, or maybe she has silk stockings on, I can't really tell. With a lion it wouldn't make much difference, anyway.

Then we hear the lion roar and he comes to the opening of the door. He stands there with his paws on the edge and looks up at all of us around the edges on top. It's really scary seeing a lion without any bars between you and him. He looks up at the light, then at the older guy with the whip. The lion starts walking toward him.

He keeps popping the whip but doesn't pop it anywhere near the lion. The lion moves over toward the sidecar and stops. The other guy, the young one, who won the race, is standing against the wall, away from the door, holding a long pole with a pointed metal sticker on the end of it. He looks as scared of that lion as I am. I know I wouldn't like to be down in a wooden hole with a lion and nothing between me and those teeth but a long stick.

The older guy keeps snapping his whip and gradually gets the lion to climb into the sidecar and sit. That whole sidecar sags with the lion in it, he's so heavy. Then, the older guy runs his hands through the mane of the lion while the lion actually rubs his big hairy head against the man's shoulder. The older guy locks a bar across the lion's front legs, over his paws, and straps him in. The lady is sitting on the motorcycle seat staring straight ahead, not looking at the lion at all. Then the older one, with the whip, comes around and kicks the starter on the motorcycle so it coughs, then roars, ready to start.

He steps back and gives a snap of his whip in the air but I think that's just for show. The lady in the purple, shining costume waves her hand, the one away from the lion, up at all of us on the top, half smiles, then starts the motorcycle going around in circles. The man with the whip stays in the center of the pit, turning around as the motorcycle gains speed then starts going up the side of the wall. It really looks as if she'll never get going fast. That lion must weigh hundreds of pounds, at least twice as much as a human being.

Then she's really up on the wall. The whole wooden bowl begins rocking as she gets higher and higher. I manage to keep my head up once when the motorcycle goes by just below us and the lion isn't more than five feet from my face; there's no bars or anything. I look at Dad and he's looking as scared as I am. It's hard to believe and I'm having an awful time keeping my head up, looking; after all, we did pay twenty-five cents. At least I ought to *look*. I'm beginning to wish she'd stop and go back down. It's not like on the merry-go-round at all when I wanted it to keep going. I'm so scared something bad will happen I want it to stop.

Finally, she begins to slow down and goes rolling onto the bottom of the pit. She sits still on the motorcycle while the older guy goes over to the lion and unhooks him. The younger one has moved toward the door opening into the lion cage; he's pulled back the wooden cover and pushed up the bars. He stands there with his pointed stick like a harpoon, still looking scared and trying not to let on.

The older guy helps the lion out of the motorcycle and holds him by the mane beside him. He doesn't seem afraid of that lion at all. But the lady gets off the motorcycle on the other side from the lion, takes off her helmet, and holds her hands up in the air, smiling a fake kind of smile and sneaking looks over at the older guy and the lion. She stays like that with her arms up and perfectly still while the older guy leads the lion toward the door out of the pit. Everybody is applauding. The lion gives a growl at the young one with the pointed stick but goes into the door without any trouble. Then, quickly, the young guy comes over when the lion's already halfway through the door and gives him a good hard punch with the pointed end of his stick. This makes the lion really roar, but he hurries through the tunnel and out to his cage.

I look at Dad. For some crazy reason I feel almost as if I'm going to cry and I don't really know why. It's probably all the excitement. Dad's face looks mad.

"There's no excuse for treating a lion that way, Dickie. He didn't have to poke him; he's just goading the poor thing. I really don't think that lion would hurt a soul; he's tame as a kitten. Cannibal's meaner than that lion by a long shot."

He puts his arm over my shoulder and we start toward the stairs with all the other people.

Mom and Laurel are waiting for us outside. Laurel has bought a little statue of Happy, one of the Seven Dwarfs. It cost twenty cents. I guess it's to help balance out the twenty-five cents I got to spend watching the Wall of Death.

Dad and I go over to look at the lion again. He's already settled down and is just sitting there staring out at the crowd as if all those things we saw inside hadn't happened at all.

Laurel is between Dad and Mom. She has hold of their hands.

"Gee, he looks so nice but he must be lonesome all by himself. Doesn't he have any family?"

Dad leans down and gives her a kiss on the top of her head between her braids.

"A lion's family is called its pride, Laurie. This lion was probably born in captivity; he's never had any family, any pride."

I turn away from watching the lion. I know he's looking right at Cannibal, and I'm sure he doesn't want to eat her or anything, he just wants to be friends.

"Is that pride like one of the capital sins, Dad? Can lions commit sins too, like people?"

"There's all kinds of pride, Dickie. There's real pride, like being proud of good work, like when we do a good job building a porch. Then there's false pride like when you think you're better than somebody else for no good reason; that's the sin one. Then there's the lion's pride, his family."

"Gee! I like the idea of a family being a pride. Let's call our family a pride. I'd be proud of our pride and I bet it wouldn't be a sin at all."

"Probably just the opposite of sin, Dickie. I hope we can always be proud of our family."

Now Laurel pulls on Dad's hand again.

"What's the opposite of a sin, Daddy? Even in first grade Sister Carmelina talks a lot about sins to us but nobody's ever said anything about the opposite of sin. Opposite means the other side, doesn't it?"

Dad looks over at Mom. He has a big smile on his face just at the edge of a laugh, but he knows Laurel's serious. Laurel's much more serious than I can ever be.

Mom straightens Laurel's collar over the top of her sweater.

"Laurel, don't you worry your head about sin. I think the opposite of sin is good deeds or maybe it's 'grace.' You can ask Sister Carmelina when we get back home."

from *Pride*

She looks at Dad again and they don't smile. I think the idea of going back isn't something they're looking forward to either.

Really, we should just up and move here to Wildwood. Imagine living all your life next to an ocean. It'd make your life seem important. At home, there's nothing but streets, pavements, houses, and lawns; only the alleys are any fun. There's nothing big and natural. I've never even seen a mountain in my life except pictures in books. It's terrible not seeing lakes or mountains or oceans. The only thing big I ever get to see is the sky and that's big but it's not enough; you can't touch it. I grab hold of Dad's other hand. I have Cannibal in one hand and Dad's hand in the other. He gives my hand a little squeeze.

"Daddy, do you mean that lion there never lived in a jungle with other lions; he's always been by himself in a cage like Cannibal in her box?"

"I don't know, but probably. Lions don't live in jungles anyway, Dickie; they live on grassy plains called savannahs."

"In *Tarzan* they live in the jungle."

"That's only in movies. I think tigers live in jungles but not lions. I could be wrong, though."

A Tale of Two
Hawkwatchers

by Pete Dunne

1931

E ric woke to the sound of his mother shaking ashes from the stove, just as
he had the morning before, and the morning before that, and every
morning that he could remember in his sixteen years. He dressed
hurriedly in the dark, partly because of the cold, partly because of the excitement.
There would be a flight at Cape May Point, today. Hawks would be skimming the
treetops: hundreds of them, maybe thousands. Normally he worked Saturdays but
he had asked for and been given the day off.

It had surprised him a little that he had gotten off so easily. The foreman at the
fish docks had cussed some and gone on for a time about how much tougher life
was when *he* was a boy. But he relented anyway, and sooner than usual. It was a
thing Eric had noticed. People seemed to go a little out of the way for him since
the *Laura B.* went down.

Hugging the wall and avoiding the boards that creaked so as not to wake his
brothers, Eric negotiated the stairs with practiced steps. A large plate of hotcakes
awaited him in the kitchen. He attacked it singlemindedly and downed scalding
coffee as fast as the limits of pain would allow.

His mother watched him over her own cup with soft gray eyes that never betrayed anger or kindness. He'd inherited those eyes — but the unkempt mane of red hair and the freckles that overran both cheeks and formed a bridge over his nose had been a gift from his father.

"Dress warm," she said. "The wind'll drive the cold into you."

Eric nodded in affirmation, mouth full of coffee.

"I packed a sandwich. It's near yer boots."

Eric's mumbled thanks echoed hollow in the mug.

The silver bell on the gun rack door rang sharp and cold in the dark despite his cautious effort. His father had put it there when Eric was a toddler — a precaution against the curious hands of children. Eric reached reflexively for his gun but hesitated as his fingers touched the stock.

It was a fine old gun, a Parker double. The bluing on the barrel had long since given way to rust. The stock was cracked near the grip from some forgotten mishap. An earlier owner had wound brass wire around it for support. Eric had bought this gun with his first earnings at Snow's fish dock and he had carried it for three seasons. But now his hand strayed down the line of metal and wood that glowed softly in the half-light cast by the kitchen door, past the carbine his grandfather had carried through the "war of rebellion," past the Springfield his father had carried through France, past other guns of lesser lineage. It came to rest upon the twelve-gauge.

It was a beautiful gun, his father's prize. Five shots, fast as a man could squeeze the trigger, chambered for standard loads or three-inch magnums, a lasting tribute to the genius of its inventor, John M. Browning.

He had fired it once before, and poorly. The stock was too long, cut to a bigger man's frame. But that was two years ago. He had the frame, now — though the man that was to fill it was still several years away.

Eric lifted the gun free, felt the supreme lightness, caught the sweet smell of solvent that still clung to the barrel a year after it had last been cleaned. His mother watched from the kitchen door. Her eyes betrayed nothing.

The stars glittered like shards of ice as Eric turned down Washington Street onto Sunset Boulevard. The wind tore the frosted breath from his lips. It was a

three-mile walk to the end of Sunset where the line of gunners would be waiting.
The hawks would begin to fly at first light and would move south along the length
of the peninsula. They would turn west when confronted by the open bay and
then, like baitfish in a weir, curl north along the shore, following the contours of
the bay. The birds would be low now, and hugging the treetops, their progress
slowed by gusty headwinds. And they wouldn't be able to see the line of gunners
waiting for them on the concrete road that cut across their path until they broke
into the open — until it was too late.

The guns would roar, shots coming so fast that it sounded like one long, endless
roll of thunder. His grandfather used to liken it to the Union artillery at Vicksburg.
And the hawks would fall to the roadway. Some would tumble like a football, end
over end. Some would arch like a catcher's throw to second. A lot of birds that
weren't hit clean would fly weakly into the trees on the gunners' side of the road.
They would starve eventually, or the foxes would get them.

By afternoon on a good day, there would be a large pile of hawks at the end of
Sunset Boulevard. The local papers would take pictures. The gunners would stand
behind mounds of fresh-shot birds and smile for the camera. Cars driving down
the road had to shift to low gears to keep from skidding on the spent shells
scattered on the roadbed. It was really something.

There were some gunners who said that *all* hawks were bad and should be shot.
But Eric knew better. He liked birds, studied them whenever he could, and read
about them in books from his grandfather's library. He particularly liked the
yellow-eyed fish hawk that nested so commonly on the Cape. He loved to watch
the adults and newly fledged young mounting higher and higher over summer
marshes, and he loved to watch them plunge into the bay for weakfish (even
though it made the commercial fishermen mad).

But the blue darter was a bad hawk. There was no denying that. They killed
songbirds. They were so quick that the little birds didn't have a chance. He had
learned from the big, two-volume book about New York birds that the scientific
name *Accipiter velox* meant "swift hawk," and that when a Sharp-shinned caught a
bird it would take it to a butchering block. He remembered that Eaton, the
orthinologist, said that you could always tell a butcher block when you found one
because of all the feathers around it. He had never seen a butcher block but he had
often seen rings of feathers scattered in the woods of Cape May where Sharp-

shinneds had eaten a kill. Yes, they were "bloodthirsty little pirates," just like Eaton and the other orthinologists said — and "should be destroyed" (Eaton said that, too).

But that didn't go for all hawks. Only Sharp-shinneds and Cooper's and Goshawks and Duck Hawks were destructive and not protected now. Killing Sharp-shinneds saved lots of songbirds, but there was another good reason to shoot them. Eric could get a nickel apiece for birds that weren't shot up too bad. Sharp-shinneds made pretty good eating. They tasted like chicken. Shells cost two for a nickel, so if he was shooting good, he could make over two cents for each bird he killed.

Of course, misses cut into the profit margin.

The street began to dance in the headlights thrown from a car coming up from behind. The car slowed as it drew abreast and a man's voice inquired: "Going to the shoot, son?"

"Yes, sir," Eric replied recognizing the voice as belonging to the editor of a local paper.

"Well, hop in then. Hand your gun to Phil there in the back."

Eric complied and noted with equal measures of pride and embarassment Phil's admiring appraisal of his gun and the care with which he set it next to the other guns propped in the back seat.

"Nice looking shotgun you have there," he said, addressing Eric. "Any chicken hawk with a sense of honor should take one look at it and just surrender to you."

"Well, I guess you better go and get one for yourself, then, Phil," chided the driver. "Way you shoot, the only way you're going to put a bird in your game bag is if he flies in there himself."

"Ha, ha, ha. Ha, ha, ha."

"Why Frank, I thought that's why you brought me along. You were goin' to drive and I was goin' to shoot 'cause you drive a darn sight better than you shoot and you can't drive worth a damn."

"Ha, ha, ha. Ha, ha, ha."

Gun talk. Men talk. It was a thing that Eric had grown up with. It was all part of fall at Cape May.

The headlights showed other cars and twenty or so men and boys at the end of Sunset, jacketed figures cloaked in anonymity by distance and darkness that fell away as the car drew near. Most were local people Eric knew or recognized. Here and there red plaid jackets marked the "sports" down from Philadelphia. The shoots were getting popular with the sporting crowd.

Light was beginning to gather the sky over the lighthouse. The stars had lost their sparkle. The clump of men drew gradually into a line flanking the road. Eric took a place at one end. He reached into his pocket, removed a shell, and pushed it through the floor plate of the Magnum 5. The mechanism snatched it impatiently from his fingers and guided it smoothly into the chamber, ready to fire. The gliding sound of metal on metal rang softly in the air. Four more shells followed the first.

Along the line, men moved their feet restlessly, but whether from nervousness or cold it was hard to say. Their eyes were turned toward the trees flanking the far side of the road, their faces drained of life by the gray light of morning.

For the first time since his arrival, Eric noticed the figure standing off to one side. He didn't have a gun, just binoculars, but he was watching the tree line just as intently as the line of gunners. Phil noticed Eric's interest and hastened over to explain.

"He's a warden hired by the *Aw-doo-bon* Society — name of Saunders. He's makin' sure nobody guns any *ill-legal* hawks. He's even trying to count all the hawks that go by. Can you imagine anyone tryin' to count all these hawks?"

Eric studied the man with heightened interest. He'd never met anyone from the Audubon Society before. The man, Saunders, turned to regard the line of gunners, noticed Eric's gaze, and nodded in a friendly fashion. Eric returned the nod and considered going over to say hello.

A shot rang down the line followed by two more in quick succession. A Sharp-shinned Hawk, naked against the morning sky, crumbled and was swallowed by the dark backdrop of trees. Scattered cheers broke out.

Eric fixed his attention on the treetops, finger on the safety, gun held at ready. He flicked a quick glance at the Audubon warden and saw him write something on a pad. Then his eyes caught movement out ahead of him.

The gun came up quick and smooth. Cheek pressed firmly on the stock, Eric swung the barrel — turning from the waist, moving the muzzle along the path of the bird. The Sharp-shinned folded its wings and began to quarter to the right in a shallow dive. Eric followed, and as the muzzle moved ahead of the bird, he pulled the trigger...

1981

... "I'll break their heads!" Carol muttered softly in the slow, even monotones that denote real anger in a person. Two more shots followed the first. Pellets, their energy spent, pattered harmlessly on and around the roof of the Higbee Beach Field Station. Carol opened her eyes with an effort, glowered at the roof — at nothing in particular — and repeated murderously, "I'll break their heads. So help me, if those guys are shooting woodcock in the no-fire zone again, I'll feed them to vultures."

Wisely, the gunners held their fire.

Carol drew herself deeper into her polarguard bag and luxuriated in the warmth, reluctant to leave it. For almost two months now she had risen before dawn, walked the short distance to the hawk watch tower at Higbee Beach Wildlife Management Area, and recorded the numbers of migratory raptors passing through. It was part of a project to understand the raptor use of the Higbee tract. For two months, she had been at her post for ten hours a day, seven days a week, identifying and recording the sixteen species of raptors that make up the Cape May flights; noting, hourly, all pertinent weather and flight-related variables; answering the queries of passing birders and hunters; and, each evening, transcribing field notes onto the impersonal and inflexible likes of computer-ready data forms.

And for the past several weeks, she had been moonlighting at the owl nets by helping to run checks and process captures. And now she was very, very tired. More tired than she had ever been in her twenty-three years.

The light seeping into the room served notice that it was past time to go to work. Carol eased one foot experimentally from the seductive confines of the sleeping bag and, like the good field researcher she was, tested to see whether the world was where she had left it several hours before. She didn't want to leap to any indefensible conclusions.

Her foot intersected a hard, flat plane, which she tentatively identified as the floor. Carol sighed. The world was still there, all right. She didn't press her luck with further experimentation. One of the first things you learn as a biologist is *never* to repeat an experiment successfully concluded. You might not be able to duplicate the results.

Carol dressed hurriedly, partly because of the cold and partly because she was late. She stumbled noisily out to the kitchen, clear across the trailer, and proceeded to smear with a soup spoon large globs of one hundred percent natural peanut butter onto whole wheat bread.

All the knives were in the sink.

As she munched, hurriedly, on what passed for breakfast on a hawkwatcher's salary, she leafed through several days' accumulation of mail. There was a letter from a popular bimonthly magazine telling her that she may already have won twenty-five thousand dollars, a letter from the finance company advising her that another college loan payment was due, a catalogue from one of those Colorado-based manufacturers of hyper-quality backpacking gear filled with equipment bearing price tags that anybody who actually uses the stuff cannot possibly afford, and, finally, a letter from New Jersey Civil Service advising her of the hiring freeze for nongame biologists.

The usual fare.

At the trailer door, she reached fondly for her trusty old binoculars and ran a finger lightly along their length. It was a fine old pair of binos, a Bushnell Insta-focus. The enamel on both barrels had long since given way to bare metal. The focus lever had cracked near the base in some best-forgotten misadventure. A little Super glue, judiciously applied, had given it several more years of life. Carol had bought this pair with her first earnings as an assistant manager at Arthur Treacher's Fish and Chips during her freshman year. She had carried them for eight semesters and one season at Cape May.

But now her hand strayed over to the soft leather case that glowed amber in the half-light of morning. The metal clasp snapped sharp and cold; the case disclosed a beautiful pair of Nikon binoculars, her prize possession — eight power with a field of 325 feet at one thousand yards, boasting a light gathering index of fifteen, a lasting tribute to the manufacturing and marketing genius of Japanese optics.

Carol lifted the binoculars free from the case and felt their supreme lightness (and caught the sweet smell of honey that still clung to the barrels after last evening's mishap at dinner).

Treacherous stuff, honey.

The clouds, rushing low overhead, were washed in lavender and salmon as Carol moved down New England Road toward the hawk watch tower. Hawks were already beginning to pass overhead, their progress slowed to a crawl by strong headwinds. Her hands moved reflexively for the counters nestled deep in the pockets of her parka. The soft gliding sound of metal on metal sounded hollow in the three-inch loft of goose down. Each muffled "click" marked the passage of another bird: Sharp-shinned Hawks in the right hand, kestrels in the left, the birds that account for sixty-six percent of the Higbee Beach flight.

Carol climbed the tower with the easy grace of a born athlete, something that even several layers of winter clothing couldn't disguise. She had been All-State in three sports in high school but had elected to pursue a career in environmental studies instead of Phys. Ed. Raptors had become her obsession during her undergraduate days at East Stroudsburg State — four years spent in the shadow of the Kittatinny Ridge, the most famous raptor corridor in North America.

She had learned all the tenets of contemporary ornithological thought postulated by Ian Newton, Leslie Brown, the Craighead brothers, and others. She had learned much about predators and the role of predation in the maintenance of a balanced environment. She knew that raptor populations were contingent upon many things, including the abundance of prey — that no species of raptor can increase beyond the carrying capacity of its prey base. She had learned that birds of prey may be used as an environmental litmus paper to test the health and stability of the whole natural structure. And she knew that birds of prey, like all creatures, have needs that must be met. Unless man is mindful of these needs, his actions may undermine them. Carol's project at Higbee Beach was part of an effort to understand the needs of the thousands of hawks that migrate through Cape May, New Jersey.

There was another thing about the way Carol moved that went beyond simple coordination and conditioned reflexes. There was an air of satisfaction about her, the kind that comes of believing that what you are doing has purpose. Carol is a professional hawkwatcher, a rare breed among mankind. Nobody watches hawks for the money. There isn't any. People become hawkwatchers because they love it. At the end of the season she will find a job inside or outside her field to tide her over. During that time, she will wait impatiently for spring — and the Sandy Hook Hawk Watch that begins in March.

Someday, there might be grad school, or a desk job, or a family, or any one of the many trappings of life. But for now, for Carol, there was only the flight — and being part of autumn at Cape May.

From her platform thirty-five feet over Higbee, she could see most of the area south of the Cape May canal. The birds moved through in pulses like blood from the heart. Several birders were searching the sorghum for sparrows; two groups of hunters were running their dogs in the woods for woodcock.

A small figure wearing a faded plaid jacket and carrying a shotgun that looked to be about two sizes too big for him worked his way up the hedge, toward the tower. Carol noted appreciatively that he carried the gun with the muzzle facing away from the tower. It looked like a gun that had seen a lot of seasons.

A new wave of birds began moving through well left of the tower. Carol brought her binoculars up quick and smooth; the Sharp-shinned counter cradled in her right hand pressed firmly against her cheek. She moved the glasses along the path of birds and clicked off Sharpies as fast as they passed through her field. A voice hailed her from below.

"Hey, what'cha doin'?"

Carol looked down into a pair of inquisitive gray eyes set against an unkempt mane of red hair and freckles that overran both cheeks to form a bridge over the fellow's nose.

"Countin' hawks," she replied, looking quickly back to the flight to pick up a few stragglers.

"Good Sharp-shinned flight today, isn't it?" the young fella invited.

Carol looked back down at him with heightened interest.

"You like watching hawks?" she inquired.

"Yeah," he replied. "I like all birds, especially Fish Hawks — I mean Osprey. I saw one about five minutes ago up the road a ways. Did you get it?"

Carol stiffened defensively, her professional pride injured.

The young hunter noticed this. "It might have been just a gull," he offered. "It was a long way off. They look an awful lot alike."

"Yeah, they sure do," Carol agreed.

"Well, I gotta get going. Good luck."

"Yeah, you too," Carol said.

She turned her eyes back to the main flight path and picked up a harrier moving low near the wood's edge, several more distant Sharpies, and a bird at the limit of conjecture that took on more and more of the characteristics of a Cooper's Hawk the closer it got, confirming her suspicions. The Cooper's Hawk made her feel good. It was a call that most people wouldn't be able to make.

She looked after the retreating figure and on impulse hailed his back.

"Hey, what's your name?"

The young hunter turned and smiled. "Eric," he said.

Beach Glass — Cape May Point

by Karen Zaborowski

She drifts toward me and bends
to scoop grains of wet sand.
She searches the loam for something
like shells, clear-white pebbles
the locals call diamonds. I see by her mouth
she will talk to me, a stranger
resting by the edge of the tide,
and my fine silence rushes away.
You can search forever and never find blue,
she says, as if I, too, need this blue thing.
She spreads her hands to show greens
and browns, cloudy edges, all ordinary.
She lifts the blue pendant which dangles
around her neck.
Once I prayed for a blue diamond

in the spot where you're sitting,

and this glass washed up to my feet,

a miracle from God.

I listen to dune grass smoothed by wind,

my roughness sanded down.

Solitude is all I ask of God, I say,

but she is drawn away

and follows her path.

A gull tosses back its head, laughs like one

dismissing a foolish idea.

It drifts on its own luck,

searching for a clamshell or a crab,

as the surf washes over my toes,

my skin — marks my belonging

a little more each time.

Contributors' Notes

Gene Ahrens has been a full-time photographer since 1966, specializing in landscapes and nature studies. He lives in Berkeley Heights, New Jersey.

J. F. Battaglia teaches writing at Bloomsburg University, about one hour east of a Pennsylvania town called Jersey Shore. He says he "knows by heart all the thin blue lines leading home."

Michael Baytoff is a freelance photographer specializing in documentary and environmental work. His photographs have appeared in numerous national magazines, including *Time*, *Natural History*, *Audubon*, and *Wildlife Conservation*. He is represented by the Black Star Picture Agency.

Kay Boyle was a short-story writer, novelist, poet, and essayist who published about fifty books, including several volumes of poetry. Born in 1903, she lived in the 1920s and 1930s as an expatriate in France, England, and Austria, and she recorded her experiences as such in several novels. She helped families of conscientious objectors during World War II and later taught at San Francisco State University, where she joined her students in protesting the Vietnam War. She twice won O. Henry awards for her short fiction, collections of which include *50 Stories* (1950) and *Life Being the Best and Other Stories* (1988). She died in 1992.

David C. Bruton formerly lived in the Beach Haven Terrace/Dunes area of Long Beach Island, and during his teens and twenties was a lifeguard on the island for nearly eight summers. "As a child I remember spending countless hours alone, and yet never alone, in the solitude of the sea and bay. I shared this world with the sea birds, the fishes, and the enormous diversity of marine and plant life.... But I lived mostly just to wake to the smell of the sea air drifting into my bedroom at sunrise and calling me to its daily mystery, a boy scientist, exploring and being young." He left there twenty years ago, he says, as houses and condos proliferated. Today he is a medical doctor living in Florida.

Elayne Clift is the author of *Demons Dancing in My Head: Collected Poems 1985-1995*; *Croning Tales*; *Telling It Like It Is: Reflections of a Not So Radical Feminist*; and *The Road to Radicalism: Further Reflections of a Frustrated Feminist*, all published by OGN Publications in Potomac, Maryland. She teaches at Yale and George Washington universities and at Emerson College. A native of Woodbury, New Jersey, she spent summer Sundays in Atlantic City. "I still go to Ocean City every year to visit an old school chum, eat Taylor Pork Roll, and walk the boards!" she writes.

A freelance photographer, **Donna Connor** has photographed numerous Atlantic City events, from Mike Tyson fights to Miss America pageants. Her clients include the Associated Press, Reuters, *New Jersey Monthly*, and *Atlantic City Magazine*. She lives in Sweetwater, New Jersey.

Karen de Balbian Verster has had numerous stories published in literary magazines and anthologies. She has written a memoir about sex and cancer called *Embracing the Angel* and is currently at work on a novel, *A Debt to Nature Due*, as well as a screenplay, *Forbidden Fruit*. She is a graduate of Parsons School of Design and has an MFA in creative writing from City College of New York. She writes: "My husband's parents spent their childhood summers at the Jersey Shore, as did he and his sister. When my husband first brought me to the Jersey Shore ... I was not impressed, but it didn't take long for it to grow on me. I crave our annual September pilgrimage that we now share with our daughter, Tirsa Avalon, who at three is just as big a fan as we are."

Stephen Dunn has published nine collections of poetry, including *Loosestrife*; *New and Selected Poems, 1974-1994*; and *Landscape at the End of the Century*. He is also the author of *Walking Light: Essays and Memoirs*. He has won several awards and fellowships, and in 1995 he received an Academy Award in Literature from the American Academy of Arts and Letters. He teaches at Richard Stockton College in New Jersey.

Pete Dunne is the director of the Cape May Bird Observatory. His essays have appeared in many birding and general publications, and his books include *Tales of a Low-Rent Birder* (University of Texas Press).

A prize-winning playwright, **Joel A. Ensana** is a former playright-in-residence at San Franciso State University. His plays have been published twice in the annual *Best Short Plays* anthology, and his short stories have appeared in *The Nebraska Literary Review*, *Evergreen Chronicles*, and other journals. A native of New Brunswick, New Jersey, he now lives in Santa Fe, New Mexico. He writes: "Some of the happiest days of my life were spent during summers with my family — Point Pleasant, Asbury Park, and Atlantic City. There were no slot machines or lounge acts — just large wooden hotels with wraparound porches, Taylor Pork Roll, [and] saltwater taffy."

Frank Finale is the co-editor, with Rich Youmans, of *Under a Gull's Wing: Poems and Photographs of the Jersey Shore* (Down The Shore Publishing, 1996), and the poetry editor of *the new renaissance* literary journal. His poems and essays have appeared in numerous anthologies and magazines, including *The New York Quarterly*, *The Georgia Review*, *The Christian Science Monitor*, and the *Anthology of Magazine Verse and Yearbook of American Poetry* (Monitor Book Company). A teacher in the Toms River School System, he has taught poetry workshops for the Ocean County Council of the International Reading Association, and in 1993 he received an award for his work in the promotion of literacy.

Ray Fisk founded Down The Shore Publishing in 1984 while working as a photojournalist for *The New York Times*, United Press International, and *The Philadelphia Inquirer*. Throughout the 1980s he covered Atlantic City, the Jersey Shore, and southern New Jersey for numerous publications, with a 1986 stint in Haiti. In 1977 he helped establish *The SandPaper* on Long Beach Island, and worked there until 1983 as associate editor and photography editor.

Christopher Cook Gilmore is the author of six published novels. He grew up in Margate, New Jersey, and learned to sail the back bays when he was five. A Margate lifeguard for ten years, he now lives in France and Morocco, but returns to Margate each summer to sail his Hobie cat.

Sandy Gingras is an artist and writer with her own wholesale design company called "How to Live." As an addition to her "How to Live on an Island" line of cards, prints, and clothing, she wrote and illustrated a gift book, *How to Live on an Island* (Down The Shore Publishing, 1996). She lives with her son, as well as a black cat and a "fat little labrador dog," next to a salt marsh on Long Beach Island. "I dedicate a portion of all my business proceeds and a (much larger) portion of my free time to environmental issues on the Jersey Shore (especially the preservation of open lands)," she says.

John Grey is an Australian-born poet, playwright, and musician. His works have appeared in numerous literary magazines, including the *Louisville Review*, *Nimrod*, and *Cape Rock*, and he has had plays produced on both coasts. His first encounter with the Jersey Shore, he says, was while accompanying his mother on a gambling trip to Atlantic City. "But, not being much of a gambler myself, I soon found myself walking the boardwalk, being intrigued by what remained of the older Atlantic City, especially the remnants of the amusement piers, another subject dear to my heart. In later visits, I did find myself in more amiable/authentic sections of the coast, including Margate and its wondrous elephant."

Thérése Halscheid has published her work in *Yankee*, *Footwork: The Paterson Literary Review*, *Snowy Egret*, and *New Jersey Outdoors*, among other magazines, and she is the author of the poetry collection *Powertalk*.

Anndee Hochman's articles, essays, book reviews, and short fiction have appeared in *Ms.*, *The New York Times Book Review*, *The Philadelphia Inquirer*, *Philadelphia* magazine, *The Toronto Star*, and other publications. Her book of essays, *Everyday Acts & Small Subversions: Women Reinventing Family, Community and Home* was published in 1994. As a child, she spent every summer at the Jersey Shore, where she rode the Tilt-a-Whirl at Million Dollar Pier, ate Fudgsicles, and, of course, played Monopoly on rainy days.

Barbara Helfgott Hyett is director of the Workshop of Publishing Poets in Brookline, Massachusetts, and cofounder of the Writer's Room of Boston Inc. She has published four collections of poetry: *In Evidence: Poems of the Liberation of Nazi Concentration Camps* (University of Pittsburgh Press, 1986); *Natural Law* (Northland Press of Winona, 1989), which includes poems about Atlantic City; the Pulitzer Prize–nominated *The Double Reckoning of Christopher Columbus* (University of Illinois Press; 1992), and *The Tracks We Leave: Poems on Endangered Wildlife in North America* (University of Illinois Press, 1996). A native of Atlantic City, she writes: "In 1984 I visited my old neighborhood with my husband and two young sons. It was late afternoon, and we arrived on the corner of Oriental Avenue and Dewey Place, my dead-end street, at precisely the moment a wrecking ball was poised at the third-floor window of number 110, the apartment I'd lived in for thirteen girlhood years. We waved and screamed until the workers stopped. A man in what seemed to be a tuxedo appeared from the cellar door (did the building have a cellar when I lived there?), told us we could go in. Worried, I told myself: *Feel nothing*, and climbed the stairs. "Razing the Tenements" is not only the record of that experience, but represents the start of the collection of poems I would write about the rise and fall of the resort that was my hometown."

Born and raised in Atlantic City, **Norman Paul Hyett** says his early life "was filled with the surreal magic that only 'The Queen of Resorts' could provide," and that he was "weaned on the smell of the ocean, nourished by boardwalk hot dog stands and saltwater taffy, and raised by the hustle of tourists" — all of which provided a unique perspective that helped him formulate his views as a counseling psychologist. "Atlantic City — 1955," he says, "speaks both to the natural wonders this city provided long before legalized gambling, and to the harshness of life endured by 'the locals.'"

Claude F. Koch is the author of several novels, as well as many poems and short stories. His work has appeared in *Janus*, *Four Quarters*, *Sewanee Review*, *Antioch Review*, and *Kansas Quarterly*, among other journals, and several of his stories have been chosen for *The Best American Short Stories* and *O. Henry Prize* anthologies. A former professor of English and director of the writing program at La Salle College in Philadelphia, he was named professor emeritus-English upon his retirement.

Robert Kotlowitz has written four novels, the first of which, *Somewhere Else* (1972), won the National Jewish Book Award and the Edward Lewis Wallant Award for fiction. His most recent work, *Before Their Time* (Alfred A. Knopf, 1997), is a memoir about World War II. The former senior vice president and director of programming and broadcasting at Channel Thirteen/WNET in New York, he retired in 1990. He lives in New York City.

Dulcie Leimbach lives in Manhattan with her husband and two children. She is a graduate of the Warren Wilson MFA program in Swannanoa, North Carolina, and a journalist. Her short stories have appeared in *Iris* and *American Fiction*. She says she "remembers visiting her Great-Aunt Clara's sprawling white house in Spring Lake, and swimming in the public pool adjacent to the beach. It had salt water, and the taste of it was shocking." She still takes the train to the town "about once a summer to swim in the ocean, where it should be salty."

Serge J-F. Levy is a New York-based photojournalist. His work has appeared in various books, calendars, magazines, and newspapers, including *Life*, *The New York Times*, *The Boston Globe*, and *The Los Angeles Times*. His photographs on commercial fishing won an award from the New Jersey Press Association.

John Bailey Lloyd, a reference librarian at Ocean County Library in Toms River, New Jersey, is the author of *Six Miles at Sea: A Pictorial History of Long Beach Island* (1990) and *Eighteen Miles of History on Long Beach Island* (revised edition 1994), both published by Down The Shore Publishing. Born in 1932 in Johnstown, Pennsylvania, he began visiting Long Beach Island in 1942 and now lives year-round in Beach Haven, in an 1879 Victorian.

John Mahoney moved to Toms River from North Jersey nearly fourteen years ago, and he says he has never regretted it. "I have many pleasant memories of my childhood vacations at the Jersey Shore," he writes. "The thrill of riding over Barnegat Bay didn't fade when I became old enough to drive my own car across. And a particular favorite song on the ol' AM radio only added to the thrill. Now, if I so choose, I can pop in an oldies CD and drive over the bridge every day. And believe me, every sojourn to Seaside brings back memories of those carefree, barefoot days."

John McPhee has written about topics ranging from the Pine Barrens to the Swiss Army to the wild reaches of Alaska. In all, he has written twenty-four books, including *Irons in the Fire* (Farrar, Straus and Giroux, 1997). He lives in Princeton, New Jersey.

Peter E. Murphy has published his poems and essays in many journals, including *The American Book Review*, *The Beloit Poetry Journal*, *Commonweal*, and *The Little Magazine*. He has won four fellowships in poetry from the New Jersey State Council on the Arts, as well as awards and fellowships from the Folger Shakespeare Library, the National Endowment for the Humanities, and the Corporation of Yaddo. He has also been a poetry consultant to the Geraldine R. Dodge Foundation and an education adviser to two Bill Moyers/PBS television series, "Power of the Word" and "The Language of Life." He lives in Ventnor, New Jersey.

Bruce Novotny is the author of *Tales of an Endless Summer: A Novel of the Beach* (Down The Shore Publishing, 1996). Born in Atlantic City just before the legendary storm of March 1962, he was for many years a local on the sands of Long Beach Island — surfing the island's beachbreaks, paddling his surf ski on Little Egg Harbor Bay, managing his family's marina business, and writing a contemporary culture column for the summer weekly *Beachcomber* in the late 1980s. He now lives in southern California, where he is pursuing a career as a screenwriter and film editor.

Barbara O'Dair works as an editor and writer in New York City. Her poem "Seaside Heights" originally appeared in the journal *Mudfish* and won the 1996 *Mudfish* Poetry Prize, judged by Thomas Lux.

Joseph Paduano is a professional photographer, instructor, and author whose work is characterized by the interplay of sunlight and shadow. His publications include a calendar, *Images of the Jersey Shore* (1983); a self-published book about the shore, *Seascapes: A Photographic Essay* (1983); and several books on the art of photography published by Amherst Media. His photographs are in the collections of the Monmouth County Park System, The Port Authority of New York/New Jersey, Price Waterhouse, the State of New Jersey, Educational Testing Service, and Johnson and Johnson.

A native of Long Branch, **Robert Pinsky** was named Poet Laureate of the United States in 1997. He is the author of several collections of poetry, including *The Figured Wheel: New and Collected Poems 1966-1996* (Farrar, Straus and Giroux, 1996), as well as two volumes of essays and the acclaimed translation *The Inferno of Dante* (Farrar, Straus and Giroux, 1994). He teaches in the graduate writing program at Boston University.

Rochelle Ratner grew up in Atlantic City and Margate, landscapes that have continually fueled her writing. She is the author of two novels and thirteen books of poetry, including *Someday Songs* (BkMk Press) and *Zodiac Arrest* (Ridgeway Press). Her first novel, *Bobby's Girl* (Coffee House Press, 1986), takes Atlantic City as its setting, as do many of her poems. She is also executive editor of *The American Book Review* and is on the board of the National Book Critics Circle.

R. C. Ringer's stories have appeared in *Witness*, *Manoa*, *Midstream*, *The Quarterly*, *Quarter After Eight*, and various other journals. "Asbury Park" is an excerpt from a novel in progress. When not writing stories, he occupies his time working at an advertising agency in New York City.

Robert E. Ruffolo Jr. is the owner of Princeton Antiques in Atlantic City. The photographs published in this book are from his collection of historical Atlantic City images.

A former reporter for *The New York Times*, **Gay Talese** contributed numerous articles to magazines (particularly *Esquire*) in the 1960s and 1970s; many of these are collected in his book *Fame and Obscurity* (1970). His other books include *Unto the Sons* (Alfred A. Knopf, 1992), which gives an account of growing up in his native Ocean City during World War II.

A native of Atlantic City, **Barry Targan** teaches creative writing at Binghamton University (SUNY). He has published three collections of stories, two novels, and two chapbooks of poetry, and his awards include two National Endowment for the Arts grants and a Rockefeller Foundation grant. His short stories have been included in *Best American Short Stories*, *O. Henry Prize*, and *Pushcart* anthologies. He and his wife, Arleen, live in Greenwich, New York.

Josephine Lehman Thomas began her professional career in 1915 as a reporter for the *Sentinel* in Ionia, Michigan. She later served as a "government girl" in Washington, D.C., during World War I; was editor of *Carpenter's World Travels*, a twenty-volume series published in 1926; and was European researcher and editor for the author and broadcaster Lowell Thomas. She married Reynold Thomas in 1931, and the payment she received from *Scribners* for *Fisherman's Wife* paid for the birth of her first child. She died in 1959.

Margaret R. Thomas (Buchholz) publishes *The Beachcomber*, a seasonal vacation newspaper in Ocean County, and during the winters she travels or writes. She has written a series of essays based on her travels in the Middle East and Europe, and her books include *Great Storms of the Jersey Shore* (with Larry Savadove; Down The Shore Publishing, 1993). She is currently compiling chronicals about Jersey Shore, and says she "still drags stuff home from the beach."

William Wharton is a painter and writer whose books include the acclaimed novel *Birdy*, which won the American Book Award in 1978 and was nominated for the Pulitzer Prize in fiction. Born in Philadelphia, the author (who writes under the pseudonym William Wharton for reasons of privacy) now lives in France.

Wendy Patrice Williams, a native of Hillside, New Jersey, lives in the San Francisco Bay area of California. She received her Master of Fine Arts degree from Mills College, California, and currently teaches English at the College of Alameda. According to the author, the area she describes in her story existed for many years alongside the U.S. military reservation at Sandy Hook; her aunt and uncle's bungalow was a few steps up the road from the U.S. Navy guardhouse. She writes: "My father's father and my dad built [a] bungalow on Sandy Hook in 1926 or 1927.... It was located a short ways up from the bridge over the Shrewsbury River between the Highlands and the Hook. Behind their bungalow was a walkway that led to a pier jutting out into the river. On this pier was an amusement park, including a roller coaster, and a dock for ferries from New York City.

"My father's sister's husband, my Uncle Bill, built a bungalow next door. Our houses became part of a small community of houses that were well in existence by 1940, part of a beach club called Sandlass's, which consisted of a stretch of sand along the Shrewsbury River, Sandlass's mansion, and the beach house. Sandlass leased his property, which included ours and other bungalows, from the government for ninety-nine years.... When I was twelve or thirteen, 1962 or 1963, the federal government reneged on the lease with Sandlass and ordered all to vacate the property. The government wanted to use our precious river beach for a dump. Well, that never came to pass, and our old property sits even now abandoned and unoccupied. The house built by my grandfather and my father was torn down, for it would not have survived relocation. My Uncle Bill and Aunt Terry's bungalow was relocated across the river [to the Highlands].... It's still there." The author would like to thank her mother, Edith Williams, for "her sharp memory of historical details about Sandy Hook."

Jason Wilson is the editor of *Grand Tour*, a literary journal devoted to travel writing. He teaches in the English department at Beaver College in Pennsylvania.

Jane Elkington Wohl lives in Sheridan, Wyoming, with her husand and three almost-grown children. She teaches in the Goddard College MFA in Writing program and is director of the Sheridan College Writing Center. Her poetry and prose have appeared in numerous journals and anthologies. "Margie and Herb," she says, was written on a visit to her parents'-in-law house in Margate, New Jersey.

Karen Zaborowski has published her poems in numerous journals, including *California Quarterly*, *Journal of New Jersey Poets*, and *U.S. 1 Worksheets*, as well as the anthology *Under a Gull's Wing: Poems and Photographs of the Jersey Shore* (Down The Shore Publishing, 1996). A recipient of a poetry fellowship from the New Jersey State Council on the Arts and a grant from the Geraldine Dodge Foundation, she teaches English at Atlantic City High School.

Acknowledgments

I would like to thank the following authors and publishers for allowing me to use the works in this book:

J. F. Battaglia: "A Day in the Life of Vincent Lucciola" used by permission of the author.

Kay Boyle: "Black Boy" by Kay Boyle, from *Fifty Stories*. Copyright © 1980 by Kay Boyle. Reprinted by permission of New Directions Publishing Corp.

David C. Bruton: "Woo" originally appeared in *The Beachcomber*. Reprinted by permission of the author.

Elayne Clift: "When Jerry Loves Jenny" used by permission of the author.

Karen de Balbian Verster: "Ashes to Ashes" used by permission of the author.

Stephen Dunn: "The Refuge" from *Loosestrife* by Stephen Dunn. Copyright © 1996 by Stephen Dunn. Reprinted by permission of W. W. Norton & Company, Inc.

Pete Dunne: "A Tale of Two Hawkwatchers" reprinted from *Tales of a Low-Rent Birder* by Pete Dunne, Copyright © 1986. By permission of the University of Texas Press.

Joel Ensana: "Voice from the Ocean" originally appeared in *Evergreen Chronicles*. Reprinted by permission of the author.

Frank Finale: "To the Shore Once More" and "The Legend of a Tree" originally appeared in *Coast* magazine. "A Walk along the Beach" originally appeared in *1991 Jersey Shore Almanac*. "Last Stop" originally appeared in *Press*. Reprinted by permission of the author.

Christopher Cook Gilmore: "Atlantic City Proof" originally appeared under the title "Rum Runners" in *Swank* magazine. Reprinted by permission of the author.

Sandy Gingras: "At the Fishermen's Bar" originally appeared in *Journal of New Jersey Poets*, Summer 1997. Reprinted by permission of the author. "The Finished Sound" used by permission of the author.

John Grey: "The Elephant, Margate" used by permission of the author.

Therése Halscheid: "Killing Time" originally appeared in *Powertalk*, a collection of earth poems by Therése Halscheid. Reprinted by permission of the author.

Anndee Hochman: "Irregular Intervals" used by permission of the author.

Barbara Helfgott Hyett: "Razing the Tenements in Atlantic City" from *Natural Law* (Northland Press of Winona, Minnesota, 1989) by Barbara Helfgott Hyett. Reprinted by permission of the author.

Norman Paul Hyett: "Atlantic City — 1955" used by permission of the author.

Claude F. Koch: "Love" originally appeared in *Four Quarters* (La Salle College), Autumn 1972. Reprinted by permission of the author.

Robert Kotlowitz: From *The Boardwalk* (Alfred A. Knopf, 1977) by Robert Kotlowitz. Reprinted by permission of the author.

Dulcie Leimbach: "Ringolevio" used by permission of the author.

John Bailey Lloyd: "A Strange Incident at Bond's Hotel" used by permission of the author.

John Mahoney: "The Wooden Gauntlet" originally appeared in *Coast* magazine. Reprinted by permission of the author.

John McPhee: "The Search for Marvin Gardens" from *Pieces of the Frame* by John McPhee. Copyright © 1975 by John McPhee. Reprinted by permission of Farrar, Straus & Giroux, Inc.

Peter E. Murphy: "Breakfast at the Wildwood Motel, 1996" used by permission of the author.

Bruce Novotny: "Beach Access" used by permission of the author.

Barbara O'Dair: "Seaside Heights" originally appeared in *Mudfish 9*, Summer 1996. Reprinted by permission of the author.

Robert Pinsky: "Long Branch, New Jersey" from *The Figured Wheel: New and Collected Poems*, 1966-1996 by Robert Pinsky. Copyright © 1996 by Robert Pinsky. Reprinted by permission of Farrar, Straus & Giroux, Inc.

Rochelle Ratner: "1962" and "Joe Jr." from *Sea Air in a Grave Ground Hog Turns Toward* ('Gull Books, 1980) by Rochelle Ratner. Reprinted by permission of the author.

R. C. Ringer: "Asbury Park" used by permission of the author.

Gay Talese: From *Unto the Sons* by Gay Talese. Copyright © 1992 by Gay Talese. Reprinted by permission of Alfred A. Knopf Inc.

Barry Targan: "Caveat Emptor" and "Old Light" from *Falling Free,* Copyright © 1989 by Barry Targan. Used with the permission of the author and the University of Illinois Press.

Josephine Lehman Thomas: "Fisherman's Wife" originally appeared in *Scribners*, July 1933. Reprinted by permission of Margaret Thomas Buchholz.

Margaret R. Thomas: "The Distant Edge of War" used by permission of the author.

Lisa Walker: "Atlantic City" reprinted by permission; © 1988 The New Yorker Magazine, Inc. All rights reserved.

William Wharton: From *Pride* by William Wharton. Copyright © 1985 by William Wharton. Reprinted by permission of Newmarket Press, 18 East 48th Street, New York, New York 10017.

Wendy Patrice Williams: "Scheinman's Deck" used by permission of the author.

Jason Wilson: "Senior Week" originally appeared in *Grand Tour*. Reprinted by permission of *Grand Tour*.

Jane Elkington Wohl: "Margie and Herb" used by permission of the author.

Karen Zaborowski: "Beach Glass — Cape May Point" used by permission of the author.

I would like to thank the following photographers for permission to print their photographs: **Joseph Paduano, Gene Ahrens, Serge J-F. Levy, Ray Fisk, Michael Baytoff,** and **Donna Connor**. In addition, I would like to thank **Robert Ruffolo Jr.** for permission to print historical Atlantic City photographs from his collection.

I would also like to thank Ray Fisk, Leslee Ganss, and Down The Shore Publishing for making this book a reality.

And, as always, I would like to thank my wife, Ann, for her constant love, support, and understanding.